"If the Anthropocene is to be understood as a condition of malaise, as David Chandler suggests in this sophisticated theoretical engagement with contemporary ontopolitics, it necessarily needs new modes of governance. While mapping and sensing might be understood as modern methods, the promise of hacking and digital activism hold out possibilities for acting that deserve much more attention in the world of new rapidly changing urban vulnerabilities. This volume, by one of the key current philosophers of resilience, offers a preliminary 'must be read' guide to these emerging political potentialities in the ruins of neoliberalism."

Simon Dalby, Balsillie School of International Affairs, Canada

"How is it possible that the new metaphysicians of the Anthropocene have greeted the threat of planetary extinction with such affirmation? This is the stirring question that drives Chandler's book. Bringing together policy questions in international relations with contemporary new materialisms, Chandler takes us beyond the entanglements of ticks, slime molds, and ocean currents to ask about the Anthropocene's ontopolitical claims and the postmodern modes of governance they affirm. The result is a stunning exposure of the pragmatic and philosophical stakes of our current condition and an urgent call to contest the affirmative ontopolitics of the Anthropocene. A must read!"

Lynne Huffer, Emory University, USA

"...Chandler's *Ontopolitics of the Anthropocene* is one of the most important pieces of analytical scholarship to come out the academy in years. It provides a new framework for understanding the world that is taking shape. Following the human own-goal of the Anthropocene, we are now suborned to let the world govern and guide us. The new orthodoxy celebrates the demise of linear causality and with it conventional modes of knowing and governing. Open to its contributions, Chandler provides an eloquent and penetrating analysis of its limits. He warns of the potential intellectual sterility of the ontopolitical alternatives it entails. Everyone should heed Chandler's urgent call to critically dissect the governing discourse of the Anthropocene and the relation to the world it creates."

Mark Duffield, University of Bristol, UK

"Chandler throws himself headlong into the global tempest of our eponymous era. What comes out the other side is a challenging and vital engagement with the Anthropocene that calls on International Relations to pay attention to the world beyond the narrow confines of our geopolitically charged, species narcissism. A must read for those of us beginning to take notice."

Jairus Grove, University of Hawai'i at Manoa, USA

"*Ontopolitics in the Anthropocene* is the culmination of David Chandler's long-running engagement with contemporary transformations in social and environmental governance. This book is essential reading for anybody interested in understanding novel practices of rule and how they shape and constrain possibilities for critical thought. As he carefully details how a post-humanist "affirmation of the Anthropocene" straightjackets our political imaginary, Chandler challenges readers to reinvent what critique might become today."

Kevin Grove, Florida International University, USA

ONTOPOLITICS IN THE ANTHROPOCENE

The Anthropocene captures more than a debate over how to address the problems of climate change and global warming. Increasingly, it is seen to signify the end of the modern condition itself and potentially to open up a new era of political possibilities. This is the first book to look at the new forms of governance emerging in the epoch of the Anthropocene. Forms of rule, which seek to govern without the handrails of modernist assumptions of 'command and control' from the top-down; taking on board new ontopolitical understandings of the need to govern on the grounds of non-linearity, complexity and entanglement.

The book is divided into three parts, each focusing on a distinct mode or understanding of governance: Mapping, Sensing and Hacking. Mapping looks at attempts to govern through designing adaptive interventions into processes of interaction. Sensing considers ways of developing greater real time sensitivity to changes in relations, often deploying new technologies of Big Data and the Internet of Things. Hacking analyses the development of ways of 'becoming with', working to recomposition and reassemble relations in new and creative forms.

This work will be of great interest to students and scholars of international politics, international security and international relations theory and those interested in critical theory and the way this is impacted by contemporary developments.

David Chandler is Professor of International Relations, Department of Politics and International Relations, University of Westminster, UK, and editor of the journal *Resilience: International Policies, Practices and Discourses*.

CRITICAL ISSUES IN GLOBAL POLITICS

This series engages with the most significant issues in contemporary global politics. Each text is written by a leading scholar and provides a short, accessible and stimulating overview of the issue for advanced undergraduates and graduate students of international relations and global politics. As well as providing a survey of the field, the books also contain original and groundbreaking thinking which will drive forward debates on these key issues.

ONTOPOLITICS IN THE ANTHROPOCENE

An Introduction to Mapping, Sensing and Hacking

David Chandler

Routledge
Taylor & Francis Group

LONDON AND NEW YORK

First published 2018
by Routledge
2 Park Square, Milton Park, Abingdon, Oxon OX14 4RN

and by Routledge
711 Third Avenue, New York, NY 10017

Routledge is an imprint of the Taylor & Francis Group, an informa business

British Library Cataloguing in Publication Data
A catalogue record for this book is available from the British Library

Library of Congress Cataloging in Publication Data
Names: Chandler, David, 1962- author.
Title: Ontopolitics in the anthropocene : an introduction to mapping,
    sensing and hacking / David Chandler.
Description: Abingdon, Oxon ; New York, NY : Routledge, 2018. |
Series: Critical issues in global politics | Includes bibliographical
    references and index.
Identifiers: LCCN 2017045732| ISBN 9781138570566 (hbk) | ISBN
    9781138570573 (pbk.) | ISBN 9780203703434 (ebk)
Subjects: LCSH: International relations–Philosophy. | Technology and
    international relations. | Internationalism.
Classification: LCC JZ1305 .C4335 2018 | DDC 327.101–dc23
LC record available at https://lccn.loc.gov/2017045732

ISBN: 9781138570566 (hbk)
ISBN: 9781138570573 (pbk)
ISBN: 9780203703434 (ebk)

Typeset in Bembo
by Taylor & Francis Books

CONTENTS

TABLES

ACKNOWLEDGEMENTS

I would like to thank the commissioning team and staff at Routledge, especially Craig Fowlie, Nicola Parkin and Lucy Frederick. I would also like to acknowledge funding support from the University of Westminster for sabbatical research leave in the academic year 2015–2016 and funding for the fieldwork in Nairobi and Jakarta that forms the backdrop to the research in Chapters 3 and 6 respectively. In Nairobi I would like to thank Monica Nthiga and the researchers at Ushahidi for offering me office space, guidance and interview time and Andy Fox, Programmes Director for Concern Worldwide Kenya. In Jakarta, I would like to thank the PetaJakarta project team, especially Etienne Turpin, Frank Sedlar and Christina Leigh Geros, for all their help, support, insights and generosity and also Yantisa Akhadi (Iyan) from the Humanitarian OpenStreetMap Team and George Hodge from the UN Jakarta Pulse Lab. I would also like to thank the Centre for Global Cooperation Research, University of Duisburg-Essen, for providing research funding during my research fellowship there in the spring of 2017, including the resources to visit and interview researchers at the Massachusetts Institute of Technology project labs. At MIT, I'd particularly like to thank Ricardo Alvarez at the Senseable City Lab and Tomas Holderness at the Urban Risk Lab.

The work presented here was informed through numerous conference panels, workshops and invited seminars, which took place during the preparation of this book, from the spring of 2016 to the summer of 2017.

Some of the most important are listed below, and I would like to thank the
organisers for their invitations and my colleagues for their contributions and
reflections: 'The Politics of Digital Technology' and 'Power and the
Anthropocene' panels, International Studies Association annual convention,
Atlanta, March 2016; 'International Politics in the Anthropocene', European
Workshops in International Studies, Tübingen, April 2016; 'Data as Things:
Dis/assembling the Stuff of Data and Data's Coming to Matter' strand,
London Conference of Critical Thought, June 2016; 9th Workshops on
International Relations (WIRE), 'Complex systems for global governance',
Brussels, July 2016; 'Ideology and Algorithmic Governance' panel, Inter-
national Association for Media and Communication Research pre-
conference, Leicester, July 2016; the 4S/EASST Conference 'Science and
Technology by Other Means: Exploring Collectives, Spaces and Futures',
Barcelona, September 2016; 'Algorithms, Racializing Assemblages and the
Digital Human' panel, *Millennium* annual conference, London, October
2016; 'Big Data as a Driver for Change: From Information Utopias to
Utopias In-Formation', Central St. Martins, London, November 2016;
'Law and the Senses II: Human, Posthuman, Inhuman Sensings' workshop,
University of Westminster, November 2016; 'The Political Economy of
Platformisation' workshop, University of Leicester, December 2016; 'Moral
Agency and the Politics of Responsibility: Challenging Complexity' work-
shop, Centre for Global Cooperation Research, Duisburg, December 2016;
UK Alliance for Disaster Research annual conference, London, January
2017; 'Resilience: Bouncing Back, Bouncing Forward and Beyond', Uni-
versity of Trier, February 2017; 'International Dissidence: Rule and Resis-
tance in a Globalized World' conference, Goethe University, March 2017;
'Putting the crowd to work' seminar, Urban Risk Lab, Massachusetts Institute of Technology, April 2017; 'Rethinking the Digital and Analogue:
Epistemologies of the Anthropocene', 'Design, Biopolitics, and Resilience
in a Complex World' and 'The controversial limits of Disaster Risk
Reduction Research and Analysis' panels, Association of American Geo-
graphers annual meeting, Boston, April 2017; 'Mapping, Mercator and
Modernity: The Impact of the Digital' workshop, University of Duisburg-
Essen, April 2017; 'Big Data and the Rise of the Digital in International
Governance' workshop, London School of Economics, May 2017; 'Digital
Objects, Digital Subjects: An Interdisciplinary Symposium on Activism,
Research & Critique in the Age of Big Data Capitalism' conference, Uni-
versity of Westminster, April 2017; 'Anthropocene Mobilities: The Politics
of Movement in an Age of Change' workshop, University of Hamburg,

June 2017; 'The Ambivalences of Abstraction' workshop, Centre for Inter-disciplinary Methodologies, University of Warwick, June 2017; the American Society for Cybernetics conference 'Resilience and Ethics: Implications', Salem, Massachusetts, August 2017.

Coming out of these engagements and discussions, some of the material here draws on and reworks some material published or in press, including: 'Intervention and Statebuilding beyond the Human: From the "Black Box" to the "Great Outdoors"', forthcoming (2018) in the *Journal of Intervention and Statebuilding*, drawn upon in Chapter 3; 'How the World Learned to Stop Worrying and Love Failure: Big Data, Resilience and Emergent Causality', published in *Millennium: Journal of International Studies*, Vol. 44, No. 3 (2016), drawn upon in Chapter 4; 'A World without Causation: Big Data and the Coming of Age of Posthumanism', published in *Millennium: Journal of International Studies*, Vol. 43, No. 3 (2015), drawn upon in Chapter 5; and 'Securing the Anthropocene? International Policy Experiments in Digital Hacktivism: A Case Study of Jakarta', published in *Security Dialogue*, Vol. 48, No. 2 (2017), drawn upon in Chapter 6.

I would also like to thank the regular contributors to the materialisms reading group meetings, held at the University of Westminster since May 2013, and the Department of Politics and International Relations for funding our wine and nibbles. This project could not have developed without the stimulation and challenges of these discussions, which were also extended to other venues and events. Last, but not least, I owe a huge debt to the intellectual support and generosity of colleagues, I couldn't name everyone but I would like to single out for thanks: Pol Bargues-Pedreny; Rex Troumbley; Etienne Turpin; Claudia Aradau; Mark Duffield; Stephanie Wakefield; Delf Rothe; Jonathan Pugh; Kevin Grove; Julian Reid; Harshavardhan Bhat; Philip Hammond; Jonathan Joseph; Nicholas Michelsen; Peter Finkenbusch; Luis Martins; Sara Raimondi; Rob Cowley; and, most importantly, Paulina Tambakaki.

PREFACE

This book is a product of my unease with the widespread affirmation of new modes of governance on the basis of what is conceptualised here as the ontopolitics of the Anthropocene. By 'ontopolitics', I mean a new set of grounding ontological claims that form the basis of discussions about what it means to know, to govern and to be a human subject. This work has been in gestation for a number of years because thinking through this radical shift, in political and philosophical assumptions at the core of governmental policy and practice, has required quite a substantial body of international and interdisciplinary research. It seems clear that fundamental questions are raised on the basis of the alleged impossibility of the humanist promise of progress, which, rather than posing a problem, is increasingly affirmed as a positive and enabling opportunity.

I initially found it hard to understand what it was about our contemporary condition that could enable the imaginary of the disappearance of humanity from the face of the earth,[1] to have an accessible 'feel good' factor,[2] or for philosophical treatises on planetary, even inter-stellar, extinction,[3] to be greeted with shows of relief, reassurance and gratitude.[4] What was it that had happened that meant Enlightenment aspirations to knowledge or to reason could be perfunctorily dismissed as barriers to seeing the rich reality of the world?[5] How was it possible for critical approaches to our present condition to be rejected merely on the basis that they still had the 'hubris' to posit the possibility of a 'collective happy ending'?[6] What was it about contemporary 'life in the ruins' or the promise of extinction that apparently offered such a wonderful 'opportunity for profound political creativity'?[7]

One thing that was clear was that discussion of whether the earth was entering a new geological epoch of the 'Anthropocene' (to be decided by the International Commission on Stratigraphy) had given this very 21st century malaise a cohering conceptual framework, which enabled a wide range of concerns with modernist political and philosophical assumptions to be articulated with a growing clarity and conceptual reassurance. Rather than seeing discussions and debates, affirming the Anthropocene, as a morbid symptom of our contemporary lack of confidence in political progress and human creativity, the cart seemed to be being put before the horse, the symptoms were seen to be the cause: the *explanandum* of the Anthropocene changed from being a question that needed to be investigated into the *explanans*, the explanation, for the rapid collapse of modernist assumptions.[8]

Making the Anthropocene the starting assumption rather than the question to be investigated assumes that the end of modernity has already occurred and that the questions modernity posed have been resolved, or rather surpassed and become irrelevant to today's concerns. This has meant that empirical evidence of catastrophic climate change and philosophical arguments displacing the centrality of the human subject have become intertwined in the assumption that we are now living after the end of modernity. Modernity is dead; so long live its 'after' ... the Anthropocene. Even asking questions about or mourning the end of modernity and its promise of progress was to be discouraged as: 'The story of decline offers no leftovers, no excess, nothing that escapes progress. Progress still controls us even in tales of ruination.'[9]

Contemporary theorists assert that modernity is over, so move along ... there is nothing to see here. Or, perhaps even more tellingly, maybe modernity never really existed anyway.[10] It all seemed rather a quick transition. Was this really it? As Drucilla Cornell and Stephen Seely note, to focus this much critical effort on debunking 'the human' and 'human agency' might be, at the very least, tactically problematic when so much may still be at stake in the multiple crises of political and planetary rule? Perhaps it is a false and 'forced choice' to choose between 'the human' and 'the world'?[11] Perhaps rethinking modernity does not necessarily involve the refutation of any possibility of political alternatives other than those based on accepting our newfound fragility and vulnerability? This book is the presentation of my investigation into the conceptual justifications for affirming the very different expectations of life and its governance in the Anthropocene. It seeks to give the analysis a material focus through framing the discussion in terms of how governance is seen to operate without the handrails of modernist ideas of rationality and progress.

The governance focus is important for conceptually thinking through the ontopolitical assumptions behind discussions of the new limits and possibilities in the Anthropocene. Sometimes it appears all too easy to dismiss contemporary theoretical engagements with the Anthropocene for perhaps lacking a clear relationship to the political. It can appear that radical philosophers and political theorists are often much happier engaging with rock formations, slime moulds, ticks and ocean currents than the implications of their theories for how policy can be developed and implemented. While a lot of theoretical approaches and trends appear to be being founded, reformulated and labelled – such as posthumanism, actor network theory, assemblage theory, second-order cybernetics, new materialisms, new empiricism, post-phenomenology, speculative realism or object-oriented ontology – there often seems to be very little clarity regarding the stakes these positions raise for politics in both theory and practice.

This is where this book seeks to open up some space for critical engagements with a rapidly emerging and important field. It seeks to explore the Anthropocene as a contextual framing both for new forms of governing and for new conceptual frameworks negotiating and constructing what it means to govern. It is a study of the ontopolitical assumptions of the Anthropocene, informing what are heuristically divided into the three modes of governance, which they enable: Mapping, Sensing and Hacking. It seeks both to provide an analytical frame for understanding how governance practices are cohered and legitimised today and also to reflect upon how contemporary theoretical approaches inform and reflect these assumptions even if they do not exactly map on to them. This book argues that the Anthropocene is not a passing fad and that its acceptance as a framing for political possibilities in the 21st century is something that needs urgent contestation.

This study of the affirmation of the Anthropocene can be read as a stand alone monograph or, alternatively, as the completion of a trilogy on governance in the international sphere. In this respect, I have been very lucky to have had the ongoing support and encouragement of the commissioning editors and publishers of the Routledge series 'Critical Issues in Global Politics' and to have worked with them over the last decade. It, of course, gives me no pleasure to see the trends outlined and discussed in my earlier work, *International Statebuilding: The Rise of Postliberal Governance* (2010) and *Resilience: The Governance of Complexity* (2014) further consolidated today. The rapid rise and consolidation of the ontopolitical assumptions of the Anthropocene – the imaginary that we are suborned to let the world govern and guide us – at least provides some conceptual clarity enabling insight into the far reaching implications of this shift. The hope of this book is that, in setting out the epistemological and ontopolitical assumptions cohering the new governance modes of the Anthropocene, the challenges facing those of us who aspire to develop a different stance towards the legacies of the Enlightenment and of modernist aspirations of progress may become clearer.

Notes

1 Weisman, 2008.
2 Lezard, 2008.
3 Brassier, 2007.
4 Mitchell, 2017: p.21.
5 'Might we see more, experience more, and understand more, by knowing less?'; Tim Ingold, 2015: p.134.
6 Tsing, 2015: p.21.
7 Mitchell, 2017: p.23.
8 Justin Rosenberg (2000: p.3) offers a similar framing, in addressing the concept of globalisation, which rehearsed some of the key ontopolitical themes at the heart of the Anthropocene.
9 Tsing, 2015: p.21.
10 Latour argues, *We have never been Modern*, 1993a.
11 Cornell and Seely, 2016: p.6.

PART I

Introduction

1

INTRODUCTION

Affirming the Anthropocene

Introduction

This book is an analysis of the ontopolitical assumptions of the Anthropocene and engages these assumptions through establishing and introducing the reader to the three distinct modes of governance grounded upon them: Mapping, Sensing and Hacking.[1] It considers each mode as providing a distinct conceptualisation of governance in a world framed as complex, entangled and unpredictable.[2] The articulation of these distinct modes of governance is my own attempt to parse and to clarify the, often unclear, forms through which political thought expresses and reflects new ways of developing policy, of engaging with problems, of deriving knowledge and of thinking about political agency in the 21st century. This is not a work on ontology, therefore it does not assert what the Anthropocene is or what humans are or are not. It operates within the discipline of international relations, in terms of its focus being the new forms of governance that Anthropocene ontopolitics are understood to engender. Its concern is a critical one; the book analyses these modes for the purposes of understanding their inner logics and their consequences for the policies and practices of governance. I do not seek to argue that these modes necessarily operate in a pure form, without overlaps or interconnections, but I do suggest that heuristically drawing out their distinctive logics is useful for understanding their development, their limits and their aporias or contradictions. I do not advocate for any particular one of these modes, nor the underlying ontopolitical claims seen to necessitate them, but seek to examine them to clarify what is at stake in the ontopolitics of the Anthropocene.

The three governance modes of Mapping, Sensing and Hacking claim to start from the empirical reality of the world as it appears rather than from assumptions of modernist progress, universal knowledge or linear causality. The ontopolitical claim informing these modes is the assertion that in the Anthropocene the world is much less addressable by modernist constructions and assumptions; it is more contingent, plural and complex: thereby less amenable to the applications of 'technological solutionism'[3] or 'lessons learned', which can be generalised and applied. Each mode reflects a shift from liberal or modernist understandings towards an affirmation of the Anthropocene, by which I mean governance discourses becoming more at home with discursive framings of contingency and complexity. With this affirmative shift, there is a sense that there is something positive in the realisation that the Anthropocene cannot be secured, governed or engaged with in traditional ways. As will be discussed below, this affirmation of the Anthropocene can be seen in Mapping (designing indirect interventions based on tracing or mapping assemblages of interactive emergence), in Sensing (with the boosting of Big Data and the Internet of Things as able to provide real time responses to 'pre-event' problems) and in Hacking (with new creative ways of engaging on the basis of repurposing, recompositioning and finding the play in already existing arrangements and practices).

This introductory chapter is organised in five sections. The next section provides an introduction to the concept of the Anthropocene and what is considered to be at stake in the discussion of the Anthropocene as a new geological epoch and, more importantly, as marking the end of modernist views of progress. The second section introduces the idea that the Anthropocene should be affirmed rather than being seen to be problematic and the following sections introduce the implications for governing in the Anthropocene without the epistemological and ontopolitical assumptions of modernity. Three arising modes of governance, grounded on the ontopolitical assumptions of the Anthropocene, are then identified with distinct logics: Mapping, Sensing and Hacking. The final section outlines the contents of the following chapters.

A new epoch

The Anthropocene – a concept coined by Eugene Stormer in the 1980s and popularised by Paul Crutzen in the 2000s[4] – is a disputed term, which refers to a new geological epoch,[5] in which human activity is seen to have profound and irreparable effects on the environment.[6] This attention to a new epoch in which humanity appears to have impacted the earth in ways which mean that natural processes can no longer be separated from historical, social, economic and political effects has powerfully challenged the modernist understanding of the nature/culture divide, separating social and natural science, destabilising the assumptions of both. Nature can no longer be understood as operating on fixed or natural laws, while politics and culture can no longer be understood as operating in a separate sphere of autonomy and freedom. These assumptions, in both spheres, were central to modernist constructions of Enlightenment progress, which is now seen to no longer exist or to have always been problematic.[7] Jeremy Davies argues that: 'The idea of the Anthropocene makes this state of being in between epochs the starting point for political thinking.'[8] As Bruno Latour, one of the most prolific and widely influential theorists articulating the Anthropocene as a break with modernity, highlights: the fact that it is science itself that appears to lead the questioning of modernist constructions of the world is highly significant, considering the impact this has for ways in which we can imagine politics and governance:

> But what is even more extraordinary is that it's the brainchild of stern, earnest and sun-tanned geologists who, until recently, had been wholly unconcerned by the tours and detours of the humanities. No postmodern philosopher, no reflexive anthropologist, no liberal theologian, no political thinker would have dared to weigh the influence of humans on the same historical scale as rivers, floods, erosion and biochemistry.[9]

This book is not directly concerned with debates and discussions around the dating of the Anthropocene as a geological era,[10] whether to start with 1492 with Columbus and the European holocaust in the Americas,[11] in 1784 with the invention of the steam engine by James Watt, which ushered in the industrial revolution, with the explosion of the atom bomb in 1945 or with the 'Great Acceleration', the spread of industrialisation across the world since.[12] The conclusion of the discussion, regardless of dating, is a shared one: that today human history cannot be understood as separate to geological history:

> The Anthropocene, as the reunion of human (historical) time and Earth (geological) time, between human agency and non-human agency,

gives the lie to this – temporal, ontological, epistemological and institutional – great divide between nature and society ... It signals the return of the *Earth* into a *world* that Western industrial modernity on the whole represented to itself as above the earthly foundation. (emphasis in original)[13]

Natural time is no longer somehow slow in comparison to the speed of human or cultural time. 'What is sure is that glaciers appear to slide quicker, ice to melt faster, species to disappear at a greater speed, than the slow, gigantic, majestic, inertial pace of politics, consciousness and sensibilities.'[14] Nature or the 'environment' is no longer to be seen as merely the 'background', but is itself a 'protagonist'.[15] Thus, the division between agential 'man' and passive 'nature' is fundamentally challenged, with catastrophic events which seemed to be exceptional or highly improbable in the past, becoming increasingly regular, even in the advanced West: 'in the era of global warming, nothing is really far away; there is no place where the orderly expectations of bourgeois life hold unchallenged sway.'[16] As Amitav Ghosh powerfully notes, expectations of normality, balance and order that defined the modern world view, appear from today's vantage point to be a terrible error or hubris: as carried to the point of 'great derangement'.[17] There is a contemporary consensus that: 'There can be no more talk of a linear and inexorable progress'.[18]

For Timothy Morton: 'In an age of global warming, there is no background, and thus there is no foreground. It is the end of the world, since worlds depend on backgrounds and foregrounds.'[19] What was taken for granted is now revealed to be much more contingent, fragile and unpredictable; for Morton, the world is no longer an object, fixed, passive and external to us, thus there can be no such thing as a human 'lifeworld' shaped within this.[20] As Latour states, the positions are reversed, the background becomes foreground: 'what was until now a mere décor for human history is becoming the principal actor'.[21] So much so that it could be said that the Anthropocene does not just overcome the culture/nature divide, 'it bypasses it entirely':[22]

everything that was part of the background has now melted into the foreground. There is no environment any more, and thus no longer a need for environmentalism. We are post-natural for good. With the end of the political epistemology of the past that insured the presence of an indisputable outside arbiter – namely, Nature known by Science – we are left without a land and without a body politic.[23]

This book is also not directly concerned with the causal drivers of the Anthropocene and debates over whether responsibility lies with the Enlightenment, with capitalism,[24] with modernity, with mass consumerism, with the organisation, industrialisation and commercialisation of agriculture, with colonialism and imperialism, with economic theory, with the extraction of and dependency upon fossil fuels, with the rise of the military-industrial complex etc.[25] In fact it is often argued that the more narratives there are, 'from many voices and many places, rather than a single narrative from nowhere, from space or from the species', the more the 'black boxes of the Anthropocene discourse' can be opened and repoliticised.[26] Regardless of where authors stand on the allocation of blame or responsibility for the contemporary condition – or whether it is named Anthropocene, Capitalocene[27] or by some other concept, such as Donna Haraway's 'Chthulucene' – the descriptive and analytical conclusions fall into a similar set of ontological framings. Whatever the driving forces, the conclusion is common across them, that there is no longer a separation between culture and nature: there is no longer an 'outside' or an 'away'. What happens 'sticks' with us, like Styrofoam cups or plastic bags that stay in the environment and do not degrade in a human lifetime.[28]

The end of the nature/culture divide is the 'end of the world'[29] as it was conceived in modernity, or by the 'moderns' (as Latour often describes those still clinging to these understandings).[30] Thus the debate, as much as there is one about the Anthropocene, could be seen to be shifting away from a discussion about the existence of the Anthropocene itself, and more about whether 'modernity' as a framework of knowing and governing ever actually existed. Bruno Latour has famously argued that 'We Have Never Been Modern', whereas for other theorists modernity as a rational and successful framework of reasoning is specifically challenged by the appearance of the Anthropocene or the 'intrusion of Gaia'.[31] Latour has, however, been criticised on the basis that, in his view, the Anthropocene, or the entanglement of humanity and nature, is only a recent discovery: plenty of non-consensual pro-environmental voices have been raised in the West[32] and this position also seems to dismiss the existence of a rich non-Western tradition of thought which was never 'modern' in terms of the centrality of the culture/nature divide.[33]

For the consideration of new ways of governing in the Anthropocene, the key point is that the Anthropocene is understood to pose fundamentally different questions about how we can know and how we can govern without the certainties and signposts of modernity. In this sense, the declaration of the Anthropocene marks a very different moment to the Club of Rome's report that launched concerns of environmentalism and over the exhaustion of natural resources in 1974.[34] As Stoner and Melanthopoulos state, it would be difficult to read back contemporary receptions of the Anthropocene into the past century, when the sense of human capacity to regulate environment impacts was much stronger.[35] The power of the Anthropocene lies not merely in the attention to the importance of acting on climate change, but also in the context of responding to climate change without the twentieth century's confidence in modernity. As Rory Rowan notes: 'The Anthropocene is therefore not simply a disputed designation in geological periodization but a philosophical event that has struck like an earthquake, unsettling the tectonic plates of conceptual convention.'[36] Bruno Latour argues:

> What makes the Anthropocene a clearly detectable golden spike way beyond the boundary of stratigraphy is that it is the most decisive philosophical, religious, anthropological and … political concept yet produced as an alternative to the very notions of 'Modern' and 'modernity'.[37]

Isabelle Stengers captures well the shift at stake, in her argument that it is 'as if we were suspended between two histories' both of which describe the world in global and interconnected terms.[38] In one history, governance frameworks are clear, based on clear evidence and with straightforward goals of economic growth and social progress. The other seems much less clear with regard to what governance requires or how to respond to ongoing processes of change. In this sense, as Haraway argues, it makes more sense to see the Anthropocene as a 'boundary event' rather than an epoch: 'The Anthropocene marks severe discontinuities; what comes after will not be like what came before.'[39] Latour eloquently describes what is at stake in this shift beyond the boundary, in the recognition of the Anthropocene:

> What is so depressing in reading the documents of the sub-commission on stratigraphy, is that it runs through exactly the same items you could have read in any 20th century listing of all the glorious things that humans have done in 'mastering nature,' except that today the glory is gone, and both the master and the slave – that is, humans as well as nature – have been melted together and morphed into strange new geological – I mean geostorical – forces.[40]

This is echoed by Nigel Clark's view that 'the Anthropocene – viewed in all its disastrousness – confronts "the political" with forces and events that have the capacity to undo the political, along with every other human achievement, by removing the very grounds on which we might convene and strategize'.[41]

As Bonneuil and Fressoz state, the Anthropocene is not a transitory crisis: 'the Anthropocene is a point of no return. It indicates a geological bifurcation with no foreseeable return to the normality of the Holocene.'[42] Clive Hamilton writes: 'it can no longer be maintained that humans make their own history'.[43] In this respect, the Anthropocene appears to confirm that we are living in an age of 'manufactured uncertainty' or 'manufactured risk', in which societal threats can no longer be seen as external but rather are immanent to social processes[44] undermining the modernist separation between security referent and security threat.[45] It is held that modernity comes up against its own limits with the end of the culture/nature divide: the end of a 'nature' of laws and regularities somehow external to human interaction. The Anthropocene is an era of 'multiple entanglements' according to Stengers, between natural or 'nonhuman' forces and human (in)action, or, as Connolly describes this, of 'entangled humanism'.[46] In the face of this entanglement, continuing to rely on modernist epistemologies, leaving us 'armed only with the results of externalized and universal knowledge' would be, we are informed, the road to 'doom'.[47]

In this more complex, contingent and inter-related world, the 'reductionist' causal connections, generalisations and 'lessons learned', which shaped the governing discourses of modernity, are no longer seen to be tenable.[48] Without the 'outside' of 'nature', counter positioned to the 'inside' of 'culture', new forms of both international and domestic governance necessarily need to be 'reflexive' and 'adaptive'.[49] Isabelle Stengers calls the end of this division the 'intrusion of Gaia', the intrusion of natural forces into every aspect of social and political governance:

> The intrusion of … Gaia, makes a major unknown, which is here to stay, exist at the heart of our lives. This is perhaps what is most difficult to conceptualize: no future can be foreseen in which she will give back to us the liberty of ignoring her. It is not a matter of a 'bad moment that will pass,' followed by any kind of happy ending – in the shoddy sense of 'problem solved.'[50]

Thus, the lexicon of international governance is beginning to carry with it an asserted recognition of the Anthropocene as a fundamental challenge to previous epistemological and ontological assumptions about how we know and how we govern/secure in a world that is no longer perceived as open to linear temporalities of cause-and-effect.[51] As Latour argues, the system of the Anthropocene or Gaia 'is anything but unified or unifying'; it is 'not a cybernetic system designed by an engineer' but the product of multiple dispersed and interacting agencies, so there is no such thing as the 'balance of nature' or the 'wisdom of Gaia'.[52] We have therefore 'permanently entered a post-natural period' where traditional science, based on stability, laws and regularities, can no longer help negotiate the problem: 'Climate scientists have been dragged into a post-epistemological situation that is as surprising to them as it is to the general public – both finding themselves thrown "out of nature".'[53]

The one thing that critical Anthropocene theorists agree on is that there can be no technical fixes. The Anthropocene is not a problem to be solved but an opportunity to be grasped. This drive to affirm the Anthropocene is particularly clear in the field of international relations, where leading theoretical journals, such as the *European Journal of International Relations*, seem keen to flag up critical work that highlights that the Anthropocene should not be confused with the problem of ecology or of climate change and thereby fitted into an extension of traditional modernist international security discourses. For example, Madeleine Fagan argues:

> Ecology offers a reordering of the world, a recreation of the world as a whole, a neutralizing of the threat to logic and sense posed by the anthropocene … This matters for thinking about security because to give the modern subject a home is to secure it; it is to reproduce the claims about universality and particularity that constitute the modern subject.[54]

The Anthropocene challenges international relations' discourses of security and strategic thinking at the most fundamental level of the subject of security itself. Modernist assumptions of securing the human against the world are held to be precisely the problem that needs to be overcome.[55] It is precisely because the Anthropocene is ontopolitically constructed as a critique of modernist discourses of problem-solving that there can be no 'comic faith in technofixes, whether secular or religious'.[56] No pretence of geoengineering solutions 'which will ensure that it is possible to continue to extract and burn, without the temperature rising'.[57] No possibility of fixed relations capable of regulation in the imaginary of 'spaceship Earth'.[58] The idea of a humanist or modernist solution, positing the idea of a 'good Anthropocene'[59] is anathema to those who seek to affirm the Anthropocene as 'after the world of modernity'. As Claire Colebrook states: 'Any "good" Anthropocene would be possible only by way of countless injustices'.[60] The modernist perspective is seen as the 'managerial variant' of the Anthropocene, where the concept could potentially be captured and 'become the official philosophy of a new technocratic and market-oriented geopower':[61]

> Whereas it should mean a call to humility, the Anthropocene is summoned in support of a planetary hubris ... [exemplified by] the Breakthrough Institute, an eco-modernist think-tank that celebrates the death of nature and preaches a 'good anthropocene', one in which advanced technology will save the planet ... sentiments characteristic of early infancy, lie at the basis of such 'post-nature' discourse, participating in the dream of total absorption of nature into the commercial technosphere of contemporary capitalism.[62]

While for Bonneuil and Fressoz eco-modernism smacks of 'early infancy', Clive Hamilton argues that this view of welcoming the Anthropocene epoch with imaginaries of geoengineering is 'reminiscent of Brian's song on the cross at the end of *Monty Python's Life of Brian*'.[63] For others, such as Richard Grusin, the imaginary of the 'heroic agency of geoengineering' is merely another failed attempt to impose 'many of the same masculinist and human-centred solutions that have created the problems in the first place'.[64] Simon Dalby asserts that any attempt to problem-solve in the manner of 'contemporary earth system science syntheses of the human transformation of the biosphere ... [with its] assumption of separation as the starting point for governing a supposedly external realm is now simply untenable.'[65]

In response to this closure, new possibilities are held to be inherent in existing communal forms of living and socio-technological forms of interconnectivity and networked community, building on new ways of making connections and seeing relationships.[66] It is this need for a fluid awareness of relations in their specific and momentary context that has enabled the new modes of governance that will be analysed here. For Anthropocene epistemologies and ontologies, the actual existing reality contains much more possibility and potential than has been traditionally recognised by policy makers and academics.[67] Thus the task is that of engaging more imaginatively with the constantly emerging present, alert to the fact that these relationships need to become a matter of care, attention and opportunity.[68]

'Welcome to the Anthropocene'[69]

This book seeks to explore the ontopolitical discourses that inform and instantiate the new governance practices of the Anthropocene, in the context of a broad demand that we accept that the way we understand the world has to change along with the way in which we act within it. The Anthropocene, in this respect, symbolises more than the threat of global warming – rather global warming is seen as the harbinger of a new awareness of our more humble position in the world: the end of the reassuring assumptions of liberal modernity. To be more precise, it is held that modernity itself was never how we understood it to be. As Bruno Latour has pointed out, modernity was a paradoxical condition, in that the more that we imagined ourselves as subjects separated from the world, developing knowledge of how we could direct and control 'natural' processes, the more humanity grew entangled within these processes. Modernity itself was the midwife to processes that were no longer 'natural' nor amenable to external control or direction by human subjects seen to have all the powers of agency while the rest of the world – of nonhumans – was seen to be merely passive objects of our intentionality.[70] As Timothy Morton argues, the awareness of human-induced climate change and of our dependence upon nonhuman agency has 'done what two and a half decades of postmodernism failed to do, remove humans from the centre of [our] conceptual world'.[71]

The Anthropocene is thus seen to call forth new modes of knowing, engaging and governing. Ways that are less human-centred or anthropocentric. Mapping, Sensing and Hacking, it will be argued here, are three such modes. It is important to realise that these modes challenge the epistemological and ontological framings of modernity, from a position of radical scepticism grounded upon a new set of metaphysical certainties. For authors, like Latour and Morton, it is held to be the advances of science itself, which has revealed the world to be much more entangled and complex than modernity imagined. Science has itself called a halt to modernity in its recognition of the Anthropocene condition. In this respect, according to Morton, global climate change could be seen as a 'saving power' or a candidate for Heidegger's 'last god', enabling humanity to come back to the world after realising the terrible errors of modernist assumptions.[72] This return to the world is not a happy but a humbling one, 'made precisely through our advanced technology and measuring instruments, not through worn peasant shoes and back-to-Nature festivals'.[73] For Ray Brassier it is science itself that has 'uncovered the objective void of being'.[74] For Morton: 'our cognitive powers become self-defeating. The more we know about radiation, global warming, and the other massive objects that show up on our radar, the more enmeshed in them we realize we are ... Increasing science is not increasing demystification.'[75]

The Anthropocene, in fact, appears to be driven by new scientific advances, understood as enabling us to overcome the limitations of modernity. As Morton argues: 'Science itself becomes the emergency break that brings the adventure of modernity to a shuddering halt'.[76] William Connolly focuses on the geo sciences revealing that the Earth's 'planetary force fields' – such as climate patterns, ocean conveyor systems, species evolution, glacier flows and air circulations – have always exhibited self-organising capacities that can go through volatile and rapid changes. Thus the Anthropocene is not new, except in the fact that human impacts amplify the non-linear and interactive effects of these forces in increasingly unpredictable ways.[77]

The Anthropocene thus spells the end of science as the cheerleader for modernist discourses of progress, rather than the end of science per se. Science as uncertainty is seen to free us from narrow or blinkered approaches that assumed a 'happy ending' in the future, based on the assumption of a telos of 'progress'. This is now off the table. It is the present not the future that is important. There is no possibility of debating what the future 'ought' to be like 'when it is the *what is* that obstinately requests its *due*' (emphasis in original).[78] There is no modernist future, regardless of whether we were ever modern or not, because we would need another five Earths 'to push our endless Frontier to the same level of development as North America'.[79]

Perhaps emblematic of this shift is Anna Lowenhaupt Tsing's book, *The Mushroom at the End of the World: On the Possibility of Life in Capitalist Ruins* (2015). Her starting assumption is the end of the modernist dream of progress, based on the division between humanity and nature: 'Without Man and Nature, all creatures can come back to life, and men and women can express themselves without the strictures of a parochially imagined rationality.'[80] The importance of the book as an exemplar of the affirmation of the Anthropocene is that it self-consciously does not set out to be 'a critique of the dreams of modernization and progress', but rather to think past their end; to take up the radical 'imaginative challenge of living without those handrails, which once made us think we knew, collectively, where we were going'.[81] The Anthropocene thus enables us to think 'after failure', 'after progress', 'after the end of the world'.

For Tsing, living with the end of modernist dreams of progress need not be a negative experience. Rather, we can come to realise that modernity itself was a barrier to living fuller lives. Our assumptions of progress, the modernist telos that striving harder would lead to collective betterment, now seem no more emancipatory than religious promises of justice in the afterlife. Precarious and contingent life in modernity's 'ruins' can be empowering and creative, full of new possibilities which modernity foreclosed. As Tsing states:

> Progress is a forward march, drawing other kinds of time into its rhythms. Without that driving beat, we might notice other temporal patterns … agnostic about where we are going, we might look for what has been ignored because it never fit the time line of progress.[82]

Her work, therefore, is constructed as a work of enablement, allowing the reader to make the transition from mourning modernity to embracing its demise:

> I find myself surrounded by patchiness, that is, a mosaic of open-ended assemblages of entangled ways of life, with each further opening into a mosaic of temporal rhythms and spatial arcs. I argue that only an appreciation of current precarity as an earthwide condition allows us to notice this – the situation of the world. As long as authoritative analysis requires assumptions of growth, experts don't see the heterogeneity of space and time, even when it is obvious to ordinary participants and observers … To appreciate the patchy unpredictability associated with our current condition, we need to reopen our imaginations.[83]

The affirmation of the Anthropocene is thus of a world that is fuller, more lively and more entangled than the soulless, simplified and atomised world of modernity. As Quentin Meillassoux argues, the Anthropocene welcomes us to the 'great outdoors',[84] what really exists rather than what exists in the stunted modernist imagination. For Tim Ingold, the question is not how to represent the world but: 'How to turn the world into something "real", how to make the world "present"'.[85] As Tsing argues: 'Precarity means not being able to plan. But it also stimulates noticing, as one works with what is available.'[86] The greatest tragedy would thereby be not the death of modernity in itself but rather the refusal to see beyond this: 'If we end the story with decay, we abandon all hope – or turn our attention to other sites of promise and ruin, promise and ruin.'[87] If we refuse to affirm the

Anthropocene, we are told that we are left only with the choice of nihilistic pessimism or with naively repeating the tragedies of the past. In fact, the Anthropocene is apparently serendipity itself, enabling us to develop just the sensitivities and new ways of affirmative thinking and being that we need to adapt to our new condition:

> What if, as I'm suggesting, precarity *is* the condition of our time – or, to put it another way, what if our time is ripe for sensing precarity? What if precarity, indeterminacy, and what we imagine as trivial are the centre of the systematicity we seek?[88]

In the ruins of modernity there is more life than could possibly have been imagined by modernist human subjects convinced of their separation from the world. Our realisation that we can no longer go on in old, modernist, ways enables us to appreciate rather than fear the Anthropocene condition. Realising our precarious condition brings us back to the world: the Anthropocene is like an unseen force, imposing a new sociability and new set of sensitivities on the basis that we are no longer separate, no longer in control, no longer not interested in other actors and agencies with which we cohabit. The Anthropocene is thereby less a world of doom and gloom and extinction than an invitation to be curious, imaginative, exploratory, playful even … as we shall see.

Ontopolitics

Ontopolitics is a key concept for this book, as the ontological assumptions of the Anthropocene are seen to necessitate new modes of governance. Whereas, for the moderns, politics carved out a separate human sphere of freedom and autonomy in distinction from nature, for the no longer moderns of the Anthropocene the situation is reversed and it is the world itself that shapes and directs the content of politics. As William Connolly has argued, 'every interpretation of political events, no matter how deeply it is sunk in specific historical events, no matter how high the pile of data upon which it sits, contains an ontopolitical dimension.'[89] Importantly: 'Political interpretation is ontopolitical: its fundamental presumptions fix possibilities, distribute explanatory elements, generate parameters within which an ethic is elaborated, and center (or decenter) assessments of identity, legitimacy, and responsibility.'[90]

For Connolly, modernist social and political thought had neglected the ontopolitical assumptions upon which it depended, treating them as a background that could be taken for granted.[91] As considered above, it is precisely these assumptions that are challenged in the Anthropocene. A new set of ontopolitical assumptions are beginning to inform contemporary social and political thought and thus the new modes of governance, which are the subject of this book. If, as Emmanuel Levinas claimed, 'political totalitarianism rests on an ontological totalitarianism',[92] then framing the politics of the Anthropocene to highlight its ontopolitical claims is a vital critical task to enable alternative perspectives to emerge.

The ontopolitics of the Anthropocene privileges the 'is' of the world over the 'ought' of attempts to carve out a separate human space. Modern politics was oriented around the problem of the 'ought', how the world could be governed or organised in ways in which humanity could prosper. The struggle (often broadly construed in terms of a continuum stretching between Left and Right) was also a contestation over forms of knowing and acting in the world. This contestation was cohered around differing assumptions of human nature, such as whether humans were rational or irrational, individualist or collective, and the extent to which states or governing authorities needed to intervene upon this basis. Today, this view of politics as a contestation over the nature of the human and how humanity can best be served is seen to be less central to contemporary concerns, and no longer as the 'be all and end all' of politics.

Perhaps an obvious analogy could be made with how the struggles of the warring kingdoms of Westeros, in the *Game of Thrones* TV series, begin to pale into insignificance in comparison to the looming collective threat posed by the coming of winter and the White Walkers. Like the coming of winter, entry into the epoch of the Anthropocene is held to displace the modernist framework and context of political contestation. Modernist politics assumed that the 'is' of the world would look after itself, i.e. that nature or the environment was just the backdrop or the stage for the great struggle between Left and Right. Today the positions seem to be reversed, winter/ the Anthropocene is seen to push the politics of Left and Right from the foreground to the background. As Nigel Clark argues, 'the impression that deep-seated forces of the earth can leave on social worlds is out of all proportion to the power of social actors to legislate over the lithosphere' (the earth's upper mantle and crust).[93] The relation between humanity and nature appears to be reversed:

> What does it mean to say that life, or the earth, or nature, or the universe are not just constellations of material and energy with which

humans forge connections, but realities upon which we are utterly dependent – in ways that are out of all proportion to life, nature, the earth or the universe's dependence on us?[94]

The reversing of the background and foreground is not entirely politically neutral. In fact, it is the aspirational politics of the Left, in its desire for greater freedom, autonomy and equality in social and economic life and for an increase in material wealth and its broader distribution, which appears to be particularly problematic. As Sara Nelson and Bruce Braun argue: 'In the context of these entanglements it is not clear what autonomy means, politically or ontologically.'[95]

As evinced in the notion of 'immaterial' production and an emphasis on the revolutionary possibilities offered by cognitive and communicative capitalism, the material conditions of this new economy of extractivism and the globalization of manufacturing remained unacknowledged ... The understanding of human potentiality ... depends on a sharp distinction between life and nonlife, human and nonhuman, and the movement's historical analysis and political imagination rely on a knowable, reliable, 'always there' nature that is neither used up nor filled with surprises.[96]

As Jason Moore has illustrated, one of the key problems for those who believe in material progress as the key to human betterment has been that capitalism did not just exploit unpaid labour power but also the productive power of nonhuman labour. Thus, for Moore, it is not only that, as Marx noted, there is a tendency of the rate of profit to fall but there is also a tendency for the rate of 'ecological surplus' to fall,[97] with the depletion of energy and mineral resources.[98] The drive to overcome boundaries to the appropriation of 'cheap nature' as well as 'cheap labour' gave capitalism a productive dynamic not based purely on the invisibility of human labour of unpaid reproduction (highlighted by feminist scholars, like Silvia Federici)[99] but also on the invisibility of nonhuman labour and resources (an invisibility which is now all too visible). What was seen to be the expansion of progress and human potential can be read as actually the extractive machine of capitalism ceaselessly seeking new untapped resources to exploit on the 'cheap'. This form of organising nature has now reached its limits, ironically because of the resistance of nonhuman 'nature' rather than a rebellion of humanity.[100] As Stengers notes: 'Today all Marxist or post-Marxist scripts

must confront a perspective of destruction that Marx could not anticipate ... which deeply perturbs any theory indifferent to the new, dramatic
restriction of our historical horizon.'[101]

Dipesh Chakrabarty argues that 'logically speaking, the climate crisis is
not inherently a result of economic inequalities'; if we had lived in a 'more
evenly prosperous and just world' then 'the climate crisis would have been
worse':

> Our collective carbon footprint would have only been larger – for the
> world's poor do not consume much and contribute little to the pro-
> duction of greenhouse gases – and the climate change crisis would have
> been so much sooner and in a much more drastic way.[102]

Similarly, part of the problem of 'population' is 'due surely in part to
modern medicine, public health measures, eradication of epidemics, the use
of artificial fertilisers, and so on' and therefore 'cannot be attributed in any
straightforward way to a logic of a predatory and capitalist West.'[103] Any
imaginary of capitalism paving the way to socialism as a more progressive
system, as Stengers argues, needs to be rejected on the basis that it 'would
instead herald the perfect socioecological storm which systematic extraction
is now unleashing'.[104]

As Amitav Ghosh asserts, colonialisation can be understood to have held
back climate change: if the European empires had been dismantled earlier,
for example, after the First World War, there is every chance that the
economies of mainland Asia would have accelerated earlier.[105] Thus the
concept of human freedom that developed with the Enlightenment is held
to disappear in the Anthropocene, as it is realised that humankind can never
shed its dependence or transcend its constraints:[106] 'the Anthropocene
challenges the modern definition of freedom, long conceived in opposition
to nature ... A freedom understood in this way sets human emancipation
against nature, against the Earth as a whole.'[107] For Chakrabarty and others,
the problem of global warming and climate change challenges political discourses of progress, based upon social justice and global equality and freedom from oppression: there is a 'growing divergence in our consciousness
of the global – a singularly human story – and the planetary, a perspective
to which humans are incidental.'[108] Nelson and Braun argue that we are
forced to accept that modernist or radical views of human autonomy and
human freedom can no longer be credible today, 'if the Anthropocene
represents the farcical realisation of human autonomy in the form of

planetary devastation – in which the 'production of man by man' appears to lead to his extinction.[109]

Taking a broader approach to problematise modernist politics in its entirety, William Connolly emphasises that the problem is epistemological rather than narrowly 'political' – or to do with capitalism per se. Modernist political frameworks of Left/Right contestation lacked an appreciation of the planetary processes, which are recognised today. While thinkers of the Right and the Left may have fundamentally disagreed over many issues they all shared a 'sociocentrism' or 'human exceptionalism', which placed humans as somehow above and separate from the world. They acted as if social, economic and political processes were all that mattered; that the 'environment' was merely the backdrop to the great human drama of social and political struggle. If the moderns considered changes caused by non-human forces and assemblages, these were considered to be set on a different and slower temporality than that of human or cultural transition and transformations:

> Sociocentrism, in individualist, nationalist, communist, neoliberal, and republican traditions, assumes that a political economy is either in charge of nature, or that the limits nature poses to it are set on long, slow time, or, in a more attenuated version, that if we lift the human footprint nature will settle down into patterns that are benign for us. Given any of these assumptions, questions of agency, explanation, and belonging in practice tend to devolve around attention to internal cultural practices.[110]

As Connolly and many other authors insist, modernist conceptions of politics, of belonging and community, of ethics and ideas of human freedom and human exceptionalism, based on modernist epistemological and ontological assumptions of reason and causal linearity all need to be reformulated and reconsidered. The contemporary consensus is that 'the Anthropocene concept obliges us to embark on a deep reconceptualisation' of the categories and concepts of political science, including the understandings of human agency, of history, of politics and of democracy:[111] 'Yet political theory, stuck in the Holocene, has been slow to recognise the Anthropocene and what it means. Most insights have come from philosophers and sociologists'[112] less tied to the assumptions and binaries of the formal political sphere of states and citizens.

This shift fundamentally alters the nature of politics and governance. Politics is no longer 'all about us' in the sense of what we might think a just or equitable world might be and instead 'all about the world itself'. Stengers captures this nicely in her view that, while the problems of the Anthropocene may be caused by the coupling of the material processes of capitalism and geological forces of nature, the brutal intrusion of the planet or Gaia means that 'Struggling against Gaia makes no sense: it is a matter of learning to compose with her.'[113] Stengers emphasises that 'there is no choice'.[114] This entails:

> cutting the link ... established [in the nineteenth century] between emancipation and what I would call an 'epic' version of materialism, a version that tends to substitute the tale of a conquest of nature by human labor for the fable of Man 'created to have dominion over the earth.' It is a seductive conceptual trick but one that bets on the earth available for this dominion or conquest. Naming Gaia is therefore to abandon the link between emancipation and epic conquest, indeed even between emancipation and most of the significations that, since the nineteenth century, have been attached to what was baptized 'progress.'[115]

For Stengers, the modernist discourse of 'progress' and of the possibility of a 'happy ending' is over, which means that if 'emancipation' is to mean anything today it will be a question of our emancipation from modernist illusions of human exceptionalism. Key to this is paying attention to the reality of the world rather than human imaginaries: 'What it is a matter of being wary of are the simplifications that would still ratify a story of progress, including the one that enables us to see the truth of what we are facing.'[116]

The ontopolitics of the Anthropocene can be simply understood as putting the nature of entangled being at the centre of politics rather than the designs or goals of the human as subject. In this respect, Anthropocene ontopolitics is very different from previous attempts to govern through the knowledge and control over life as constituted through modernist science. Powerful critiques of modernist forms of governing through the sciences of 'life', 'population' or 'race' in the frameworks of biopolitics have been informed by or in response to the work of Michel Foucault.[117] However, in the Anthropocene, as considered above, biopolitics as a form of modernist command-and-control seems particularly inadequate as a way of managing risk and contingency.[118] In contrast to biopolitics, which seeks to govern on the basis of the knowledge of biological or ecological life and its optimisation (variously understood),[119] Anthropocene ontopolitics seeks to govern in the face of the loss of modernist epistemological assumptions:[120] governing thereby seeks to adapt or respond to the world rather than seeking to control or direct it.

Mapping, Sensing and Hacking

Modernist forms of politics assumed that governance could be centrally directed on the basis of 'command-and-control' understandings. Power was understood to operate hierarchically on the basis that knowledge could be centralised and operationalised in universal and linear ways. Traditionally the ways in which governmental power was understood and operationalised have differed with the development of social, historical and productive processes and the outcomes of ideological contestation and political struggle. Perhaps the most influential description of the modes of governmental power has been that of Foucault's analysis of the exercise of authority directly, through 'sovereign power' and in more distributed ways, through 'disciplinary power' through social institutions, and in the form of 'biopower', understood as a more positive attempt to manipulate and develop social and biological forces. As analysed above, the Anthropocene appears to bring to a close the human-centred, subject-centred or anthropocentric understandings of power and governmental agency. The three modes of governance analysed in the rest of this book all depart from a modernist framing and seek to govern adaptively or responsively in ways which increasingly appear to become at home in the Anthropocene condition.

Mapping

The governance mode of Mapping is the first major challenge to modernist forms of knowledge and power, through the shift in focus from the subject of power (the ideas and understanding of governing agencies) to the importance of the object of governance itself. Mapping assumes that causality is non-linear and that knowledge is not universal; in other words, the same external stimulus may produce different responses depending on the social, historical and economic relations of a particular entity or society. It is therefore these internal relations that require tracing or mapping as a precondition for any policy intervention into these processes. In Mapping as a mode of governance, grounded in the ontological assumptions of the

Anthropocene, governance interventions cannot impose or direct outcomes from above but only work indirectly to shape or enable the processes of interactive emergence. Mapping can thus be understood as autopoietic as the process is internally generated: internal or endogenous relations are key to enabling adaptive and effective responses to external stimuli. Mapping approaches of 'bottom-up' immanence therefore inform a wide-range of governing practices and philosophical perspectives, from neo-institutionalist understandings of contingency, context and path-dependencies, to the adaptive cycles and panarchies of ecosystem resilience and the more radical conceptions of assemblage theorists, seeking to map and to understand nested assemblages of non-linear causal chains of emergence.

Sensing

While Mapping is a distinctive governance mode in that it works on the assumption of non-linear causality, Sensing is distinctive in shifting the emphasis of governance from causality to correlation. This is fundamental as Sensing no longer carries the modernist baggage of problem-solving based on understanding the 'root causes' even if these are constructed in complex and non-linear ways. Whereas Mapping can be grasped as autopoietic, as the focus is on self-growth, based on adaptive 'bottom-up' processes of interaction, Sensing can be grasped as homeostatic, seeking to maintain the status quo. Sensing lacks an ontology of depth and works on the surface of appearances, seeking to respond to the emergent effects of processes rather than to intervene at the level of causal chains of understanding. Sensing as a form of governance, based on correlation rather than causation, depends upon the ability to see things in their process of emergence. It is for this reason that new technologies are often crucial to the deployment of Sensing with an imaginary that sensing responses can become increasingly real time, thereby not preventing problems from arising but minimising their impact or disturbance.

Hacking

Hacking as a mode of governance is neither autopoietic nor homeostatic but sympoietic in its understanding that life is entangled from the start. For Hacking it is the process itself that comes first rather than the separations of self and other, subject and object or human and nonhuman. Like Sensing, Hacking lacks a concern with the depth of processes of emergence and of attempting to trace and map causal interconnection, but what sets it apart from Sensing is that Hacking is a much more interactive and affirmative engagement with the unfolding of the Anthropocene. Hacking as a process of sympoiesis seeks to enable the creativity of the Anthropocene rather than merely to resist it or limit its effects.

All three governance modes – Mapping, Sensing and Hacking – reject modernist perspectives of progress and their universal knowledge assumptions as well as the modernist binary divide of culture/nature, seeing the human subject as relationally embedded or entangled rather than as an autonomous rational subject distinct from the world. I would suggest though, that the three modes are distinct in charting the shift from modernist to non-modernist assumptions of the Anthropocene condition. Mapping approaches highlight the importance of adaptation to the risks and threats posed by the Anthropocene and often assume the possibility of governance interventions in processes of emergence. Sensing focuses more on accepting the Anthropocene condition and responding to threats and problems in ways that minimise or efface them, rather than attempting to prevent or solve them in some way. Hacking goes furthest in affirming the opportunities provided by the Anthropocene, encouraging new forms of creative experimentation and in developing a greater awareness of new possibilities.

TABLE 1.1 Modernity, Mapping, Sensing and Hacking

Modernity	rationality	linear causality	culture/nature divide	progress
Mapping	autopoiesis	non-linear causality	depth/immanence	adaptation
Sensing	homeostasis	correlation	surface/effects	responsive-ness
Hacking	sympoieisis	experimenta-tion	entanglement/becoming with	radical openness

Structure of the book

This book is organised in five parts. Part I is this introductory chapter. Part II provides an introduction to the governance mode of Mapping. In Chapter 2, the developing of Mapping as a specific form of governance is analysed through the transition from neoliberal or neo-institutionalist frameworks of differentiation to contemporary approaches of assemblage thinking. Neoliberal thought has classically been concerned with the limits of governance and the unknowability of complex processes of interaction. It is argued that in the late 1970s neoliberalism shifted from the critical margins to informing governmental understandings of different path-dependencies with non-linear outcomes, central to neo-institutionalist policies of development intervention. In the same period, similar understandings of system interaction and emergent outcomes developed in ecosystem theories of resilience and system adaptation. Mapping thus developed as a specific mode of governance based on the importance of internal or endogenous processes of adaptive learning and development and the necessity of intervention, not directly or from the 'top-down' but indirectly, from the 'bottom up'. Chapter 3 draws out the development of Mapping through an attempt to 'drill down' to understand the complex processes of emergence and then increasingly shifting to seeing these limits of depth as a necessary ontological barrier to knowledge, leading to an appreciation of multiple worlds and forms of phenomenological access.

Part III of the book considers the second governance mode of Sensing. Chapter 4 analyses Sensing as a response to the limits of Mapping. Where Mapping focuses on indirect forms of intervention on the basis of an ontology of non-linear or process-based causality, Sensing works on the surface of appearances, on the level of the actual, without causal assumptions. The chapter engages with the alternative forms of knowledge generation through the use of correlation to datafy relations in order for processes of emergence to be seen in real-time. Without causal assumptions, Sensing as a mode of governance thus moves further away from a modernist framework of understanding and lacks a temporality of progress or problem-solving, instead seeking to slow-down or hold-back emergent effects, ameliorating their effects through responsive actions. Chapter 5 draws out these points in relation to one of the key driving forces of Sensing, the development of Big Data analytics. It discusses the epistemological and ontopolitical claims of Big Data as the ability to develop sensing capacities and the use of data-driven discourses of resilience to promote non-modernist understandings of government as self-responsiveness and self-regulation. While Mapping discourses encounter the problem of depth it is suggested that Sensing discourses of the homeostatic modulation of effects encounter the problem of developing alternative possibilities.

Part IV provides an introduction to Hacking as a third form of governance in the Anthropocene. Chapter 6 describes Hacking as an experimental practice seeking to repurpose and re-envision relations. Hacking can be seen as a response to the limits of Big Data Sensing in that rather than passive or automated responses to emergent effects, Hacking discourses seek to engage proactively through new participatory practices, seeing disturbances as opportunities for experimentation rather than merely as problems in need of solutions and for a return to the status quo. Chapter 7 provides a more conceptual framing of Hacking as a distinct governance mode based on an ontology of sympoiesis, of 'becoming with', rather than either an autopoietic or homeostatic framing. Hacking works with the emergent effects, as does Sensing, but seeks to see new creative possibilities through interactive processes. In this way, Hacking is process-based, like Mapping, but is future-oriented, seeing human freedom as not subject-based but process-oriented in enabling the unfolding of change. Whereas both Mapping and Sensing seek to hold back the Anthropocene, Hacking as a mode of governance seeks to affirm and to intensify the process of transformation.

Part V reflects upon the stakes of Anthropocene ontopolitics. Chapter 8 analyses the implications for critique and draws out the distinction between the critiques of modernity on the basis of its alienating and dehumanising framing of the gap between man and nature and the contemporary affirmation of Anthropocene ontopolitics which seeks to reify and intensify this gap rather than to overcome it. This distinction is fundamental for understanding the affirmative power of Anthropocene ontopolitics in its transvaluation of reason into the affirmation of unreason, which no longer resides in human social, political and scientific limitations – the lack of knowledge or understanding of the world, which therefore can potentially be corrected – but in the contingent processes of life itself and therefore forms the ontopolitical grounds for new modes of its governance. Chapter 9 provides a brief summary conclusion of the argument of the book.

Notes

1   I capitalise these terms, when they designate modes of governance.
2   See, further, Chandler, 2014d.
3   Morozov, 2013.
4   See Crutzen and Stoermer, 2000; also Crutzen, 2002; Crutzen and Steffen, 2003.
5   The previous understanding was that earth was in the epoch of the Holocene, which began at the end of the last Ice Age, 12,000 years ago. The Holocene is understood to be an epoch of relative temperature stability, which enabled the flourishing of human progress: the naming of the Anthropocene as a new epoch calls attention to how human impacts on the earth have brought this period of stability to an end. At the time of writing the International

Commission on Stratigraphy had not reached a formal decision on the naming or dating of the Anthropocene as a new epoch.

6 Working Group on the Anthropocene, 2017. These impacts include the emissions of 'greenhouse' gases leading to global warming, the collapse of biodiversity including debate about whether we can speak of a 'sixth extinction', the acidification of the oceans and changes in biogeochemical cycles of water, nitrogen and phosphate. The earth system scientists of the Resilience Centre in Stockholm list nine planetary boundaries: stratospheric ozone depletion; loss of biosphere integrity (biodiversity loss and extinctions); chemical pollution and the release of novel entities; climate change; ocean acidification; freshwater consumption and the global hydrological cycle; land system change; nitrogen and phosphorus flows to the biosphere and oceans; and atmospheric aerosol loading. Four of these are currently operating beyond the safe operating space and two are not yet quantified (Stockholm Resilience Centre, 2017).

7 Latour, 2014; Clark, 2010; Haraway, 2015; Proctor, 2013; Swyngedouw, 2011; Macfarlane, 2016; Bonneuil and Fressoz, 2016.

8 Davies, 2016: p.5.

9 Latour, 2013b: p.77.

10 Any attempt to quantify an ontopolitical shift in understandings via geological markings or historical events is inevitably going to be unsatisfactory as it is impossible to demarcate a change empirically, when the key aspect is the changing interpretation of the facts rather than the facts themselves. It is this interpretative shift that is the subject of this book.

11 Lewis and Maslin, 2015.

12 For discussion, see Bonneuil and Fressoz, 2016: pp.14–18.

13 Ibid.: pp.32–3.

14 Latour, 2013b: p.129.

15 Ghosh, 2016: p.6.

16 Ibid.: p.26.

17 Ibid.: p.36.

18 Bonneuil and Fressoz, 2016: p.21.

19 Morton, 2013: p.99.

20 '…there is no meaningfulness possible in a world without a foreground-background distinction. Worlds need horizons and horizons need backgrounds, which need foregrounds… We have no world because the objects that functioned as invisible scenery have dissolved. (Morton, 2013: p.104)

21 Latour, 2013b: p.4; see also p.63; p.100.

22 Ibid.: p.78.

23 Ibid.: p.125.

24 See Moore, 2015.

25 See the extensive discussion in Bonneuil and Fressoz, 2016, who provide seven, in depth, historical narratives.

26 Bonneuil, 2015: p.29.

27 See Moore, 2016.

28 Morton, 2013: p.1; p.60. As Myra Hird and Alexander Zahara note (2017: p.123) 'waste constitutes perhaps the most abundant and enduring trace of the human for epochs to come'.

29 Ibid.: p.7.
30 See, for example, Latour 1993a; 2010a; 2013a.
31 Morton, 2013: p.19; Stengers, 2015; Ghosh, 2016.
32 Bonneuil and Fressoz, 2016: pp.72–9.
33 Danowski and Viveiros de Castro, 2017.
34 In 1972, hardly any voices challenged the modernist view that the crisis could be managed through predictive modeling and improvements in global governance, enabling a new 'global equilibrium', 'a condition of ecological and economic stability that is sustainable far into the future' (Club of Rome, 1972: p.24); Friedrich Hayek and C S Holling (both of whom will be considered in the following chapter) were two of the very few dissenting theorists who contested what they saw to be the 'hubris' at play in imagining that a stable equilibrium was possible (Walker and Cooper, 2011: p.149).
35 Stoner and Melanthopoulos, 2015: p.20.
36 Rowan, 2014: p.447
37 Latour, 2013b: p.77
38 Stengers, 2015: p.17.
39 Haraway, 2016: p.100.
40 Latour, 2013b: pp.76–7. As Claire Colebrook notes (2017: p.16), discussion of the Anthropocene, 'lends more weight to Walter Benjamin's claim that every document of civilization is a document of barbarism.'
41 Clark, 2014: p.28.
42 Bonneuil and Fressoz, 2016: p.21
43 Hamilton, 2015: p.35.
44 Giddens, 1994: p.4; Beck, 2009b.
45 Baldwin, 1997; Chandler, 2010.
46 Connolly, 2017.
47 Latour, 2013b: p.9.
48 See, for example, Mitchell, 2009: pp.ix–xiii; Prigogine and Stengers, 1985; Cilliers, 1998.
49 Voss and Bornemann, 2011; Berkes et al., 2003.
50 Stengers, 2015: p.47.
51 See Fagan, 2017.
52 Latour, 2013b: p.81.
53 Ibid.: pp.81–2.
54 Fagan, 2017: p.308.
55 See Hamilton, 2017.
56 Haraway, 2016: p.3.
57 Stengers, 2015: p.8; see also Stengers, 2017: 'whatever the geoengineering method, it would require that we keep extracting and mobilizing the massive necessary resources, to keep on feeding the climate manipulating machine...' (p.384).
58 Latour, 2013b: p.66.
59 See, for example, Revkin, 2014.
60 Colebrook, 2017: p.18.
61 Bonneuil and Fressoz, 2016: p.xiii; p.49.
62 Ibid.: p.86.
63 Hamilton, 2015: p.41; see also Hamilton, 2013.

64 Grusin, 2017: p.ix.
65 Dalby, 2017.
66 For example, Gibson Graham and Roelvink, 2010.
67 See, for example, Sharp, 2011; Grosz, 2011: p.77, p.183.
68 In this regard, the implications of the Anthropocene accord closely with perspectives forwarded by a wide range of critical theorists associated with posthuman, new materialist and speculative realist approaches among others (for example, Braidotti, 2013; DeLanda, 2006; Coole and Frost, 2010; Barad, 2007; Bennett, 2010; Connolly, 2013; Harman, 2010).
69 See Economist, 2011.
70 Latour, 1993a; 2004a.
71 Morton, 2013: p.181.
72 Ibid.: p.21.
73 Ibid.: p.36.
74 Brassier, 2007: p.25.
75 Morton, 2013: pp.160–1.
76 Ibid.: p.21.
77 Connolly, 2017: p.4.
78 Latour, 2013b: p.126.
79 Ibid.
80 Tsing, 2015: p.vii.
81 Ibid.: p.2.
82 Ibid.: p.21.
83 Ibid.: pp.4–5.
84 Meillassoux, 2008: p.50.
85 Ingold, 2015: p.135.
86 Tsing, 2015: p.278.
87 Ibid.: p.18.
88 Ibid.: p.20.
89 Connolly, 1995: p.1.
90 Ibid.: p.2.
91 Ibid.: pp.2–4
92 Cited in Campbell, 2005: p.131.
93 Clark, 2010: Kindle location 220–1.
94 Ibid: Kindle location 917–18.
95 Nelson and Braun, 2017: p.224.
96 Ibid.: p.229.
97 Highlighted as a 'metabolic rift' by McKenzie Wark (2015; p.xiv): 'where one molecule after another is extracted by labor and technique to make things for humans, but the waste products don't return so that the cycle can renew itself.'
98 See, Moore, 2015: p.226.
99 See, for example, Federici, 2012.
100 See discussion in Read, 2017.
101 Stengers, 2017: p.383.
102 Chakrabarty, 2015: p.49; see also Chakrabarty, 2009.
103 Ibid.: p.50.
104 Stengers, 2017: p.387.

105   Ghosh, 2016: pp.109–10.
106   Ibid.: p.119.
107   Bonneuil and Fressoz, 2016: p.40.
108   Chakrabarty, 2015: p.55.
109   Nelson and Braun, 2017: p.233.
110   Connolly, 2017: p.20.
111   Hamilton et al., 2015b: p.9
112   Ibid.
113   Stengers, 2015: p.53.
114   Ibid.: p.58.
115   Ibid.
116   Ibid.: p.67.
117   See, for example, Foucault, 1981, also 2003; 2008; for more recent and contrasting frameworks, see, Agamben, 1998; 2005; Esposito, 2008; 2013; Mbembe, 2003.
118   See, for example, Dalby, 2013.
119   For an excellent introduction see Lemke, 2011.
120   As Elizabeth Povinelli notes (2017: p.54) 'Certain tokens (human animals, nonhuman animals, plants, rocks and minerals…) of certain types (life, nonlife) no longer seem as self-evidently distinct as they once did… we might say that the disclosure of this ontological world is being redisclosed by the emergence of a new condition of knowledge.'

PART II
Mapping

2

AFTER NEOLIBERALISM

Mapping assemblages

Introduction

Mapping is perhaps the most analysed of the three modes of governance, heuristically drawn out in this book as illustrative of the ontopolitics of the Anthropocene. While the critique of, and distance from, modernist governance assumptions is clear in the other two modes, Mapping as a mode of governance has a more conceptually mixed trajectory, which takes discourses of Mapping from neoliberal critiques of classical liberal modernist assumptions through to the contemporary philosophical concerns of computational assemblages and object-oriented ontology. This chapter thereby analyses the development of Mapping as a mode of governance, starting with a brief engagement with the neoliberal critique of modernist assumptions of the human subject and of rationalist claims to knowledge and the development of this framework of thinking in the field of systems ecology and philosophically through the approach of assemblage theory. The next chapter analyses in more depth the debates around Mapping as a mode of governance in the international sphere, in which the epistemological limits to intervening in non-linear processes are at the heart of policy concerns.

The first point that should be established is that Mapping has little in common with traditional cartography; in fact, it is an explicit critique of this approach to the conceptualisation of both time and space, viewing these as outcomes of relational processes rather than as the containers in which they operate. J. B. Harley, in his influential work, which helped establish the field of critical cartography, accurately describes the limited nature of mapping in modernity with its emphasis on the 'true' map:[1] 'Its central bastions were measurement and standardization and beyond there was a "not cartography" land where lurked an army of inaccurate, heretical, subjective, valuative, and ideologically distorted images.'[2] For critical approaches to cartography, 'the map is an authoritarian image', removing life and context, and thus facilitating managerial, bureaucratic and autocratic modes of governance, distanced from the complex reality on the ground.[3] For Latour, the map as an 'immutable mobile' was key to the homogenising and universalising drive of modernity, enabling the abstraction of knowledge and the creation of 'objective' space:

> Even the very notion of scale is impossible to understand without an inscription or a map in mind. The 'great man' is a little man looking at a good map. In Mercator's frontispiece Atlas is transformed from a god who carries the world into a scientist who holds it in his hand![4]

Mapping in modernity constituted space as an empty container filled with distinct autonomous parts, side-by-side as separate entities, without context or relation: it created a fictional world amenable to subject-centred human rule.[5] As Benjamin Bratton states:

> Lines that are linked, folded, and looped become a frame, keeping things in or out … The modern nation-state is itself also [a] function of a cartographic projection that conceives the Earth as a horizontal plane filled with various allotments of land

thus there is 'no stable geopolitical order without an underlying architecture of spatial subdivision'.[6] Mapping was thereby a process of 'emptying out' space of its constitutional relational dynamics and its replacement by a 'universal spatial order based on mathematical formalization and geographic interchangeability': a 'groundless materialism' of 'false equivalences' that could be 'divided up like an algebraic equation'.[7]

Mapping conceptualised as a mode of governance, grounded upon the ontopolitics of the Anthropocene, is very different to this modernist understanding. Rather than the two-dimensional flat or universal space of modernity, Mapping develops an understanding of space as a product of inter-relationality. Therefore, as Doreen Massey noted: 'we understand space as the sphere of the possibility of the existence of multiplicity in the sense of contemporaneous plurality; as the sphere in which distinct trajectories coexist; as the sphere therefore of coexisting heterogeneity'.[8] For Mapping as a mode of governance, space, actively produced through plural interaction, is understood as a relational outcome, which can be mapped only through seeking to concretise it as a specific or unique set of contingent relations.

In this sense, following from Kitchin and Dodge, Mapping is not seen as a fixed or objective representation of the world but as an iterative and processual attempt to visualise a particular set of relationships to facilitate problem-solving.[9] Rather than abstracting from the world – as if a single map could be 'viewed as a universal and essential solution to a range of questions (that there can be a "best" or "most accurate" map that all people understand and use in the same way to address a range of problems)'[10] – mapping is seen as deconstructing universal forms of representation and causality, bringing knowing closer to reality. Mapping is thus conceived here as processual rather than as representing fixed points or relations. Where this framing differs from that of Kitchin and Dodge is that the relational problems addressed in mapping are not merely spatial but also temporal. Mapping as narrative tracing can deal with relations in time as well as space.[11] Mapping becomes central in the Anthropocene precisely in recognition of the appreciation of relationality and differentiation.

Mapping is therefore an important governance mode to grasp as it reverses the imaginary of classical liberal assumptions of universal or flat 'Newtonian' space and instead emphasises the spatial, contextual and relational development of social, economic and political institutions, ecosystems and, in its logical development, all entities and assemblages.[12] It is opposed to reductionist understandings of the world, which empty it of relationality and historical specificity. Mapping has thus powerfully entered social and political theorising to explain difference and non-linear outcomes, for example, why the introduction of markets or democracy might make problems of conflict or development more intractable, or how social and political institutions affect the impact of social and environmental changes. Rather than taking appearances for granted and assuming the power of agential forces (either human or nonhuman) or properties of fixed entities, pragmatic, institutional and mapping approaches see these appearances as concealing the work of relation and translation.

This chapter analyses Mapping as the first governance mode of the Anthropocene as it develops through a clear and well-articulated critique of modernist or linear understandings of governance and provides a field for negotiation and experimentation in terms of what it might mean to govern without the clear goals and top-down mechanisms of 'command-and-control' or assumptions of universal or linear frameworks of cause-and-effect. Key to Mapping is the notion of 'emergence': the understanding that causality is not the unfolding of fixed essences or relationships but a process of complex interaction in which outcomes are non-linear. Non-linearity means that outcomes are mediated, i.e. that they depend not merely on 'inputs' into the system but rather how these inputs, in terms of information, interaction, system disturbances etc., are perceived, understood and responded to. Mapping thereby develops as the study of the internal relations and interactions of the object of policy intervention (in the sphere of international relations this object would be states or societies subject to policy interventions in the diverse spheres of economic, political, social and environmental problems). Mapping bears the clear legacies of its modernist heritage and is very much premised on assumptions of governmental agency. However, this agency is no longer exercised from the 'top-down' but the 'bottom-up'. In neoliberal or neo-institutionalist thought, the mapping of these relations and interactions is often termed 'process-tracing' or the charting of 'path-dependencies', to reveal the contingent nature of interactive processes and the possibilities for intervening to adjust or manipulate these.

This chapter is organised in two main sections. The first provides the reader with an introduction to neoliberal thought as a critique of modernist universal assumptions of knowledge and of the potential for governance, through direct or 'top-down' intervention based on linear understandings of causality, i.e. that the same policy inputs will lead to the same policy outcomes. Mapping comes into being through the understanding that the object of governance needs to be grasped in its historical and sociological specificity. It is the internal relations, or the way that states and societies are 'wired', that is key to how they respond to international policy interventions. Mapping is an attempt to grasp this specificity. The second section then examines the extension of this framework from a focus on subjectivity and choice-making to the workings of life itself, perhaps most widely articulated in terms of second-order cybernetics and the approach of assemblage theory, where the focus is upon endogenous system-interactions in response to external disturbances. Here Mapping as a science is developed in the field of systems ecology, most famously in the work of C. S. Holling on ecological resilience, the adaptive cycle and nested panarchy. The latter part of this section introduces the reader to more contemporary approaches to

Mapping as articulated in assemblage theory and object-oriented ontologies in order to highlight the problem of ontological depth, which will be further engaged with in Chapter 3.

Mapping – governing non-linearity

Mapping, as a mode of governance, is not novel in its articulation of limits, or in its scepticism of universal knowledge or linear causality. As Foucault states, all liberal forms of governing require the articulation of internal limits to rule as part of the process of reflective self-knowledge of what it means to govern – the construction of the limits to knowledge or to governance is inseparable therefore from a study of what it means to govern in a liberal way.[13] What is distinct about Mapping is that non-linear or entangled causality is no longer seen as merely constituting the limit to the world of governmental reason but instantiates the basis of governmental reason itself. This only becomes possible through a number of transformations and inversions in neoliberal reasoning, particularly in relation to the key sphere through which limits were internalised or brought into governmental reason: that of political economy, held to produce its own parallel mechanisms of 'truth' as a limit to those generated by liberal governmental reason.[14]

Thereby Mapping, which focuses on tracing non-linear processes and interactions, can be seen as a distinctive mode of governance. This way of grasping contingent relations as an object of governance and integrating non-linearity into governmental reasoning is often understood as originating in neoliberal constructions of the limits to 'command-and-control' governance agency. These limits were established on the basis of a challenge to the social and historical abstractions of classical liberal or modernist political thought, which was seen to exclude contingency and to assume universal, rational and linear modes of reasoning on the basis of the fixed laws of nature and understandings of linear causality. It is thereby useful to trace the emergence of non-modern conceptions of governance through engaging with the internal development of, and transformations within, neoliberal discourse as neoliberal approaches moved from the position of marginal critique to becoming an important operating methodology of governance: 'actually existing neoliberalism'.[15]

Mapping as a limit to governing

Empirically, the rise of neoliberal and neo-institutionalist understandings in the social sciences, especially in political economy, can be seen as an ideological response to the extensions of state intervention from the 'top-down' in order to deal with the economic and social crisis of the inter-war period, the New Deal in the US, Keynesianism in the UK and, of course, the totalising Stalinist and Nazi regimes that came to power in Russia and Germany.[16] Neoliberalism, as a response, cohered theoretically in the post-war period, suggested that top-down interference could only lead to the erosion of liberal freedoms. Neoliberal thought did not initially articulate a governing methodology, but rather argued for the limits of governmental knowledge. Classical neoliberal formulations argued that the knowledge necessary for policy interventions in interactive and entangled life was not of the type acquired under the modernist sciences with their assumptions of universal regularities of cause-and-effect. It was only in the late 1970s and early 1980s that rather than separating the realms of governmental reason (governing over rational and autonomous subjects of rights and interests) and an external realm of unknowable and ungovernable interactions (the social and economic sphere, subject to laissez-faire non-intervention), neoliberalism brought interaction and contingency into governmental reason itself.[17]

The driving concern of Friedrich von Hayek, often considered the archetypal neoliberal theorist, was the need to counteract the Keynesian influence of state-led development perspectives. These were seen as dangerous approaches to governing intervention in the market, which could reinforce the claims of socialist and communist parties, seeking power on the basis of the possibility of a state-led transformation of socio-economic conditions.[18] For Hayek, knowledge of reality was not that of scientific and technological laws but other forms of adaptive knowledge learnt by imitation and cultural transmission:

> Rules for his [man's, the individual's] conduct which made him adapt what he did to his environment were certainly more important to him than 'knowledge' about how other things behaved. In other words: man has certainly more often learnt to do the right thing without comprehending why it was the right thing, and he still is often served better by custom than understanding.[19]

Hayek argued that there was no relationship between technical and scientific progress and liberal modernist assumptions of governmental reason, which assumed that technical and scientific knowledge provided government with a greater ability to control or direct policy outcomes.[20] While Cartesian or Newtonian imaginaries of fixed separations might work for the development of abstract technical and scientific 'laws' with some (although limited) application in the natural sciences, the social world was not amenable to understanding through such conceptual fabrications and crude tools of reasoning.[21] In the face of 'real' interactive and entangled processes, modernist frameworks thus vastly overrated the power of human reasoning.[22]

For Hayek and classical neoliberal thought, while governments were denied access to knowledge of interactive and interconnected processes, the market was able to indirectly make accessible the complex interactions of socio-economic life. The market (as the 'truth' of contingent interactive and epistemologically inaccessible life) was idealised as the intermediary connecting local and specific knowledges, through prices as indicators. Prices played a fundamental role of revealing or giving access to the plural reality of entangled life and also acting as a guide to future behaviour – how one should adapt to and learn through this reality. No theory or external knowledge was required to learn the 'truths' revealed by the price mechanism. Hayek argued that 'the unavoidable imperfection of man's knowledge and the consequent need for a process by which knowledge is constantly communicated and acquired' depended upon market signals, interconnections and outcomes, which demonstrated 'how a solution is produced by interactions of people each of whom possesses only partial knowledge'.[23]

The inability to know complex processes was seen to be a major barrier to any plan for government policy intervention within the social order. Mapping thereby first develops as a conceptual schema not for governing or intervening but precisely the opposite: as a case against governance interference. This case was built upon the understanding of immanent and self-organising processes without a conscious designer, planner or controller. It was emergent interaction, which was key to the social order and the long processes of cultural and societal interaction, establishing contextual norms and rules through trial and error over time. This is captured well in the key concept of 'path-dependencies': endogenous and self-reinforcing feedback loops of social interaction, which can lead to very different social and institutional outcomes, which, once established or stabilised, are held to be very difficult to overcome.

Mapping and difference

Hayek sought to introduce difference as ontologically prior to universality and to emphasise the non-linearity of human socio-political organisation on the basis of interactive evolutionary characteristics, which become self-amplifying to produce different regimes of order. In his *The Sensory Order: An Inquiry into the Foundations of Theoretical Psychology* (1952) he emphasised the importance of understanding human subjects themselves as unique, differentiated and emergent outcomes of complex evolutionary processes.[24] According to Hayek, behavioural responses depended less on the universal 'reality' we were confronted with than on the previous psychological pre-conditioning of our minds.[25] Human consciousness, in fact, prevented engagement with the world in a universal reasoned and rational way.[26]

Just as individuals were held to respond in differential non-linear ways, which fed-back and magnified differences in behavioural responses, so too did nations and states, depending upon their endogenous eco-social conditions. For neoliberal development economists, these path-dependencies meant that, even if the world was becoming more interdependent and globalised, the impacts of these universalising tendencies would be non-linear – differences in eco-social developments would be magnified rather than becoming ameliorated.[27] For neoliberal theorising, all distinct systems could self-reproduce different forms of emerging order despite seemingly universal starting conditions. Interactive and iterative processes meant that small differences could over time produce different socio-economic orders – in the same way as evolution produced differences in species if they were isolated from each other, such as Darwin's finches on the Galapagos.

Neoliberal understandings of the endogenous production of order developed not to guide policy governance, in terms of the need to intervene in the interactive social processes, but to justify and legitimise international inequalities on the basis of cultural and eco-social differences, held to reproduce problematic path dependencies that prevented societies from rationally adapting to market signals. As John R. Commons described institutional economics back in 1936, it was based on understanding the importance of social and cultural mediation – 'man's relationship to man' – which was ignored in classical liberal economic theory, 'based on man's relation to nature', assuming an abstract, universal, rational, autonomous subject.[28] Commons suggested that there was a 'nationalistic theory of value': that these national collective institutions meant that it was a fiction to think of the market as universal in its operation; as much of a fiction as the belief in the universal individual subject of classical liberal political and economic theory:

> Even the individual of economic theory is not the natural individual of biology and psychology: he is that artificial bundle of institutes known

as a legal person, or citizen. He is made such by sovereignty which grants to him the rights and liberties to buy and sell, borrow and lend, hire and hire out, work and not work, on his own free will. Merely as an individual of classical and hedonistic theory he is a factor of production and consumption like a cow or slave. Economic theory should make him a citizen, or member of the institution under whose rule he acts.[29]

Commons therefore stressed that rather than treating humans as automatic pursuers of fixed interests, real life behaviour had to be understood as shaped by institutional forms, especially those of custom and social norms.[30] Individuals freely and rationally made choices and decisions but on the basis of their cultural contexts and understanding. Individual will is both an act of volition and conscious rational choice but also a product of historical and social context, shaped and constructed on the basis of existing or habitual norms and values.[31]

The work of Commons and other institutional economists, on the differential mapping of contextual relations, was developed further by Herbert Simon, who directly challenged the assumptions of the rational decision-making capacity of the classical liberal subject, dethroning the autonomous rational subject – *homo œconomicus* – from economic rational choice theory. In his argument, there was no such thing as perfect information or perfect rationality, merely 'bounded rationality' where not all the facts can be known or all the possible options considered. The decisions made with 'bounded rationality' were still rational, i.e. made on the basis of a freely willed conscious decision, but they no longer resulted in furthering the collective good or in optimal outcomes. This critique of the rationality of the classical liberal subject was to have immensely powerful consequences, in being the intellectual basis upon which the governance mode of Mapping – tracing the difference that differences make – could be instituted.

The crucial facet of Mapping for neoliberal institutionalism is that differences in outcomes can be understood as agential – conscious, subjective choices – rather than as structurally imposed outcomes. The important research focus is then the relations and interaction between the individuals making the decisions or choices and the institutional frameworks (formal and informal) determining or structuring these choices. Choices, which appeared to be irrational or suboptimal, were understood firstly in terms of institutional blockages at the level of custom, ideology and ideas and then in terms of the formal institutional blockages, the incentives and opportunities available to enable other choices. The key to the self-responsibilisation of the neoliberal subject was therefore not the liberal assumption of rational autonomy, presupposing equality, but the neoliberal view that this 'autonomy' explained differential outcomes, presupposing and reifying inequality.[32] As Michel Foucault noted, the work of these neoliberal or neo-institutionalist theorists was not primarily concerned with economic theory but was closely tied to sociological framings and drew on legal and historical problematics, raising 'a whole series of problems that are more historical and institutional than specifically economic.'[33]

Mapping was transformed once it became a governmental practice of 'actually existing neoliberalism'; from an epistemological problematic of the inability to know a world of complex interaction into an ontopolitical problematic of knowing and governing in a world that was seen as immune to modernist 'command and control' conceptions of power. Where political programmes of intervention through social or political engineering posited social differences as amenable to 'top-down' change, neoliberal approaches stressed agential choice in concrete conditions. It was precisely the agential nature of choice-making which made developmental processes non-linear or unpredictable. Thus the critique of the modernist ontology of fixed relations in the external environment was intimately tied to conceptions of distributed agency. While, for neoliberal frameworks, the focus was upon explaining (and justifying) socio-economic differences and inequalities, as will be analysed here, this sensitivity to agency and interaction as drivers of difference and contingent or non-linear outcomes is central to the development of Mapping as a mode governance grounded in the ontopolitics of the Anthropocene.

Mapping and policy intervention

Neoliberal approaches were only confronted with the need to be responsible for policy outcomes after the gradual implosion of the Left/Right framework of politics, and the post-war consensus that supported this, in the late 1970s and 1980s. It is in this period that 'actually existing' neoliberalism developed as a set of understandings of how contingency might be governed. Perhaps the clearest expression of the problem of adapting neoliberal understandings to policy intervention is that articulated by Nobel Prize-winning economist and neoliberal World Bank policy advisor Douglass North. North acutely posed the dilemma: 'Hayek was certainly correct that our knowledge is always fragmentary at best … But Hayek failed to understand that we have no choice but to undertake social engineering'.[34]

Neoliberal thought found 'social engineering' deeply problematic as the policy interventions of governmental power necessarily appeared to imply the need for knowledge of how social processes operated and the development of instrumental means-ends understandings in support of promised policy outcomes.

Mapping was now no longer merely articulating processes of differential development but was to become a mechanism for tracing these relational interactions and for enabling interventions able to redirect these processes. Mapping was to become vital for the success of neoliberalism as a mode of governance. If the problems were the social, economic and ideational path-dependencies that resulted in sub-optimal choice-making then Mapping was to carve out a sphere through which these processes could be 'corrected'. Thus for North:

> Understanding the cultural heritage of a society is a necessary condition for making 'doable' change. We must have not only a clear understanding of the belief structure underlying the existing institutions but also the margins at which the belief system may be amenable to changes that will make possible the implementation of more productive institutions.[35]

This active and interventionist framing of neoliberalism has been analysed well by Foucauldian governmentality theorists, and others, who have described these forms of regulatory and technical intervention, extending the role of the state in areas of socio-cultural life held to be the preconditions shaping the environmental and ideational context for social and economic decision-making.[36] These new indirect forms of intervention necessitated an understanding of deeper and deeper sets of relational interaction: and thus Mapping as a mode of governance was consolidated. In fact, it could be argued that this mode of indirect governance intervention, on the basis of building adaptive capacity, is so well established today that it is rarely considered as a neoliberal construct, but rather a pragmatic recognition of the determining role of contextual, institutional and cultural realities.

In the international sphere this shift was broadly consolidated in the last years of the 1990s, with greater disillusionment with universalist or 'liberal' approaches suggesting that Western or international actors could resolve problems of development, democracy and peace through the export of liberal institutions. As policy-makers shifted away from understandings of the ease with which liberal values and institutions could be exported, so they discovered the importance of societal-interactions and the contexts in which local agencies operated on the ground. In response to the so-called 'Liberal Peace' approach,[37] neoliberal or neo-institutionalist approaches argued instead for Mapping as a governing methodology, clearly expressed, for example, in Roland Paris' book *At War's End*. [38] Paris argued that the export of liberal institutional frameworks could not be expected to work as a 'quick fix' when the deeper relations of interaction within these societies were not compatible with their operation. Any lack of fit would potentially result in unintended and illiberal outcomes.[39] Thus institutional and socio-cultural interactions were seen as prior concerns to be mapped and addressed to enable any 'translation' of Western institutional forms.[40]

Mapping approaches thereby sought to understand problems as a result of maladaptive dependencies or blockages to system adaptivity. Therefore, external governance interventions sought to map social, cultural and institutional interactions and effects in order to design interventions into these internal processes. Mapping was able to become the first new governance mode, based on the non-modern assumptions of the Anthropocene, as this approach could easily cut across the nature-culture divide, considering ever more aspects which shaped interactive outcomes to explain why some societies were better able to cope with problems of conflict, disaster and social and environmental change than others. This process of including more and more factors has extended to trace a wide range of emergent outcomes, which were previously excluded as 'natural'. Thus, it is common today to argue that disasters and 'natural' catastrophes have, throughout history, had endogenous social roots, being products of human decision-making and non-linear path dependencies.[41] It is for this reason that the United Nations, in 2009, voted to change the designation of the 'International Day for Natural Disaster Reduction' to remove 'natural' from the title.

Under the auspices of the Anthropocene, international organisations such as the UN, the World Bank and the IMF have been central to bringing Mapping understandings of assemblage to bear in the formulation of extensive good governance regulations, on the basis that 'natural disasters' are contingent products of internal systems of socio-economic and political relations.[42] For example, the 2005 Hyogo Agreement and 2015 Sendai Agreements brought disaster risk awareness into mainstream governmental planning processes, on the basis of the need to think less linearly about planning, development and construction, education, social welfare and other measures, which previously had not taken into account the unintended consequences of their approaches. One of the most interesting aspects of the Sendai preparations was the argument that disaster risk reduction was itself a problematic concept and that, instead of risk reduction, policy-thinking should shift to the proper recognition and integration of emergent effects, the argument being that risk cannot be 'reduced' as all actions have interactive outcomes that need to be assessed and calculated: thus the new paradigm is that of disaster risk 'management', in recognition of the relational embeddedness of all policy actions.[43]

Mapping as assemblage theory

Mapping as a set of immanent or endogenous understandings of non-linear outcomes perhaps receives its clearest conceptualisation in the approach of assemblage theory, which is seen to move 'away from the anthropocentrism' of modernist thought.[44] In international theorising, assemblage theory has become increasingly discussed as a critical methodology focusing upon immanent and emergent understandings of causation.[45] Philosopher Manuel DeLanda argues that a theory of interactive assemblages (and thus of Mapping as a mode of governance) can be derived from ideas dispersed across the work of Gilles Deleuze and Felix Guattari.[46] Assemblage theory is understood as overcoming scientific framings, which tend to either focus on the parts (reductionism) or the wholes (structuralism) rather than interactions and relations. As Ben Anderson et al. state:

> By beginning from the claim that 'relations are exterior to their terms', assemblage thinking allows us to: foreground ongoing processes of composition across and through different human and non-human actants; rethink social formations as complex wholes composed through a diversity of parts that do not necessarily cohere into seamless organic wholes; and attend to the expressive powers of entities.[47]

The conceptualisation that 'relations are exterior to their terms', derived from Deleuze, is conceptually central as relations are not reduced to mere intermediaries between autonomous entities but neither are entities constituted or fully determined by their relations. Relations are the key to the understanding of the contingent emergent effects of interaction. DeLanda, the leading theorist taking Deleuze's work further in this area, argues that the key to non-linear understandings (and thereby the precondition for Mapping) is the ontopolitical assumption that the internal organisation of an assemblage or entity is more important that the external or extrinsic factors, which 'are efficient solely to the extent to which they take a grip on the proper nature and inner processes of things'. One and the same external set of policies or causal actions 'may produce very different effects'.[48]

This point is the cornerstone for Mapping as a mode of governance grounded on the ontopolitics of the Anthropocene. If developments, whether societal, economic or environmental, were the outcomes of complex interplays between different and overlapping processes of interaction and contingency, policy interventions would make little sense as the process would be too complex to make meaningful intervention possible. Turning Mapping from a framework of knowledge scepticism into a policy approach of governance intervention methodologically required the construction of a conceptual division between the internal processes within the assemblage and the external stimuli or information, which were necessarily processed and adapted to in contingent ways. It would necessarily be the internal relations, which were open to mapping as a methodology of understanding and for intervention to shape outcomes. For this reason, some form of assemblage thinking was necessary for actually existing neoliberalism to develop as a coherent mode of governmental reason. As we will see in later chapters, analysing the modes of Sensing and Hacking, this view of internal relations as the key determinant to outcomes is distinctive to Mapping as a mode of governance.

Ecological resilience

The framing of assemblage thinking which has been perhaps most instrumental in facilitating and cohering Mapping approaches, especially in the terminology of resilience, has been ecologist C. S. Holling's work on complex interaction in the field of ecology. Jeremy Walker and Melinda Cooper, in a well-cited article on the genealogy of resilience, emphasise the interconnections between the neoliberal thought of Friedrich Hayek and the assemblage approach of ecological systems theory developed by Holling, noting that: 'Holling and Hayek, writing in the early 1970s, were simultaneously preoccupied by questions of epistemic limits to prediction and assertions of ecological limits to growth.'[49] Thus Mapping as a mode of governance develops and gains coherence through parallel discussions in ecology, considering how ecosystems' relations of interaction enable them to withstand or adapt to external pressures.

Holling, in his path-breaking 1973 paper, 'Resilience and Stability of Ecological Systems', distinguished 'ecological resilience' from traditional understandings of 'engineering resilience'.[50] For Holling:

> If we are examining a particular device designed by the engineer to perform specific tasks under a rather narrow range of predictable external conditions, we are likely to be more concerned with consistent nonvariable performance in which slight departures from the performance goal are immediately counteracted. A quantitative view of the behaviour of the system is, therefore, essential. With attention focused upon achieving constancy, the critical events seem to be the amplitude and frequency of oscillations. But if we are dealing with a system profoundly affected by changes external to it, and continually confronted by the unexpected, the constancy of its behaviour becomes less important than the persistence of the relationships. Attention shifts, therefore, to the qualitative and to questions of existence or not.[51]

Whereas 'engineering resilience' was concerned with quantitative measuring, derived from classical physics understandings of fixed relations, 'ecological resilience' was more concerned with the qualitative nature of changing relationships within a system. The assumption being that systems are likely to be 'transient' or changing all the time, rather than operating around a fixed or 'natural' equilibrium that would be 'returned' to.[52]

Not only did Holling question the idea of a natural equilibrium, he fundamentally challenged the dominant idea that space was a pre-existent universal container, in which causal relations operated in a linear fashion.[53] As in the discussion above, regarding the neoliberal framing of difference, ecological theorising sought to distinguish between different autonomous systems. Holling therefore emphasised that it was vital to 'recognize that the natural world is not very homogeneous over space, as well, but consists of a mosaic of spatial elements with distinct biological, physical, and chemical characteristics that are linked by mechanisms of biological and physical transport.'[54] Thus for understandings of ecological resilience, the differences of context make all the difference: there could be no universal understanding of causal interaction nor of the outcomes of policy intervention, as the internal relations of the system were key to the responses, which would necessarily be non-linear: ecological resilience 'emphasizes variability, spatial heterogeneity and nonlinear causation'.[55]

Mapping was therefore an essential precondition for any form of governance intervention seeking to make a system more sustainable or resilient, as there could be no 'reductionist' view that external actors could assume a linear causal outcome, or transfer lessons from one system to another.[56] It was the internal relations that were decisive. In language very similar to those deploying neoliberal or neo-institutional forms of intervention in international relations, Holling saw reductionist approaches, which assumed linear causality, to have counterproductive and sometimes disastrous effects:

> crises and surprises… are the inevitable consequences of a command-and-control approach to renewable resource management, where it is (implicitly or explicitly) believed that humans can select one component of a self-sustaining natural system and change it to a fundamentally different configuration in which the adjusted system remains in that new configuration indefinitely without other, related, changes in the larger system.[57]

Ecological resilience exhibited very similar concerns with regard to mapping and non-linearity as those exercised in neoliberalism as a framework of intervention. Intervention could not be direct or goal directed with a modernist telos but only indirect, enabling systems based on their own internal relations and interactions:

> A management approach based on resilience, on the other hand, would emphasize the need to keep options open, the need to view events in a regional rather than a local context, and the need to emphasize heterogeneity. Flowing from this would be not the presumption of sufficient knowledge, but the recognition of our ignorance; not the assumption that future events are expected, but that they will be unexpected. The resilience framework can accommodate this shift of perspective, for it does not require a precise capacity to predict the future, but only a qualitative capacity to devise systems that can absorb and accommodate future events in whatever unexpected form they may take.[58]

Ecological resilience requires the mapping of internal system relations in order to understand how the system copes with and responds to external pressures. One aspect of internal system relations which was vital was a mapping of the 'adaptive cycle': composed of a 'front loop' – a period of production and accumulation but of increasing rigidities – and a 'back loop' – of experimentation and reorganisation. The stage of the cycle influences responsiveness:

> The reshuffling in the back loop of the cycle allows the possibility of new system configurations and opportunities utilizing the exotic and entirely novel entrants that had accumulated in earlier phases. The adaptive cycle opens transient windows of opportunity so that novel assortments can be generated.[59]

Thus, Deleuze can be read to have captured well the processes of the adaptive cycle where there are tendencies towards rigidity and organisation as well as towards fluidity and disorganisation, which he analysed in the terminology of 'territorialisation' and 'deterritorialisation'. As already discussed in terms of assemblage theory, ecological approaches to resilience also view systems as nested scales of interaction:

> These scales represent ecosystems, which are defined here as communities of organisms in which internal interactions between organisms determine behaviour more than do external biological events. External abioitic events do have a major impact on ecosystems, but are mediated through strong biological interactions within the ecosystems. It is through such external links that ecosystems become part of the global system.[60]

Thus the process of Mapping is a nested one, where interaction takes place both within systems, or assemblages, and between them. In ecological resilience thinking, mapping becomes generalised as way of tracing cross-scalar interactions in what is often conceptualised as a 'panarchy'.[61] Panarchy offers a vision of complex social-ecological systems as nested sets of adaptive cycles that correspond to sub-systems operating at particular organisational scales and speeds. Change at higher levels of the panarchy is slower and more rare than at the faster and smaller levels. As Kevin Grove argues, in his in-depth study of Holling's work in the formulation of contemporary understandings of governance in resilience discourses:

> the process of self-organized adaptation results from nothing more or less than the non-linear interactions of key elements within sub-systems that are bounded by processes occurring at larger scales – even as these

processes are themselves impacted through complex relations with other social, economic and biophysical systems.[62]

Thus, as a mode of governance, Mapping reconfigured sustainability from a linear problem of optimising scarce resources into a non-linear problem of systemic adaptation to emergent social, economic and environmental conditions. Mapping resilience works to enable system governance on the ontopolitical assumption of a nested hierarchy of interactive relations in which assemblages are primarily self-organising as autopoietic systems at the same time as being impacted by external stimuli. As an example of how a 'panarchy' of nested assemblages of systems with their own adaptive cycles can bridge the level from the micro to the global, DeLanda uses the development of the world market, where local or regional market-places form assemblages of interaction at a local level but at the same time will impact upon and be impacted by national markets and, at an even higher level of assemblage, global market-places will be impacted by and impact on national markets.[63]

Work in the complexity sciences and in ecology, which heavily influenced Deleuze, was important for the extension and development of Mapping, taking governance beyond the initial neoliberal focus in understanding bounded rationality. In this shift, Mapping moves from being a question of epistemology (the focus on subjectivity and socially constructed understandings) to one of ontology (the material entanglements of interactive life). It is important to clarify the nature of this shift. As we saw in the section above, for neoliberal and neo-institutionalist thought, the problem is epistemological, in that sub-optimal decisions are taken due to different and distinct path-dependencies that create barriers to adaptation. For neo-institutionalist thought, these lie at the level of formal institutions, for example, property laws or barriers to trade, and at the informal or cultural level. Thus interventions, as in those of peacebuilding or disaster risk management, seek to adapt or alter these institutions to enable better or more efficient outcomes. The solution is seen to be indirect work on shaping the choice-making environment.[64] This adaptation takes place on the assumption that there is a hierarchy of institutional 'fits', in this case that democracy and markets work best but that they depend on lower institutions having the right 'fit' in terms of cultural and religious values etc. Mapping as neoliberal or neo-institutional problem solving seeks to shape or influence these institutions according to preconceived (Eurocentric or Western) ideas of 'what works'.

Mapping, as developed through the generalisation of ecosystems theory of resilience or as assemblage theory, is concerned with ontology more than epistemology, or, to put this another way, seeks to drill down in much more detail to the reality of the world in its plurality, flux and difference, rather than seeking to align maladjustments or 'sub-optimal' systems to an ideal model. While for neoliberal or neo-institutionalist models – for 'actually existing neoliberalism' policies of governance intervention – there is an assumption of what the correct outcome is, in terms of an efficient economy and social, economic or democratic 'progress', this is less the case for Mapping understood as an ontological theory of interaction. For assemblage theory, differentiations lead to further differentiations but there can be no external goal of 'progress' to pre-set goals, only the careful management or modulation of interactions to attempt to balance and ease the strains of adaptation as an ongoing process.

Onto-Cartography *and* The Stack

Two works that provide useful contemporary examples of how Mapping as a mode of governance can be conceptualised via the ontopolitical assumptions of the Anthropocene are object-oriented theorist Levi Bryant's book *Onto-Cartography* (2014) and design theorist Benjamin Bratton's *The Stack* (2015). These works highlight how Mapping can be understood as a political rationale of governance intervention that is grounded in a distinct framework of ontopolitical reasoning. The key focus, as we have seen, for Mapping, is how differences emerge through processes of interaction which are internal to systems, be they societies, ecosystems or markets. Traditional forms of governance as the intervention of a transcendent subject or sovereign, equipped with the powers of direction and control, are seen to fail because transcendent forms of power necessarily operate with a 'vertical ontology',[65] in top-down or linear ways which cannot grasp the specificity of the plural and fluid contexts of the systems which they seek to intervene in. Thus governance is not a straightforward problematic and, as we have seen, neoliberal and neo-institutionalist policy-making sought to use Mapping as a way of developing a mode of indirect governance intervention, attempting to manipulate and change the contexts of decision-making or the processes of interaction in more 'bottom-up' ways.

Mapping is crucial for 'flatter', 'horizontal' or 'immanent' ontologies of assemblage and systems interaction because agency cannot be centralised, but rather is understood as distributed across numerous systems and actors.

For Bratton, *The Stack* is an 'accidental megastructure' of systems of plane-tary scale computation, with multiple levels of both vertical and horizontal interaction, each with its own immanent processes of interactive emer-gence.[66] It is important to clarify that this 'distributive' agency is not a property of individual systems, actors or agents but is emergent, relational and interactive; as Bratton argues the real outcomes are 'undesigned acci-dents'.[67] This is necessarily the case as, in a nested framework of assemblage, each assemblage is itself made up of internal relations or interaction, all the way down. Thus the interaction between assemblages, systems or agents is always producing contingent or non-linear outcomes. Therefore, in every interaction only one outcome emerges out of the many potential possibi-lities. This process of interactive emergence is thereby necessarily 'bottom-up' as every interaction depends on a previous chain of interactions. It is this process that gives neoliberal or neo-institutionalist approaches their histor-ical and sociological depth and enables Mapping, as a mode of governance, to overcome the modernist divides of culture and nature, through expand-ing the breadth and depth of the interactive processes that need to be mapped to enable governance intervention. As Bryant states:

> This is the basic thesis of onto-cartography and geophilosophy. If we are to understand why assemblages take the form they take, we must investigate how corporeal and incorporeal, human and non-human, inorganic, organic, and social machines intersect and interact with another ... In arguing that culture is itself a formation of nature, that it is continuous with nature rather than separate, geophilosophy hopes to ... better understand why social ecologies take the form they take and, *above all, to multiply our sites of intervention to produce change.* (emphasis added)[68]

Bratton's work focuses explicitly on the need to map the shifting assemblages of more-than-human interaction as ubiquitous more-than-computational regimes (of overlapping layers, claims and networks of computational, social, human and concrete forces)[69] increasingly become the key site of governance through competing visions of 'platform sovereignty', where specific technologies and techniques emerge with 'the ultimate effect of how increasingly powerful techniques of perception, sensing, detection, parsing, and processing all react together to enforce design and retrain governance in their own images' as this agglomeration of 'platform systems not only reflects, manages, and enforces forms of sovereignty; it also generates them in the first place'.[70] Mapping is the key to enabling governance interventions in a world of complex and emergent assemblages; these interventions thereby need to be recursive, understanding that there is no 'system' as such but rather 'an accumulation of interactions between layers in an emergent structure [that] is producing the scale, dimension, and contours of this supercomputational geography in the first place'.[71]

While Bratton focuses upon the importance of assemblage approaches in capturing the possibilities implied in complex processes of interaction, Bryant's work focuses upon the forms governance intervention can assume. Bryant lays the ontopolitical basis for the extension of Mapping as a mode of governance capable of 'producing more just, equitable, and sustainable worlds', on the grounds that assemblage thinking, as outlined above, enables governing actors 'to constructively intervene in worlds so as to produce better ecologies or assemblages'.[72] Bryant proposes the methodology of 'onto-cartography' as the 'mapping of assemblages' across space and time, because: 'The first step in producing any sort of change or new assemblages lies in having a good map.'[73] In a formulation very similar to that used by the neoliberal and neo-institutionalist economists who sought to argue that there was no such thing as capitalism as an abstraction but only different 'capitalisms' produced on the basis of different societies' internal relations of interaction, Bryant argues:

> The problem isn't that things such as patriarchy, capitalism, society, racism, and so on aren't real, but rather that they don't explain. Rather, they are the very things to be *explained*. These terms are all shorthand for *assemblages*. They are generic terms for extremely complex relations ... It is those *assemblages* ... that cause things, not these terms. Onto-cartography aspires to get at the organization of these assemblages. It aims at the concrete. Its question is 'how is this assemblage put together, what are the interactions ...?' rather than 'how do we overcome capitalism or "patriarchy" or "racism" or "ontotheology"?' ... Working on the premise that these things exist in and through assemblages, cartography strives to map those assemblages to determine privileged and strategic points of intervention that would lead to change or destroy these things.[74]

Bryant suggests that Mapping can operate in four ways.[75] Firstly, he argues for 'topological maps', drawing closely on the ecosystem resilience approaches outlined earlier: identifying the key systems and how their ecologies operate; the hierarchies of assemblages; and the feedback loops between them. The second type of mapping is 'genetic' or historical, providing a history of the present, which can defamiliarise the way the world appears and open up new possibilities or see alternative paths that could have been taken. The third approach, of 'vector maps', considers how tendencies may develop in the future on the basis of the key influences in the present. The fourth approach, of 'modal maps', follows the opposite tack, not based on the likely future if there would be no intervention but on possible alternative futures, which could be actively produced through intervention based on the understanding of assemblages and their interaction.

Once the various forms that Mapping can take are laid out, it becomes clearer that Mapping as a mode of governance, grounded in a specific ontopolitics, tends to constantly open itself to the problem of depth or infinitude, which will be further examined in the next chapter. As Bratton argues, the complex interplay between layers in *The Stack* assemblage means that there is no possibility of designing interventions in linear ways, there 'is no more innocent outside, now only a theoretically recombinant inside'.[76] Bratton notes that the recursive forms of governance intervention by design look a lot like the 'basic principles of second-order cybernetics';[77] as a cybernetic landscape, the 'design brief' for interventions is both shaped by and shapes emergent outcomes which means that 'we need a diagram of the global Stack that we have as it actually is ... to give a technical specificity to our speculations on geopolitical and geosocial alternatives'.[78] However, even if perfect knowledge of the infinite variables were available, any reflection upon the 'totality that emerges unintentionally' would necessarily involve always playing catch-up: governing as responsive adaption to these immanent logics.[79] Importantly, this necessarily implies that interactive outcomes themselves can't be designed; at most, the means and processes can be shaped adaptively in response to past results.[80]

Thus the problem of the autopoietic process of adaptive intervention through governance as design is that it has difficulty managing the immanent interplay between equilibrium and emergence. Here it will suffice to introduce the problem through Bryant's engagement with the problem of the 'unintended consequences' of governance interventions, where it is always possible for 'the cure to turn out to be worse than the sickness':

> In devising a modal map ... it is important to take contingencies into account as much as the desired outcomes. This requires a knowledge of the topography of the system into which we're intervening, the nature

of the machines [systems of assemblages] that populate that topography, and how they're likely to react to these [interventions].[81]

What is interesting is the use of the conception of 'contingencies', which need to be taken into account. Presumably if Mapping was able to fully grasp the inner workings and interactions of networked assemblages, 'contingencies' would not arise. If 'contingencies' and 'unintended consequences' were to emerge then logically the solution would be to undertake Mapping more intensively. As Bryant states: 'onto-cartography seeks not to diminish our points of social and political intervention, but to multiply them'.[82] This would make sense and seem to express the inner logic of Mapping as a mode of governance: not governing through centralised direction from above would seem to inevitably lead to conceptions of micro-governance through interventions 'from below' and their micro-management through every level and its interactions. What starts out as a 'light touch' or indirect recursive process of 'designing for design' appears to end up requiring a much more interventionist process of regulation and monitoring than that assumed by 'top-down' 'command-and-control'.

Conclusion

This chapter has elucidated the ontopolitical assumptions underlying the emergence of Mapping as a mode of governance, firstly through the neo-liberal framework of the limits to knowledge, secondly as the framework for governance intervention, seeking to map societal interactions in order to intervene and redirect the processes and outcomes, and, thirdly, as a method of locating the productive source of potential policy solutions. Thus mapping can take different forms as an applied framework, nevertheless the common thread is that of assemblage theory, with a clear distinction made between the entity (and its internal relations) and the external perturbation or disturbance which provokes non-linear responses or outcomes and thus reveals the processes of interaction. The distinction between the earlier neoliberal and neo-institutionalist approaches, and those of systems ecology and more contemporary approaches, for example, those of Bryant and Bratton, is that the governance framework expands from a consideration of shaping the 'choice-making environment' of individuals to a broader, ontological framing of the processual becoming of life itself.

The distinction between the earlier, subject-centred, framework of Mapping seeking to enable more efficient or adaptive rational choice-making and the less, subject-centred Mapping of assemblage thinking, *Onto-Cartography* and *The Stack* is that the agential problematic of radical constructivism becomes ontologised. It is not only thought that is contextually shaped and 'bounded' in its rationality but the processes within which thought itself operates. Thus the world is composed of assemblages 'all the way down', without an outside. The Mapping problematic of adaptation thereby shifts (or, more accurately, could be seen as providing a conceptual continuum) from adaptation to a fixed or ideal path or set of practices to adaptation as a necessarily ongoing process of becoming without goals.

This framing then can be taken in two directions. The following chapter considers how Mapping with its ontology of depth negotiates the difficulties of tracing the everyday or local interactions to enable policy interventions from the 'bottom-up'. Chapter 4 considers how the limits of Mapping have led to a focus on developing capacities of sensing and responsiveness to the peturbations or disturbances themselves rather than mapping the assemblage through tracing internal interactions and inter-relations. While Mapping is the first proper non-modern governance mode of the Anthropocene, as this book emphasises, it also begins to transition governmental thinking away from the aspiration to transform or alter processes through the mechanism of intervention.

Notes

1 Harley, 1989.
2 Ibid.: p.5.
3 Ibid.: p.14.
4 Latour, 1986: p.27.
5 Latour, 2016: p.7
6 Bratton, 2015: p.24.
7 Ibid.: p.30.
8 Massey, 2005: p.9.
9 Kitchin and Dodge, 2007.
10 Ibid.: p.12.
11 See, for example, on mapping and narrative, Caquard, 2013.
12 See further, Massey, 2005.
13 Foucault, 2008: pp.10–22.
14 Ibid.: p.35.
15 'Actually existing neoliberalism', following Neil Brenner and Nik Theodore (2002), is understood as a highly interventionist and regulatory set of practices, which flag up a discrepancy between neoliberalism in theory and neoliberalism as a set of diverse policy practices.
16 In this sense, what is at stake in modern neoliberalism, according to Foucault, is not a revival of pro-market sympathies or the economic need to 'free the

economy' but rather a political mistrust of the extension of a certain form of governing intervention seen as producing a crisis for liberal forms of rule (Foucault, 2008: pp.68–70; 116–118; 130–134).

17 Foucault, 2008: p.131.
18 Plehwe, 2009.
19 Hayek, 1978a: p.8.
20 According to Hayek, 1960: p.22: 'The conception of man deliberately building his civilization stems from an erroneous intellectualism that regards human reason as something standing outside nature and possessed of knowledge and reasoning capacity independent of experience.'
21 Hayek, 1978b.
22 Hayek, 1978a: p.22; see also 1945: pp.521–2
23 Hayek, 1945: p.530.
24 Hayek, 1952.
25 Mirowski, 2002: pp.232–40.
26 Hayek, 1952: p.25.
27 See, for example, Douglass C. North, 1990; 1999; 2005.
28 Commons, 1936: p.242.
29 Ibid.: pp.247–8.
30 Forest and Mehier, 2001: p.592.
31 Ibid.: p.593.
32 See further, Chandler and Reid, 2016.
33 Foucault, 2008: p.135.
34 North, 2005: p.162.
35 Ibid.: pp.163–4.
36 See, for example, Collier, 2005; Castree, 2007; Dean, 2010; Foucault, 2008; Barry et al., 1996.
37 See further, Campbell et al., 2011.
38 Paris, 2004.
39 For a more extensive discussion of policy developments in the field of peace-building, see Chandler 2017.
40 As Bruno Latour argues (2013a: p.332) 'democracy can't be parachuted from the bay of a US Air Force plane': 'If the universalization of knowledge remains a hypocritical pretense as long as we fail to extend the laboratories and colleagues that make it possible to bring knowledge into existence, the universalization of freedom is only a gratuitous injunction as long as we don't take pains to build the artificial enclosures, the "greenhouses", the air-conditioned equipment that would finally make the "atmosphere of politics" breathable.'
41 Tierney, 2014: p.36.
42 See, for example, the World Bank, 2010; 2015.
43 UNISDR, 2014; Lavell and Maskrey, 2014: p.278.
44 Acuto and Curtis, 2014: p.2. They argue in the introduction to their edited collection that assemblage theory can be read to cover a variety of different approaches with multiple intellectual roots.
45 See, for example, Anderson et al., 2012.
46 DeLanda, 2006: p.3.
47 Anderson et al., 2012: p.172.
48 DeLanda, 2006: p.20.

49 Walker and Cooper, 2011: p.144.
50 Holling, 1973.
51 Ibid.: p.1
52 'An equilibrium centered view is essentially static and provides little insight into the transient behavior of systems that are not near the equilibrium. Natural, undisturbed systems are likely to be continually in a transient state; they will be equally so under the influence of man.' Ibid.: p.2; see also Holling, 1986: p.76.
53 On the distinction between 'Newtonian' conceptions of space as homogenous and alternative 'topological' conceptions of space as agentially constituted through interaction, see, for example, Bryant, 2014: pp.143–7; Morton, 2013: pp.55–68.
54 Holling, 1973: p.16.
55 Holling, 1986: p.72. It is not the intention here to engage with the whole range of concepts developed by Holling and his associates in their work on ecosystem resilience, for a detailed study see Grove, 2018.
56 Folke, 2006.
57 Holling and Meffe, 1996: p.330.
58 Holling, 1973: p.21.
59 Holling, 2001: p.397.
60 Holling, 1986: p.77.
61 Holling, 2001; Gunderson and Holling, 2002.
62 Grove, 2018.
63 Ibid.: pp.17–18.
64 These approaches are dealt with in more detail in Chandler, 2010.
65 Bryant, 2014: p.237.
66 Bratton, 2015: p.367.
67 Ibid.: p.9.
68 Bryant, 2014: p.255.
69 Bratton, 2015; p.11.
70 Ibid.: p.8.
71 Ibid.: p.27.
72 Bryant, 2014: p.257.
73 Ibid.
74 Ibid.: p.258. Bryant uses a formulation very close to that of Bruno Latour (2004).
75 Bryant, 2014: pp.259–67.
76 Bratton, 2015: p.38.
77 Ibid.: p.47.
78 Ibid.: p.65.
79 Ibid.
80 Ibid.: p.342.
81 Bryant, 2014: p.273.
82 Ibid.: p.280.

3

FROM THE 'BLACK BOX' TO THE 'GREAT OUTDOORS'

Introduction

The previous chapter introduced the governance mode of Mapping as a framework of intervention that sought to understand the internal relations of the object of governance rather than basing policy-making on the power, knowledge-capacities or ethical values of the governing or intervening agency. This framing opened up systems or societies being intervened in to external regulatory regimes but posed the problem of ontological depth and complexity: the problem of external or governing knowledge of these contingent relations and interactions. This chapter continues the analysis to focus on the use of technological aids to 'drill down' deeper to attempt to acquire the knowledge necessary and the perceived limits to this exercise in the sphere of international policy intervention. It draws upon contemporary discussion of the problems confronting practices of international policy intervention to highlight how the shift from direct 'top-down' to indirect 'bottom-up' interventions has facilitated the movement from external perspectives or 'subject-centred' methodologies to more speculative or 'object-oriented' frameworks. It seems that the inner logic of Mapping as a mode of governance reveals the paradox of seeking to maintain the capacity for designing governing interventions for adaptation towards desired goals at the same time as working within an immanent ontology of emergence.

While the previous chapter considered the turn to 'ontology' and away from a neoliberal focus on subjectivity alone, through the assemblage approach to the world as multiply constituted through differentiating chains of interaction, the understandings analysed still assumed an external observer or governing agency operating external to these processes and able to intervene to design interventions capable of influencing and redirecting processes of emergent outcomes. It is this external positionality, central to the genealogy of Mapping as a mode of governance, which will be the key concern of this chapter. It analyses how an increasing orientation towards problems, understood as concrete relational assemblages of interaction, has enabled the transformation of Mapping as a mode of governance, in response to the recognition of complexity as a barrier to policy-making interventions. In doing so, it highlights the influence of posthumanist and speculative approaches beyond the marginal realms of continental philosophy and positions these perspectives as increasingly cohering and reflecting mainstream policy debates and discourses. The lack of attention to this shift in the policy realm is brought into focus through reading the reconstruction of international interventionist discourses in terms of Mapping as a distinctive mode of governance.

Two stages are heuristically drawn out: the initial turn towards Mapping as an ontology of assemblages (as discussed in the previous chapter); and then the renegotiation of Mapping as a mode of governance, as it is increasingly realised that the position of an external observer or governing actor, external or 'objective' in relation to these processes, is increasingly difficult to sustain. Increasingly, problems are addressed in ways that seek to grasp them through the alternative perceptions and responsivities of other actors and agencies, seeing them as emerging outcomes of concrete interactive processes that are not accessible to external agencies (this, as will be analysed in the following chapter, can be read as marking a passage towards Sensing as an alternative mode of governance). This has fundamental epistemological and ontological implications, which indicate how Mapping can be seen as an attempt to grasp non-linear causal relations in order to 'problem-solve' or design adaptive interventions to steer systems towards a desired outcome but also move beyond this to focus on the positive potentials of emergence, beginning to see problems as opportunities for learning more about local capacities and abilities.

This chapter is organised in four sections. The first considers how Mapping, as a form of governance, is operationalised in contemporary international relations discourses, orientated to a 'realist' approach, starting with problems understood as contextual and specific rather than amenable to generic, or 'off the peg', solutions. The second section considers the difficulties of gaining the necessary knowledge or of 'drilling down' sufficiently to understand assemblages of interaction and to design interventions in processes of emergence 'from the bottom-up'. The third section focuses on the recognition of these limits to external projects of Mapping as a framework of policy intervention, seen increasingly in terms of moving beyond the problem of 'correlationism'. The final section considers how these limits thus become reworked and problems appear as invitations to learn more about and to explore the richness of a world in which interactive processes of emergence are beyond the powers of governmental knowledge and interventionist mechanisms.

Rethinking policy discourses of international intervention

Mapping as a mode of governing has been key to providing coherence to a range of discussions on policy reform in the international arena, particularly in relation to the design of international policy intervention.[1] Mapping seeks to start from the problem understood as the product of a concrete context of interactions, as an assemblage with specific limits and possibilities, rather than importing causal or conceptual frameworks of generic understanding and solving the problem 'from the outside'. In this respect, the focus shifts from the understanding and perceptions of external interveners to the project of accessing the problem itself. This process of accessing the problem is increasingly perceived to be dependent upon the way it is constructed by the actors and agents involved, whether this is societies operating in different contexts or cultural frameworks or even more-than-human collectives and nonhuman forces and agencies.[2] The importance of this shift lies in the fact that earlier approaches to mapping assemblages in order to design interventions assumed an expansion of existing frameworks of knowledge, from the subject position of an external actor. International experience of policy interventions, however, begins to suggest that problems cannot be resolved through such an extension and require instead a way of working with the problem 'from the inside': through grasping the depth of the problem from the perspective of other ways of being and relating to the world.

This chapter analyses debates on policy understandings within the discursive framing of Mapping to bring together two discussions in the field of international relations – the pressing need to reform the frameworks and understandings of international policy intervention[3] and work on the speculative or object-oriented 'turn'[4] – which have rarely been considered together. On the one hand, policy discussion of the problems and limits of international policy interventions have tended to be couched in rather traditional and technical policy terms, focusing on questions of policy coherence, lessons learned and problems of state or commercial influence[5] although a few exceptions have linked the debate to broader epistemological and ontological issues, in a world seen to be increasingly dynamic and complex.[6] On the other hand, intellectual engagement with a range of new materialist, actor network, speculative realist and object-oriented approaches has often been limited to the fringes of critical theory, in specialist book series or journals[7] and generally regarded as useful for informing and developing critical approaches rather than (as deployed here) as an increasingly dominant lens through which problems and policy interventions are reworked and cohered on the basis of the ontopolitical assumptions of the Anthropocene.

The policy discourses of Mapping illustrate a growing policy convergence in international approaches to policy-intervention, increasingly covering the fields of peace and security, development and environmental sustainability, and humanitarian emergency,[8] cohered through the United Nations' 2030 Sustainable Development Agenda.[9] As the UN Secretary-General recommends:

> A common understanding of context, needs and capacities should then lead to a common 'problem statement'. The problem statement should identify priorities in meeting immediate needs but also reducing vulnerability and risk over several years; the capacities of all available actors, particularly national and local, to address those priorities; and where international actors can support existing capacities, complement and scale them up, and improve the circumstances of the most vulnerable.[10]

This radically challenges the traditional 'top-down', institutionally-driven or supply-centred policy approach because the 'problem' is not necessarily seen as amenable to resolution through any existing set of institutional skills or policies. The need to start engagement with a concrete context or problem on the basis of the priorities of 'the most vulnerable' and a clear view of the capacities of all the actors further challenges and complicates any idea of a quick fix or a simplistic provision of pre-packaged solutions. However, as will be analysed, this shift towards Mapping interventions has much more radical implications, challenging the initial assumptions made about the potential for designing indirect forms of intervention.

As the Overseas Development Institute has highlighted, the shift towards Mapping as a mode of governance is driven by the perception that international agencies face a deep crisis of legitimacy; one that goes to the heart of their identity and the belief that international policy interventions can be neutral or objective in the desire to problem-solve and to capacity-build, 'regardless of context or culture'.[11] This idea of Western ethics, expertise and knowledge as applicable universally was crucial to humanitarian discourses and to liberal internationalist approaches to peace and development assistance. However, it is seen to be problematic today and to represent a 'Western ethos' that others would wish to 'question or reject':[12]

> large parts of the current way the West conducts its ... business – the charity model, the near-monopoly of the UN agencies, the compulsion to create parallel structures, the reluctance to properly engage with and respect local authorities and cultures, the tendency to privilege international technical expertise over local knowledge and capacities, with 'exogenous "solutions" meeting endogenous "challenges" and "needs"' – [come] into question.[13]

The focus of this chapter is not so much the critique of the practices of policy intervention per se[14] but the contemporary articulation of a set of responses in terms of the need to overcome the division between 'external' and 'internal' forms of knowing and agency. They highlight the development of Mapping as a problem-oriented approach from 'black-boxing' problems as if the internal context and relations of societies did not matter to what could be called 'the great outdoors', seeing the failure to grasp complex interaction as an invitation to explore and learn the mysteries of the world. This can be seen as a two-stage process. Firstly, there is the growing recognition of the limits of 'bottom-up' forms of Mapping, as an attempt to drill-down deeper into social processes to enable external forms of knowledge and control. Secondly, there is a shift to enabling alternative ways of perceiving and responding: understanding problems as emergent and interactive processes that need to be grasped 'from the inside'.

This two-stage process transforms the assumptions of interventionist policy-practice and expands the problem downwards and outwards to more complex sets of relations and interactions. In this process of expansion the knowledge of external interveners appears to be increasingly less relevant and the distinctions and separations between actors, entities and policy areas are increasingly ameliorated. Perhaps counterintuitively, the loss of the modernist framework for external intervention is increasingly perceived to be positive, as previous approaches become understood to have failed to grasp problems adequately and to have limited the effectiveness of international policy interventions. As will be concluded, in this discursive framing, interventionist practices of Mapping no longer construct problems as amenable to easy external solutions, rather problems – understood as emergent interactive processes – enable international interveners to see the world in other, much richer, ways. Mapping as an extensive process of governing for an adaptive goal and Mapping as a limitless exploration or discovery of emergent outcomes of interaction become two sides of a coin, which can be easily flipped.

The limits of assemblage theory

Over recent years, the refocus of international policy intervention on preventive approaches, risk and vulnerability, rather than merely on post-crisis response, has posed new strategic and tactical questions of how to engage with societies, communities and individuals.[15] In fieldwork in Nairobi, in May 2016, I was able to interview a number of international agencies concerned with developing new 'bottom-up' Mapping approaches to understanding problems and vulnerabilities, based on designing indirect forms of intervention for community engagement and empowerment rather than traditional 'top-down' policy assistance at the level of state institutions. As one interlocutor (the programmes director for Concern Worldwide, Kenya) explained, the shift in perspectives to an 'assemblage' approach begins to transform the relationship between international agencies and the societies they are engaging with. These societies were now revealed to be much more densely rich and differentiated – much more lively – than in the hierarchical, traditional approaches, which worked with broad and reductive categories which only touched the surface of the problem:

> It was the issue of addressing extreme poverty which really changed things for us. We could no longer act as if could just solve problems. It forced us to engage with outlying areas of risk and inequality, which before we were not interested in. We were just saving lives ... Now we needed to develop contextual analysis: to really drill-down to the

community. To ask: 'What are the differences here?' To really delve into the risks, vulnerabilities and mitigating factors. This really broadened the way we understood communities.[16]

This shift towards Mapping, starting with an understanding of context and local community interaction, sought to refocus perspectives and to challenge the subject-centred or Eurocentric positionality of international interveners.[17] Starting from drilling-down to the specific concrete nature of the relational interactions through which problems and vulnerabilities emerged – for example, the vulnerability of an elderly person in a middle class housing estate or pockets of extreme disadvantage or vulnerability to particular price or climate changes in areas which may otherwise have coping strategies – enabled a new set of interconnections to be mapped out and described.

International agencies and lead operatives have jumped at the chance to shift from exporting policies, already fixed externally, to in-depth and open-ended engagements with the aim of long-term community empowerment.[18] It is here that Mapping as a mode of governance demonstrates its close affinity to other relational approaches, such as philosophical pragmatism, probably most fully articulated in the work of John Dewey in his classic work *The Public and Its Problems.*[19] Here, Dewey challenged rationalist understandings of the public as already fixed and pre-formed and instead understood publics as emerging in response to the effects of indirect social and material interconnections which appeared in terms of problems which needed to be addressed. This disruption of classical liberal binaries between publics (or subjects) and emerging problems (or objects of concern) is key to understanding the attraction of the Mapping approach for indirect intervention into processes of interactive emergence. Problems thus do not just appear for publics, but reflect and enable the construction of publics in different ways. Problems and publics are thus intertwined or co-constructed in an assemblage of emergent effects, which require Mapping as a mode of governance.

However, it does not seem to be easy to turn assemblage thinking into a viable form of adaptive governance. The essential problem appears to be that of the barriers to access and understanding, required by Mapping, despite an increasing awareness of the need to differentiate and prioritise by drilling-down further (getting more micro-level information) and enabling interventions to be more aligned with complex processes of interaction both within and between assemblages. This is why new digital technologies are often held to be key to the reform of international practices,[20]

highlighted in the fact that the need to integrate new technological innovations is a constantly recurring theme for international agencies. The UN
Secretary-General, for example, has urged that: 'Data and joint analysis must
become the bedrock of our action. Data and analysis are the starting point for
moving from a supply-driven approach to one informed by the greatest
risks and the needs of the most vulnerable.'[21]

Methodologically, the attempt to overcome the problems of international
intervention mirrors broader philosophical and political concerns, within
politics and international relations, over the narrowness of the modern
Western episteme.[22] In this regard, Bruno Latour has done much to flag up
the radical consequences for knowledge of the application of digital technologies in constituting the world with a much flatter social ontology,
essential for the grasping of complex interactions required by Mapping,
through drilling down to the concrete context without reducing reality to
broad categories in which differences and distinctions are submerged from
vision. As Latour states:

> one is tempted to treat an entity differently from its context only
> because of a lack of access to the list of attributes that make up that
> entity. At the very least, the digitally available profiles open new questions
> for social theory that don't have to be framed through the individual/
> collective standpoint.[23]

Awareness that the context is key rather than the entities within it has
meant that approaches of digital mapping, or the use of social media for data
analysis, are held to work very differently to traditional surveys and interviews, even if they have inevitable technical limitations. In this context,
Venturri and Latour note: 'The advantage of the new methods is that they
allow *tracing the assemblage* of collective phenomena instead of obtaining
them through statistical aggregation. The question of representativeness is
thus posed in an entirely different way.' (emphasis added)[24] They make a
valuable point regarding the flatter ontology of digital approaches for
Mapping, no longer relying on reductive categorisations and generalisations
(as considered in the previous chapter). Drilling down to understand how
problems emerge in concrete contexts is not about producing 'representative' knowledge that can be generalised but engaging with the context itself
through 'tracing the assemblage'.[25] Here, knowledge is held to be concrete
and context specific, enabling external actors and agencies to trace and to
design interventions in processes of interaction.

The problem is that it seems that, whatever level of technological drilling-down or deeper forms of surveillance may be deployed, it is not possible to capture all the potential variables within any given assemblage. It appears that any system of surveillance could never be complete or able to grasp processes of interaction in their emergence. It is therefore little wonder that many commentators doubt that the aspirations for digitally enhanced modes of access to relations, both within and between assemblages, can be fulfilled.[26] As one of the managers of Ushahidi (a major digital platform provider) informed me, technology itself can only ever be part of the solution to international interveners attempting to access the processes and interactions revealing hidden vulnerabilities. She suggested that 90 per cent of the answer lay with enabling community knowledge rather than with digitally enhancing external capacities. Surveillance, no matter how far it drills down, still needs to have the knowledge of the variables to be traced, measured or monitored and can only reach those individuals or communities which are open to such surveillance: just working at the level of community leaders or requiring the use of smart phones for digital tracing is not able to overcome the limits of these 'bottom-up' methodologies when deployed in the Mapping paradigm of intervention:

> We need the appropriate use of technology; who the audience is is very important and has to drive strategy ... maybe the use of radio programmes or focus groups, we need to innovate our own approaches based on things that people have access to already, not just fancy dashboards and smart phone applications.[27]

On the ground, it seems that international actors and policy agencies have much less faith in the promise of Big Data technologies than the boosters in the media and academia.[28] Sharing the sceptical mood of policy agencies are those commentators who suggest that even with new data-generating approaches the most vulnerable will be missed or the problems will only be flagged when it is too late, indicating that 'external' approaches of knowing more about the processes of 'bottom-up' interaction and emergence will always be limited. As Nat O'Grady writes, the data categories used for cross-checking risk factors will always be too wide in scope and not targeted enough, thus increasing rather than ameliorating 'the problem of rendering invisible those most vulnerable'.[29]

It, in fact, seems to be logically inevitable that any attempt to start from the perspective of the knowledge and technical mechanisms of international agencies and policy actors will constitute new forms of exclusion and marginalisation. Starting from subject-centred perspectives (of acquiring greater, more varied or more interactive knowledge) inevitably exposes external actors to accusations of being too Eurocentric or Western in their views and not being open-enough to the systems and societies in which they are engaged. These forms of criticism cannot be avoided by seeking to develop and innovate technologically, whether it is through Big Data, open source mapping technologies or other means, as whatever the nature of the innovation and no matter how extensive its application and how efficient it may be in delivering information, real and complex life can never be adequately captured.[30]

The application of new technologies increasingly reveals the nature of the problem to be different to how it was previously imagined: they reveal communities to be much more differentiated and reveal that causal chains are often much more mediated and less linear than previously understood. Acquiring greater knowledge of depth, intricacy and complexity inevitably questions previous knowledge assumptions as well as bringing attention to the epistemological limitations of Mapping as an external attempt to know societies and processes in real-time depth.[31] The density is overwhelming. The problem for international actors tasked with policy intervention is that discussion and reflection upon the epistemological limits of knowledge is bound up with their own external, Western positionality.[32] They, in fact, appear to exemplify the contemporary epistemological crisis, which (as discussed in the introductory chapter) appears as the Anthropocene condition.

Contemporary debates over the limits to what international actors can achieve thus construct policy interventions as a performative epistemology:[33] the failure of policy-making is seen to directly manifest the limits of a Western way of knowing. This failure is driven by the conflation of epistemological limitations with a Western, Eurocentric or colonial positionality. This positionality is then held to have historically been elitist, hierarchical and exclusionist. The inability to drill down to the required level of depth, to grasp the rich interactive density of complex relational processes, then gives the lie to Western claims of objectivity or of epistemic superiority. All interventionist actors (who, by definition, in Mapping as a mode of governance, are external agents intervening with instrumentalist intentionality) are caught in the problem of their inability to see the problem in the ways in which it may appear to those more closely involved, despite their claim to be objectively addressing it. Contemporary political, scientific and philosophical sensitivities necessarily bring international aspirations 'back down to earth', in the knowledge that interveners cannot escape their own socially, politically and technologically mediated frameworks of understanding. It appears that they cannot step outside of their positionality, even with the nicest and most generous of intentions (or with the most reflexive awareness of the recursive processual nature of assemblages and emergent causality).

Beyond correlationalism

Mapping, while appreciating non-linear and emergent causality and the importance of an ontology of assemblages, appears to be unable to overcome the epistemological limits of international policy-intervention. Mapping, as a 'problem-solving' discourse, appears trapped in a modernist deadlock, still reproducing 'objective' Western understandings in the attempt to externally 'resolve' problems. However, I argue here, this experience has opened the possibilities for these limits to be legitimised or worked around through the further development, or intensification, of Mapping as a mode of governance. In response to the problems of legitimising knowledge claims, policy innovators are increasingly shifting perspective towards a richer understanding of Mapping approaches to knowledge generation. Problems are increasingly recast as ones of phenomenology rather than merely epistemology. Rather than directly understanding problems of interactive assemblages and emergent causality but only addressing them in indirect forms, the approach is becoming more epistemologically mediated or indirect. Access to the problem is sought through the understanding or perceptions of other agencies or actors. As a programme manager for Ushahidi stated:

> Especially marginalised groups are very important to the data revolution, with their buy-in and their opinion, we will really be able to make a difference. Design-thinking needs to emphasise the need to place ourselves in her [the vulnerable or 'at risk' subject's] shoes – what are the language barriers, what tools does she have access to?[34]

Driven by the Mapping paradigm, approaches to international policy intervention have increasingly developed their instruments of knowledge gathering – from surveys, with their broad categories, to the narrower attempts to shift to in-depth surveillance on the basis of disaggregating categories to ever more micro-levels and the use of Big Data technologies to attempt to grasp changes in greater relational specificity. However, these approaches have distanced interveners from their policy objects rather than bridging the knowledge gap. This is because these approaches have all started from the position, needs and understanding of the external actors. The fundamental shift, raised here, is from the emphasis upon 'drilling down' to the need to start from an understanding of how vulnerable subjects and communities themselves relate to and perceive the world, by 'putting themselves in their shoes'.

It is at this point that the necessary limits to 'bottom-up' or assemblage approaches of designing adaptive policy interventions appear to become much clearer. The problems are then no longer the purely epistemological ones of extending modernist forms of knowledge deeper into social and cultural processes of interaction by fine-tuning techniques of data gathering and breaking down categories of analysis or speeding up the feed-back from digital recording and sensing equipment. None of these approaches enable international interveners to put themselves 'in the shoes' of those they seek to empower or capacity-build. A fundamental gulf opens up between the agency of the international policy-actors and the problem itself, whether this is understood as providing information and assistance or in terms of knowing more about capacities, choices and needs. Mapping as a mode of governance initially emphasised the need for intervention to be indirect; with this shift, inevitably, governing and knowing agency also increasingly becomes understood as more widely distributed.

The shift to Mapping as a mode of governance, seeking to design interventions in processes of interaction, appears to have the additional implication of making assemblages much more opaque, or rather infinitely complex, than initially imagined, thus forcing problems to be increasingly recast as phenomenological rather than merely epistemological. The point of the distinction is the vantage point or positionality of the knowledge that is required. An epistemological problem can be solved through an expansion of existing frameworks of knowledge, from the subject position of an external actor (in this case the international agency concerned). A phenomenological problem cannot be resolved through such an extension and requires indirect access through the ways of thinking and relating internal to the policy target or problem itself. The question is then no longer: 'How can we understand more?' or even 'What do they want?' or 'What do they need?' but an entirely different presentation of the problem, from the opposite position, from the side of the object of knowledge: 'How do they think?' 'How do they see the world?' 'What language do they use?' 'How do they use it?' 'What tools do they use?' 'What instruments or technologies do they use to make sense of the world?' The knowledge sought is how phenomena appear – how information is processed and things are perceived – to others.

In this way, the extension of the assemblage approach of Mapping to overcome the phenomenological barriers of the modern or Western episteme closely begins to resemble that of object-oriented ontologies, in that its object is always obscure: it withdraws or recedes from the direct or unmediated view of the external actor.[35] The more that the external intervening agency or actor thinks that it grasps the problem in the governance mode of Mapping – understands the processes involved, locates the most vulnerable, finds the mechanisms of mediation, interpretation and translation – the more the problem recedes or withdraws; and it is clear that what was mistakenly taken as knowledge of the problem was merely a self-projection of the categories and understandings of the external actor itself. Rather than coming closer to the problem, to addressing causes and removing barriers, the problems appear to be further away, or, more precisely, to have much more relational depth.

The critique of earlier policy approaches within the mode of Mapping is precisely that they were based on projections of Western understandings: of a liberal, modernist or Eurocentric episteme, which made 'God's eye view' assumptions that the epistemological barriers to problem-solving could be overcome while ignoring the possibility of phenomenological barriers to knowledge.[36] In the work of object-oriented ontology or speculative realism, this problem of ignoring phenomenological barriers is often termed 'correlationism', a problematic, first coined by Quentin Meillassoux,[37] which is seen to stem from Kant's transcendental idealism. Phenomenological barriers to knowledge are not taken seriously as it is assumed that we never have access to the inner world of experience of other subjects or objects, only to the world as we perceive and experience it, trapped within our own phenomenological world of perception. Thus problems are always understood within our own set of correlations between the world and ourselves.

Problems are always 'problems for us', never constructed in the ways in which they may appear for other forms of being or ways of existing. The perceived need to overcome or to bypass these limits has been increasingly raised by decolonial approaches[38] and these fit well (in this regard) with the concerns of speculative realist or object-oriented theorists. For example, Levi Bryant states:

A phenomenology-of investigates how *we*, us humans, encounter other entities. It investigates what entities are *for-us*, from our human perspective. It is humanist in the sense that it restricts itself to our perspective on the beings of the world ... The problem is not markedly different from that of understanding the experience of another person. Take the example of a wealthy person who denounces poor people as being lazy moochers who simply haven't tried to improve their condition. Such a person is practicing 'phenomenology-of', evaluating the poor person from the standpoint of their own experience and trying to explain the behavior of the poor person based on the sorts of things that would motivate them. They reflect little understanding of poverty. [39]

The key problematic for Mapping, as a mode of governance, is thus that of not taking alterity seriously enough:[40] the study of different assemblages of interaction from the God's eye view of a Western observer or governance agency appears to risk affirming the modernist worldview (of 'phenomenology-of') rather than questioning the hegemonic Western assumptions about the objective or scientific nature of knowledge. This links back to the neoliberal starting assumptions (considered in the previous chapter) that the problem of divergences from a desired outcome could be resolved through adaptive techniques of intervention, based upon the assumption that the world was single and uniform and that it was the socio-cultural understandings and responses that were problematic.[41] While Mapping approaches use assemblage theory to emphasise the nested assemblages of geology, history and socio-economic development to explain suboptimal choices, as Mario Blaser argues, the side-effect of Mapping approaches is that differences become minimalised and the modernist view of objectivity naturalised in a process of 'Sameing' rather than Othering.[42]

Martin Holbraad writes that pointing out these phenomenological limits (to Mapping approaches) enables the move from the neoliberal question of why others 'get stuff wrong' to the opening up of a challenge to rethink the analytical concepts of international actors and agencies themselves.[43] This turn to 'phenomenology-for' is an ethical challenge to take alterity seriously by starting from taking literally (rather than metaphorically) what interlocutors say. Similarly, for Blaser (drawing on the work of actor network and posthumanist approaches of Latour, Law, Haraway, Mol and others) the turn to 'phenomenology-for' would have profound implications for Mapping as a mode of governance as it would challenge the assumption that realities are 'out there' rather than continually and multiply enacted or performed.[44] Here the work of Annemarie Mol is seen as particularly useful; 'understanding ontology as performance or enactment brings to the fore the notion of ontological multiplicity', where different stories and practices are neither describing something existing ultimately 'out there' nor are they mistaken or metaphorical, but actually enact or 'world'.[45]

This reversal of positionality in relation to the problem increasingly links new developments in policy practices with posthuman, speculative or object-oriented approaches. In international policy discourses, assemblage theory approaches of Mapping thus increasingly seek to go beyond correlationism, beyond merely the projection of a Western external, or modernist, framing of problems and solutions in order to access the problem through a 'phenomenology-*for*-them' approach to grasp the problem 'from the inside'; or 'to put itself in their shoes'. As Meillassoux puts it, this shift can be understood as an exciting challenge of entering 'the great outdoors',[46] no longer forced to be constrained by traditional frameworks of gaining access to problems. This was certainly how it has been put to me in my field work with international policy-making agencies (as illustrated above) who have been keen to move away from even indirect interventions of adaptation to an assumed outcome or goal and instead seek to enable others to explore the societies concerned and to enable them both to construct and to address problems themselves.

It cannot be emphasised enough that previous approaches to international policy-intervention are seen to have black-boxed societies, being too little interested in their internal workings and relationships and instead focusing on surface appearances and offering policy advice and assistance on this basis. The opening up of this black box has provided the dynamic driving and transforming Mapping approaches to designing policy-intervention, which increasingly seek to draw from the rich plurality of the new worlds opened up in the problematisation of a narrow assemblage approach. In fact, as articulated here, it becomes clear that there are two stages of the opening up of the problem. The first stage, external and subject-centred, seeks to drill down, operating within the legacy of the modernist episteme, pluralising the variables and localising the factors (as described above and in the previous chapter). The second stage begins to shift to a less modernist framework, intensifying the assemblage approach further, with a pluralising or flatter ontology, speculating upon multiple ways of knowing or perceiving reality, or of being in the world.

The attempt to address problems in the way they may appear to others, rather than to seek to resolve them on the terms on which they appear to external actors, is often unclear (in the remaking of international Mapping discourses of policy-intervention) because this means dealing with the alien nature not of objects but of communities constituted as vulnerable or 'at risk'. Thus Meillassoux's 'great outdoors' becomes recast as an open-ended engagement with the 'other', with the 'local' or with 'grass-roots communities'.[47] The fact that the other can never really be known is not a problem but, on the contrary, positive and enabling, and 'expands possibilities for opening to "new" understandings of difference'[48] where external actors can 'value cultural difference independently of claims to have or know culture, attend directly to the process of constituting culture, and open to other ways of knowing human difference'.[49]

Regardless of the 'bottom-up' terminology through which this shift is recast, the phenomenological framing is the same: Mapping policy interventions increasingly start from the internal perceptions of actors closer to the problem itself and its articulation in its concrete 'local' context. The problem is then posed in terms of the ways of knowing and interacting of the 'local', vulnerable, marginalised or most at risk. The more the 'project design' starts from the perceptions of the 'other' or the ways in which the problem emerges 'for-itself' the more it is alleged that it will be possible for empowering interventions to be effective and to draw out innovative solutions.[50] Thus Mapping as a mode of governance seeks to see more intensively 'from the inside' of problems, understood as nested sets of constructed worlds of interaction where how other actors and agents see and understand these interactions is vital to grasping the world in its 'ontological multiplicity'. This provides a major challenge to the approach of drilling down to access and open up problems to an external understanding, as in the neoliberal and ecosystem resilience approaches to Mapping as a mode of governance which retain the baggage of the modernist episteme.

Working from inside the problem itself

Mapping approaches thus increasingly problematise the external approaches and technical fixes of modernist problem-solving in both its direct and indirect guises, attempting to grasp the problem on its own terms instead: on the basis of its own unfolding relationships to the world and the ways of knowing contained within these material and embodied processes. This shift also appears to be reflected in contemporary resilience discourses, where the mantra is increasingly that of rejecting external 'technical' or 'engineering' approaches of 'bouncing back' and instead cashing in on the 'resilience dividend' by using the failure of modernist approaches as an opportunity to see the world differently (as will be considered further in the next chapter).[51] In a world held to be more interconnected and less linear, the subject-centred knowledge of international policy-interveners is no longer knowledge. The focus on moving beyond drilling-down and instead seeing 'from the inside', through understanding interactive responsivities, enables the construction of problems in less correlationist ways: in ways which can perceive problems in their 'bottom-up' emergence, through attempts to 'follow the actor' or to 'follow the data'. The closest academic thinking generally comes to making the links between these disparate debates and discussions about how to design policy interventions in autopoietic processes, largely immune to external direction, is through the general concept of 'resilience'. However, without any methodological or philosophical insight into the underlying ontopolitical assumptions driving these discussions, there is as yet very little clarity even when a unifying signifier is introduced.[52] Debates over the nature of resilience as a policy methodology thus echo those within the mode of Mapping with little certainty over what counts as expertise, the nature of knowledge claims and the possibility of pursuing policy goals.[53]

The focus on the need to approach new modes of governance intervention from bottom-up perspectives, on the one hand, appears to draw the focus and attention of policy-makers down into a seeming black-hole; on the other hand they enable the world to be re-envisioned through the webs of relations and interconnections which are simultaneously revealed through moving beyond the assumptions of external knowledge implied by assemblage approaches. For Mapping, it is exactly the recessive, withdrawn or intractable nature of the problems addressed, their failure to be captured by external 'problem-solving', that forces policy-makers to see the nature of the interactions and connectivities which construct the world itself. In this way, every problem constructs or maps the world differently, through its emergence as a set of material and cognitive interactions and relationships. As a policy director for an international agency explained to me: 'This really pushed people. We realised that we couldn't operate in little bubbles. The people, the NGOs, private agencies, government actors, we all had expertise in different areas... There was a need to link everything together.'[54]

It may at first glance appear counterintuitive but the focus on the epistemological barriers to seeing the problem in its own relational emergence necessarily implies a much flatter, more diversified and interconnected approach to enabling adaptive policy intervention than top-down provisions of policy advice and assistance. The view of policy directors on the ground thus echoes closely the ontological framing of Bruno Latour:

> The point of this navigation is that it does not start with substitutable individuals ... but individualizes an entity by deploying its attributes. The farther the list of items extends, the more precise becomes the viewpoint of this individual monad. It begins as a dot, a spot, and it ends (provisionally) as a monad with an interior encapsulated into an envelope. Were the inquiry to continue, the 'whole world', as Leibniz said, would be 'grasped' or 'reflected' through this idiosyncratic point of view.[55]

Policy interventions become more about discovering the world in its intricate complexity than about applying pre-established forms of expertise. In fact, it could be argued that this was already the emerging trend in the late 1980s, when discussion of 'holistic' and 'integrated' approaches became fashionable,[56] only for this to be submerged by the clamour for emergency responses in the militarised and 'exceptional' interventions *ex nihilo* of the 1990s and early 2000s.[57] However, there is the vitally important proviso, the return of integrated approaches takes place not on the basis of the modernist unity of science but on the rejection of a unified approach on the basis of the subject: the new unity takes place on the basis of the rich (intensive and extensive) complexity of the problem itself. Each problem invites a different way of seeing the world through its lenses; a world of indirect experiential learning that can only be grasped by moving beyond disciplinary expertise and taking alterity seriously.

The world constituted through Mapping as a mode of governance is a very different world from that conceived in earlier approaches to international policy intervention. Attempts to grasp the specificity of problems in their unfolding interrelations necessitate the reconstruction of the world as a continuous process of working inside the problem, which at the same time continues to recede or to appear in more and more complex and interrelated ways.[58] If this is the case, pre-existing knowledge and approaches will inevitably be inadequate and the more 'objective' or 'scientific' they are, the less adequate they will be. This may seem counterintuitive, but the 'bottom-up' attempt to grasp a problem in terms of the 'phenomenology-*for*' or 'from the inside' necessarily challenges the assumptions of 'correlationist' science, which can only ever grasp appearances at the level of universal generalities rather than from the alternative Mapping perspectives of the actors and agencies involved.

Thus, Mapping as a mode of governance necessarily develops a flat ontology: all problems have the same ontological status.[59] All problems thus offer new opportunities to explore 'the great outdoors' – the depth and intensity of interactivity; to think in other ways and reflect differently upon the world as it is. Ian Bogost develops a useful analogy when he talks of the need for 'tiny ontology' and suggests that all objects are like black holes of infinite density. The useful aspect of this framing is that there are two sides to being:

> On the one side of being, we find unfathomable density, the black hole outside which all distinctions collapse into indistinction. Yet, on the other side, we find that being once again expands into an entire universe worth of stuff ... Things are both ordinary and strange, both large and small, both concrete and abstract. [60]

Bogost, following the lines of enquiry of other object-oriented theorists, such as Bryant, Harman and Morton,[61] seeks to give being two aspects: on the one side an infinite density of complexity that always withdraws or recedes from view and can never be entirely accessible but on the other side being expands into infinity, like the explosion of the Big Bang. Things, objects – or 'units of being' in Bogost's ontology – are thus worlds among worlds, infinitely entangled. Drawing from object-oriented approaches, such as Bogost's, can be insightful for the analysis of Mapping approaches to international policy-intervention. What does it mean to understand the problem 'for-itself' or from the perspective of other actors and agencies? We can see already, as a logical necessity, that the problem evades the modernist grasp, or subject-centred understanding of mapping assemblages, on two levels.

Each level responds to the two aspects of its being. Firstly, the problem recedes: no matter how much external actors attempt to 'drill-down' to the specificity of the context it seems that they will never grasp the infinite complexity of causation and emergence. The 'hidden' vulnerabilities, which intervening agencies seek to address, will, to a certain extent, always be hidden despite the development of new techniques of digital and algorithmic surveillance. Secondly, the problem reappears as a demand to remove the distinctions and to bridge the many policy 'silos' of international policy intervention. The discovery of depth, multiplicity and interconnection means that the approaches of development, security, humanitarianism, resilience, human rights etc. become increasingly merged together. These two linked processes are infinitely expanding: exploring problem-solving 'from the inside' reveals new depths and complexities which increasingly dissolve the distinctions of the policy areas and fields of traditional forms of policy interventions.

Paradoxically, in the governance mode of Mapping, the world of international policy intervention is a doubly disappearing one: the problems increasingly dissolve into deeper and more complex and differentiated processes of interaction and at the same time the existent policy mechanisms, distinctions and fields of expert knowledge increasingly dissolve into indistinction. A further paradox can be added to this: the assemblage theory approach, discussed in the previous chapter in its first, subject-centred iteration, thus becomes increasingly indistinguishable from its more object-oriented displacement as both become increasingly totalising. Both approaches to Mapping, those with the 'God's eye view' and those without it, are caught in the infinity of depth of processes of emergence. This means that interventions with the aim of micro-managing adaptation towards desired goals blur into (or can easily flip back and forth with) journeys of discovery, listening to and learning from the 'other'.

Conclusion

This chapter has sought to bring clarity to the discussion of the limits and possibilities of the practices of Mapping as a mode of governance, using the example of international policy intervention. The problems of international intervention have been the focus of the discussion as they bring to the surface the demand for Mapping as a response to the difficulty of maintaining the legitimacy of the internationalist imaginary of intervention from a universalist, detached, or objective perspective (even if it were possible for policy interventions to be free from the blinkers of power or ideology). Understanding the 'conditions of impossibility' for traditional or modernist conceptions of international intervention – the inability to legitimate the separations and cuts necessary to demarcate a distinct or separate policy sphere – shines an important light on the frameworks through which policy interventions are understood and contested today. It also suggests that to dismiss posthumanist, speculative realist or object-oriented approaches, as somehow not 'policy relevant' would be to miss the broader context in which both academic and policy processes are evolving on the basis of the ontopolitical assumptions of the Anthropocene.

Ian Bogost suggests that the problem of speculative realism and object-oriented approaches has been their inherently abstract presentation and that the task for philosophy today is to develop a practice, to search for a 'pragmatic' or an 'applied' speculative realism.[62] As demonstrated by the discussion above, this perhaps inverses the problematic: rather than philosophy emerging as an abstract theory unrelated to the world, and practices following later, it would appear that the practices and discourses of the policy world also facilitate shifts in philosophical perspectives. Perhaps it is policy-makers looking to legitimise new frameworks and approaches which have, in part, driven this shift to seeing problems as continually withdrawing from reach, while at the same time calling for the end of distinctions in policy areas and approaches and highlighting the need for local communities to 'own' their own problems and solutions. The policy world of international intervention seems to be a very real example of 'pragmatic' or 'applied' speculative realism, as the governance mode of Mapping develops in ways that appear to increasingly displace views of Western expertise and generalisable knowledge.

In the development of Mapping as a mode of governance, problems – ontopolitically cast as effects of complex chains of non-linear causation – appear as invitations to discover the mystery of the world in its 'weird' interconnectivity. Mapping thus can appear to be resuming its original formulation in neoliberal theory as knowledge scepticism – as a speculative framework of limits to governing knowledge – rather than as a programme of policy intervention. This retreat from 'actually existing neoliberalism' is clearly indicated in the dissolution of both the problem and the knowledge capacities of governing intervening actors. It is possible that the question of ontological depth will always pose a problem for Mapping as a mode of governance, as all entities, assemblages or objects are composed of relations of interaction 'all the way down'.[63] In the language of object-oriented theorists, all objects or entities can be seen as existing in two dimensions, in terms of their 'virtual proper being', i.e. the range of affordances or capacities that they are potentially capable of, and their 'local manifestation', those capacities or affordances which are actually expressed or developed: their forms of appearance.[64] While Mapping appears to be unable to intervene successfully in complex processes of emergence, the experience of practising Mapping as a technique of intervention seems to powerfully affirm the ontopolitical assumptions of depth, complexity and distributed agency at the heart of Anthropocene discourses.[65]

Mapping thus appears to confirm the end of modernist constructions of policy-making while not necessarily being able to formulate an adequate replacement, continually hovering between aspirations to achieve adaptive policy goals or, alternatively, to explore novel forms of emergence. The rest of this book engages with the two other modes of governance based on the ontopolitical assumptions of the Anthropocene: Sensing and Hacking. Both can be understood as responses to the limits of Mapping. Hacking (as will be considered in Chapters 6 and 7) can be seen as a logical extension of Mapping, aspiring to take up the invitation to explore the 'great outdoors' of interactive creative possibility, but without the constraints of seeking to derive knowledge of these processes or to design interventions in order to adapt them. Sensing (as will be analysed in the following two chapters) retreats from the difficulties of ontological depth and interactive complexity, focusing on real-time responsiveness to the effects of emergent processes. We turn next to Sensing.

Notes

1 The project presented here deploys some material from field investigations with leading international agencies in Nairobi in May 2016. The interview material is taken from unstructured interviews with a number of international agencies working in the field of rights, development and conflict management.

2 Posthumanist phenomenology is often seen as starting with Thomas Nagel's famous essay, 'What Is It Like to Be a Bat?' (1974) or with Deleuze and Guattari's popularisation of Jacob von Uexküll's 'ethology' (Deleuze 1988: pp.124–6), drawing attention to how our perceptions of the world are very different to those of other actors and agencies. This approach pluralises the world, enabling the world to be seen as constituted through many multiple ways of being, decentring the human as an all-knowing actor. A variety of related approaches – such as speculative realism, object-oriented ontology, actor network theory, new materialism and post-phenomenology – have extended the pluralising perspectives of critical, gender, feminist, black and decolonial studies to the nonhuman, thus radicalising perspectivism; see, for example, Bogost, 2012; Bryant, 2011; Ihde, 2009; Morton, 2012; Harman, 2016.

3 By practices of international policy intervention, I refer to the broad range of policy activity based upon furthering the needs of development and security through strengthening institutions at both state and societal levels.

4 The speculative or object-oriented 'turn' is used here as shorthand for the development of approaches which problematise modernist divides, such as those between culture and nature, human and nonhuman, mind and matter, and subject and object, through a focus on the material relationality of embodiment in a shared world (see, for example, Coole and Frost, 2010; Bennett, 2010; Barad, 2007), taken furthest in a range of theorists associated with the

developing fields of speculative realism and object-oriented ontology (see Gratton 2014, for a useful introduction and Wolfendale 2014 for a critique).

5 For example, Barnett and Weiss, 2008; Weiss, 2013; Chandler and Sisk, 2013.
6 See Ramalingam, 2013; Heins et al., 2016.
7 See, for example, Acuto and Curtis, 2014a; Millennium, 2013; Salter, 2015; 2016.
8 UN, 2015a; 2015b; 2015c.
9 UN, 2015d. The UN Secretary-General argues (UN, 2016a: p.29): 'We must [move]... beyond short-term, supply-driven response efforts towards demand-driven outcomes... international providers will need to set aside such artificial institutional labels as "development" or "humanitarian", working together... to assess what skills and assets they can contribute in a given context, at a particular time (short, medium and long term) and towards a specific outcome.'
10 UN, 2016a: p.33.
11 ODI, 2016: p.5.
12 Ibid.
13 Ibid.: p.23.
14 There is a large and well-established critical literature on the reproduction of international interests, hierarchies and exclusions through the interventionist impulse, informed through a broad range of conceptual and methodological frameworks (see, for example, Bennett et al., 2016; Collinson, 2016).
15 See discussion in COIC, 2016; Oxfam, 2016.
16 Programmes Director, Concern Worldwide, Nairobi, 9 May 2016.
17 On the 'epistemic avatars of Eurocentrism', see Sabaratnam, 2013.
18 See UN, 2016b.
19 Dewey, 1991.
20 UN, 2014; Meier, 2015; Mayer-Schönberger and Cukier, 2013.
21 UN, 2016a: p.31.
22 The modernist or Eurocentric episteme, which is being rejected, is usually understood as deterministic and reductionist, assuming Cartesian divisions (between subject and object, mind and matter, and culture and nature) and seen as exemplified in the fixed deterministic laws of classical Newtonian physics (see further, Barad, 2007; Mitchell, 2009).
23 Latour, 2012: p.595.
24 Venturini and Latour, 2010: p.94.
25 See ALNAP, 2016.
26 Read et al., 2016; O'Grady, 2016.
27 Programme manager, Ushahidi, Nairobi, 11 May 2016.
28 See also the discussion in Chapter 6.
29 O'Grady, 2016: p.78.
30 Critics have argued that new scanning and mapping technologies may distance humanitarian actors even more from these societies (Scott-Smith, 2016; Duffield, 2016; Meier, 2015) or that they may reproduce epistemological blind spots and exclusions in different forms (Read et al., 2016; Kitchin, 2014; Aradau and Blanke, 2015).
31 See, for example, Finkenbusch, 2016.
32 See Bargues-Pedreny, 2016.
33 See Pickering, 2010.

34 Programme manager, Ushahidi, Nairobi, 11 May.
35 See, for example, Harman, 2016.
36 See, for example, Chandler, 2017.
37 Meillassoux, 2008: pp.5–7.
38 See, for example, Mignolo, 2011; Mignolo and Escobar, 2010; Shilliam 2015; Wynter, 2003.
39 Bryant, 2012.
40 Candea in Carrithers et al., 2010: p.175.
41 Holbraad in ibid.: p.181.
42 Blaser, 2013: p.549.
43 Holbraad in Carrithers et al., 2010: p.184.
44 Blaser, 2013: p.551.
45 Ibid.: p.552; see also Mol, 2002.
46 Meillassoux, 2008: p.7.
47 See, for example, MacGinty and Richmond, 2013.
48 Brigg and Muller, 2009: p.136.
49 Ibid.: p.138.
50 See, for example, Bahadur and Doczi, 2016.
51 Rodin, 2015; Pelling, 2011; Haas, 2015.
52 Brand and Jax, 2007; Bourbeau, 2015.
53 See Chandler 2014a; 2014c.
54 Programme manager, Ushahidi, Nairobi, 9 May 2016.
55 Latour, 2012: p.599.
56 Macrae and Leader, 2001.
57 See Chandler, 2017.
58 I first came across the problematic of depth in Mapping discourses, in November 2009, when I took part in an ESRC funded seminar series 'Changing the Subject: Interdisciplinary Perspectives on Emotional Well-Being and Social Justice', at Nottingham University in the UK. The problem at issue was the sub-optimum choice-making of teenage boys and girls from economically deprived areas of the city of Nottingham (such as the high levels of teenage pregnancy and low levels of university take-up). It was argued that the problem stemmed from low levels of confidence and self-esteem and early school years intervention was advocated for. One of the Labour Party MPs from the area contributed his view on the problem, highlighting its depth, and suggested that pre-school intervention might be better, and that it would be better-still, 'if intervention were possible while they were still in their mother's womb'. The audience agreed. Apart from the poisonous view of a working class cultural environment, the view of how to tackle social and economic problems is notable in the desire to trace causation downwards in a never-ending ontology of depth.
59 Analogous to Levi Bryant's object-oriented onticology of the 'democracy of objects' (2011). Latour calls this process 'irreduction' in that 'Nothing is by itself either reducible or irreducible to anything else' (1993b: p.169), no problem can be reduced to another problem; all problems constitute the world in infinitely multiple ways.
60 Bogost, 2012: pp.22–3.
61 Bryant, 2011; Harman, 2009; Morton, 2013.
62 Bogost, 2012: p.29.

63 Bryant, 2014: p.38.
64 Bryant, 2014: pp.40–1. Or as Graham Harman puts it, reality is irreducible or inaccessible as it is 'objects wrapped in objects wrapped in objects' all the way down: 'We never reach some final layer of tiny components that explains everything else, but enter instead into an indefinite regress of parts and wholes. Every object is both a substance and a complex of relations.' (Harman, 2005: p.85)
65 '...our discourse and maps and plans regarding things are not those things. There is an irreducible gap.' (Morton, 2013: p.133; see also p.48)

PART III

Sensing

4

THE RISE OF THE CORRELATIONAL MACHINE

Introduction

Mapping as a mode of governance, as considered in the previous two chapters, has an ontology of processual emergence and depth. In contrast, Sensing works on the surface, on the 'actualist' notion that 'only the actual is real'.[1] As Roy Bhaskar, the originator of the philosophy of critical realism, has argued, 'actualism' can be seen to be problematic in that hierarchies of structures and assemblages disappear and the scientific search for 'essences' under the appearance of things loses its value.[2] However, if it is understood that causal laws are so mediated by non-linear assemblages, each with their own contingent relations and processes, all the way down, then it would make sense to think less about 'drilling down' in ever more technically exhaustive ways and, instead, to think more about engaging with surface appearances. Once causality appears to have lost its 'modernist' linearity, the question of causation increasingly appears to be more a matter of metaphysics than one of relevance for governance, which needs to be much more pragmatic in relation to problems and concerns.

It is for pragmatic reasons that Sensing as a mode of governance appears to be increasingly rivalling Mapping as a way of coping with and being responsive to the pressures of the Anthropocene condition. Mapping tends towards 'solutionism' or adaptive 'problem-solving' though internal processes of transformation and learning lessons, acquiring new forms of (plural and differentiated, context-specific) knowledge. Mapping offers the promise of resilience, framed as 'bouncing back better' and learning retrospectively, but Sensing is increasingly becoming a rival as the key governance mode for resilience. Sensing accepts that little can be done to prevent problems (understood as emergent or interactive effects) or to learn from problems and that aspirations of transformation are much more likely to exacerbate these problems rather than solve them. Rather than attempt to 'solve' a problem or adapt societies, entities or ecosystems, in the hope that they will be better able to cope with problems and shocks, Sensing seeks to work on how relational understandings can help in the present; in sensing and responding to the process of emergence. Where Mapping works on the depth of processes, Sensing seeks to work on the surface, on the actual.

This chapter is organised in four sections. The following section introduces Sensing as the governance of effects rather than causation, focusing on the work of Ulrich Beck and Bruno Latour in establishing the problematic of contingent interaction, rather than causal depth, as key to emergent effects, which can be unexpected and catastrophic. The second section considers in more depth how Sensing puts greater emphasis on relations of interaction rather than on ontologies of being, and links the methodological approach of Sensing closely to actor network assumptions that disavow structures of causation. The final two sections analyse how correlation works to reveal new agencies and processes of emergence and how new technologies have been deployed in this area, providing some examples of how the shift from Mapping causal relations to Sensing effects has begun to alter governmental approaches.

Sensing and the governance of effects

Sensing, as a mode of governance, understands problems in terms of their effects rather than their causation. Today, as noted in the previous chapter, analysts are much more likely to highlight that the complexity of global interactions and processes mitigate against ambitious schemas for intervention, aimed at finding the root causes of problems or developing solutions through ambitious projects of social and political engineering from the ground up.[3] In a more complex world, depth ontologies can appear to be reductionist and are easily discredited by the growing awareness that any forms of external design intervention or social engineering will have unintended side effects. It is in the attempt to minimise these unintended consequences that the focus of policy-makers has shifted to Sensing, focusing on the responsive governance of effects rather than seeking to address ostensible root causes. For example, rather than seeking to solve conflict or to end it (resulting in possibly problematic unintended consequences) international policy intervention is increasingly articulated as 'managing' conflict, developing societal strategies to cope better and thereby limit its effects.[4] Focusing on managing effects rather than engaging with non-linear causative chains makes the forms and practices of policy intervention quite different.

The link between conceptual discussions of governance and epistemic questions of knowledge is usefully highlighted by developing Giorgio Agamben's framing of a shift from a concern with causation to that of effects, which he understands as a depoliticising move.[5] Debates about addressing causation involve socio-political analysis and policy choices, putting decision-making and the question of sovereign power and political accountability at the forefront. Causal relations (even non-linear ones) assume power operates in a hierarchy or panarchy of systems, with policy outcomes understood to be products of conscious choices, powers and capacities. Agamben argues that, whilst the governing of causes is the essence of politics, the governance of effects reverses the political process:

> We should not neglect the philosophical implications of this reversal. It means an epoch-making transformation in the very idea of government, which overturns the traditional hierarchical relation between causes and effects. Since governing the causes is difficult and expensive, it is more safe and useful to try to govern the effects. [6]

The governance of effects can therefore be seen as a retreat from Mapping as a mode of governance, which dominated interventionist approaches of the 1990s and early 2000s, in terms of both resources and policy goals. However, the shift from causation to effects involves a shifting conceptualisation of intervention itself; it is this conceptual connection that is the central concern of this book, which seeks to introduce the distinct ontopolitical assumptions informing new modes of governing in the Anthropocene. The mode of Sensing — governing through attempting to enhance system and community responsivity to effects — shifts the focus away from the formal public, legal and political sphere to the capacities and abilities of systems or societies for responsiveness to changes in their environmental context. The management of effects involves redistributing agency, understood as responsive capacity, and thereby evades the question of the responsibility or accountability for problems or the need to intervene on the basis of government as a form of political decision-making.[7]

Policy interventions have shifted from the governance mode of Mapping to that of Sensing as governing agencies have sought to respond to the effects of indeterminacy and risk as inherent in the complex and inter-dependent world rather than understanding problems in a modernist telos of solutionism and progress. Thus the rearticulation of problems in terms of effects rather than causation fits well with Anthropocene sensibilities described in the introductory chapter. Problems in their emergence are the ontological product of complex feedback loops and systemic interactions that often cannot be predicted or foreseen in advance. Surprising and catastrophic effects thereby call for new ways of thinking and governing: ways that go beyond modernist linear and non-linear cause-and-effect assumptions and that can potentially cope with unexpected shocks and unseen threats.

As 'effects' become more central than causes, 'solutions-thinking' becomes less useful and potentially a barrier to responsiveness, this is because 'problem-solving' tends to affirm current practices and approaches rather than emphasising the need to be alert to emergent effects.[8] The promise of 'solutions' seems to deny our entangled responsibilities and commitments while greater sensitivity to effects enables us to become increasingly aware of them. Initially, the leading theorist to problematise 'problem-solving' approaches was perhaps Ulrich Beck, who argued that the risk of unin-tended effects could no longer be bracketed off, compartmentalised or excluded in the Second Modernity.[9] Beck argued that unexpected feedback effects from policy-making were an inevitable result of globalisation and interconnectivity, suggesting that the boundaries of liberal modernity – between the state and society and between culture and nature – were increasingly blurring. Surprises and shock events could no longer be treated as exceptions to the norm, to be quantified and insured against.[10]

The radical awareness of interconnectivity and feedback effects, articu-lated by Beck, was initially presented as purely negative: as a factor to be addressed, and potentially minimised, through governing under the 'pre-cautionary principle'.[11] The awareness of entanglements leading to unin-tentional effects thus began to integrate concerns of contingency into the practices of governance. The precautionary principle of Beck's still had a modernist legacy, in the positing of a potentially knowing and controlling subject able to manage unintended effects. But, as the assumptions of modernity began to ebb away and discourses of globalisation morphed into those of the Anthropocene, this subject increasingly had to act more humbly and cautiously, testing and experimenting rather than assuming cause and effect modalities.[12] Unfortunately, Beck focused on the regulation of effects through ways of predicting or imagining the consequences of human actions, which seemed logically impossible to foresee. For example, even if scientists reached a consensus on the safety of a new procedure or initiative before its application, scientific experimentation in the laboratory cannot reproduce the same conditions as those of real, differentiated and complex life. This then led critics, like Bruno Latour, to convincingly argue that, once included, effects could not be prevented or minimised through precautions but instead had to be followed through 'all the way' (Latour's thesis will be considered in greater detail below).[13]

Towards the end of his life, Beck (in line with the times) shifted the presentation of his approach, articulating the appreciation of effects as enabling governance rather than as merely constraining it.[14] There were also positive feedback effects of the entanglements of culture and nature, indicating the need to adequately understand the new anthropogenic manufacture of risks – such as global climate change. Thus, the awareness of the catastrophic effects of climate change and other risks could be seen to be potentially positive.[15] For Beck:

> Anthropological shocks provide a new way of being in the world, seeing the world and doing politics. The anthropological shock of Hurricane Katrina is a useful example … Until Hurricane Katrina, flooding had not been positioned as an issue of environmental justice – despite the existence of a substantial body of research documenting inequalities and vulnerability to flooding. It took the reflection both in the publics and in academia on the devastating but highly uneven 'racial floods' of Hurricane Katrina to bring back the strong 'Anthropocene' of slavery, institutionalized racism, and connect it to vulnerability and floods. This kind of connecting the disconnected is the way the cosmopolitan side effects of bads are real, e.g. the invisibility of side effects is made visible.[16]

The flooding of New Orleans illustrated how devastating emergent effects could be, but had the consequence of enabling governing authorities to know the connection between risks that were thought to be natural or external with racial, social and economic inequalities which were thought to be purely social. This necessitated the bringing together of governance expertise on the basis that the natural and the social were intermingled and that the politics of race was not disconnected from the politics of ecology.[17] In the same way, the natural and the social sciences needed to be brought together in rethinking how to engage with the world beyond this posited culture/nature divide.[18] For Beck, this 'Metamorphosis is not social change [it] … is a mode of changing the mode of change. It signifies the age of side effects. It challenges the way of being in the world, thinking about the world and imagining and doing politics.'[19]

A new form of governance thus emerges from the inclusion of effects: the understanding of crises and disasters as no longer purely natural or purely social but as contingent and emergent processes beyond governing control:

> Metamorphosis is deeply connected with the idea of unawareness, which embeds a deep and enduring paradox. On the one hand, it emphasizes the inherent limitations in knowledge … [N]ano-technology, bio-engineering, and other types of emergent technology contain not only knowable risks but also risks we cannot yet know, providing a window of fundamental limitations to society's ability to perceive and govern risks.[20]

Beck's understanding of the Anthropocene as 'the age of side effects'[21] nicely encapsulates how the contingent and unforeseeable emergence of effects has been captured and incorporated into governance under discourses of Sensing. Beck had not much more to offer than that the 'imagination of a threatening future' would focus attention on the ways in which contingent processes interacted. Although Beck had established the importance of Sensing as a mode of governance, he did not follow this framing through to its logical conclusion.[22]

Bruno Latour has sought to go beyond the limits of Beck's work in this area, seeking to trace the effects of human actions in real time feedback loops; requiring less of the imagination and more of science and technology for Sensing. Latour has deployed the radical discourse of understanding problems in their emergence to great effect, having long waged war on modernist binary understandings, particularly that of the separation of culture and nature. For Latour, just as humanity has become more entangled with nature than ever before, ecologists have sought to emphasise the need for separation to protect 'nature' and modernist science aspires to know the world/'nature' as somehow a separate and fixed reality.[23] Therefore, along similar lines to Beck's later work, global warming is not so much a sign of the failure of modernity but an enabler of new forms of governing in the Anthropocene. The unknown and unintended consequences of humanity's historical footprint on the planet could only be construed as problematic in modernist terms if people still bought into modernity's linear fantasy of 'progress'.[24] Instead, the awareness of emergent effects such as climate change reveals the entanglements of humanity and the environment and is a critical wake-up call to radically reorganise the governance of the planet on the basis of a more inclusive understanding that 'nature' cannot just be left alone, but must be 'even more managed, taken up, cared for, stewarded, in brief, integrated and internalized into the very fabric of policy'.[25]

Sensing is crucial for Latour's project of enfolding the unintended effects of planetary interaction into the everyday governance of the Anthropocene. This cannot be done by Mapping, with an ontology of depth, as the effects of interaction are concrete and contingent and thus depend on the ability to trace the surface of interactive relations through seeing effects, to follow the unintended and unforeseen consequences of human actions 'all the way'. Latour thus enthuses:

> the principle of precaution, properly understood, is exactly the change of *zeitgeist* needed: not a principle of abstention – as many have come to see it – but a change in the way *any action* is considered, a deep tidal change in the linkage modernism established between science and politics. From now on, thanks to this principle, unexpected consequences are *attached* to their initiators and have to be followed through all the way.[26]

Latour's subject is the initiator of actions and thereby responsible for the interactive consequences of this initiation.[27] For Latour, the consequences of human actions can be traced through seeing or being sensitive to the network formed through their effects.[28] Thus Sensing as a mode of governance does not seek to drill down to discover the ontology of assemblages and processes of emergence but to trace these links on the surface, in the sphere of the actual. The need to be responsive to effects also drives debates establishing the networks of entanglement of the Anthropocene, calling for greater sensitivity to the everyday feedbacks that bring these relations and interactions to light.[29] For some authors, extreme weather events or outbreaks of new viruses, for example, indicate networked interactions spanning the globe, revealing contingent linkages, interconnections and feedback loops.[30]

The ability to see or sense the actual effects of relational interactions becomes more enabling, the more connections can be established or imagined across greater distances and across more varied forms of interactive life. These complex and intricate feedback loops also call for greater technological capacities for Sensing. Thus, these tasks can be accomplished, according to Latour:

> by crisscrossing their [the loops'] potential paths with as many instruments as possible to have a chance of detecting in what ways they are connected ... laying down the networks of equipment that render the consequences of action visible to all the various agencies that do the acting ... '[S]ensitivity' is a term that applies to all the agencies able to spread their loops further and to feel the consequences of what they do come back to haunt them ... but only as long and as far that it [humanity] is fully equipped with enough sensors to feel the feedbacks.[31]

Latour's framework sees the ability to sense effects as crucial to revealing the unseen and unknown interconnections of the Anthropocene, involving the technology and regulatory mechanisms necessary to 'trace and ceaselessly retrace again the lines made by all those loops' with a 'strong injunction: keep the loop traceable and publically visible' so that 'whatever is reacting to your actions, loop after loop ... weighs on you as a force to be taken into account'.[32]

New sensorial forms of governance are given a material political form as a new set of political competencies and responsibilities are established: 'Such an accumulation of *responses* requires a responsible agency to which you, yourself, have to become in turn *responsible.*'[33] Unlike the governance mode of Mapping, Sensing does not seek to make causal claims,[34] the emergence of effects can be traced to reveal new relations of interaction and new agencies or actants to be taken into account but there is no assumption that effects can be understood and manipulated or governed through transcendental policy goals[35] – real time responsive forms of management through Sensing increasingly focus on the 'what is'[36] of the world in its complex and plural emergence.

The fact that the 'what is-ness' of the world is not a concern with a modernist ontology of being and causation is often neglected in considerations of Sensing as a mode of governance, so it will be considered here and in more detail in the following section. Latour, in the 'Facing Gaia' lectures, argues that nature has to be understood in 'post-epistemological' terms.[37] By this he means that modernist forms of representation, reduction, abstraction and exclusion cannot know a world that is plural, lively and interactive. This is post-epistemological because knowledge can no longer be extracted from its concrete context of interaction in time and space. In this framing, knowledge, to be 'objective' – to be real – has to be plural, fluid and concrete.[38] This is very similar to Donna Haraway's understanding of 'situated epistemology', which rejects modernist drives to extract knowledge, i.e. to turn knowing into abstractions from real emergent processes through methods of scaling up, generalising and universalising, fixing knowledge apart from its plural, changing and overlapping context of meaning.[39] In this way of rethinking knowledge, the modernist divisions between subjective and objective and qualitative and quantitative are dissolved.[40]

The multiple concrete of emergence articulates a very different ontopolitical vision to that informing Mapping as a mode of governance. Here, there can be no divisions between interacting assemblages in a panarchy of speeds, size and influence. Latour's is a flat ontology, where speed, size and scale are momentary and contingent products of interaction rather than constructing and shaping path-dependencies. As Latour repeats, in a world of unknowable contingencies 'it is the *what is* that obstinately requests *its due*'. [41] This 'empirical' displacement of causal understandings can also be intimated from Beck's later work. Beck imagined the development of real time empirics as able to evade both the dangers of critical immanent approaches, which tended to reproduce the knowledge scepticism of postmodernism, and the hubristic knowledge claims of transcendental frameworks of cause-and-effect. Thus, the world could be governed in its complex emergence, through focusing on effects as the starting point for governance:

> Seen this way, climate change risk is far more than a problem of measures of carbon dioxide and the production of pollution. It does not even only signal a crisis of human self-understanding. More than that, global climate risk creates new ways of being, looking, hearing and acting in the world – highly conflictual and ambivalent, open-ended, without any foreseeable outcome. As a result, a compass for the 21st century arises. This compass is different from the postmodern 'everything goes' and different from false universalism. This is a new variant of critical theory, which does not set the normative horizon itself but

takes it from empirical analyses. Hence, it is an empirical analysis of the normative horizon of the self-critical world risk society.[42]

In the governance mode of Sensing, the focus on empirical analysis to facilitate real time responsiveness enables emergent effects to discursively frame governance without an external subject 'setting the normative horizon'. This new 'normative horizon' is one imagined as set by the world itself – and accessed through the development of new mechanisms and techniques sensitised and responsive to the world in its emergence. The post-epistemological implications of frameworks of Sensing seem to underlie the fascination with Big Data approaches as a way of generating increasingly sensitive real-time responses to emergent effects, as will be analyzed in more detail in the next chapter. [43]

Objects and relations

As already intimated in the consideration of Latour's work in the previous section, Sensing can be usefully engaged with as a mode of governance that necessarily shares the ontopolitical assumptions of actor network theory (ANT) and can be informed by a consideration of the long-running engagement between Bruno Latour (the leading proponent of ANT) and Graham Harman (a leading speculative realist) over the conceptualisation of this approach.[44] Harman takes Latour to task precisely for the 'actualism' at the heart of the ANT approach, stating that, for Latour, momentary relations are more important than the substance of entities (or 'actants'):

> For Latour an actant is always an event, and events are always completely specific: 'everything happens only once, and at one place.' An actant ... is always completely deployed in the world, fully implicated in the sum of its dealings at any given moment. Unlike a substance, an actant is not distinct from its qualities, since for Latour this would imply an indefensible featureless lump lying beneath its tangible properties ... And unlike a substance, actants are not different from their relations. Indeed, Latour's central thesis is that an actor is its relations. All features of an object belong to it; everything happens only once, at one time, in one place.[45]

This focus on relations in the actual, in the present rather than on the potential, or possibilities, which may lie latent or virtual in entities, ecosystems or assemblages, is crucial to the distinction with the depth ontology of Mapping:

> Since Latour is committed to a model of actants fully deployed in alliances with nothing held in reserve, he cannot concede any slumbering potency lying in the things that is currently unexpressed. To view a thing in terms of potential is to grant it something beyond its current status as a fully specific event.[46]

As Harman argues, 'Latour is the ultimate philosopher of relations' and in this way inverts the assemblage theory of DeLanda,[47] described in Chapter 2 as the ontopolitical essence of Mapping as a mode of governance, which understands assemblages as never fully actualised, enabling the possibility for intervention to bring forward alternative paths of emergence. For Harman, and object-oriented ontologists, ANT falls down for its lack of distinction between objects and their relations, which he argues acts by 'flattening everything out too much, so that everything is just on the level of its manifestation', and therefore, the approach 'can't explain the change of the things' or the hidden potential of alternative outcomes.[48] For actor network theory the emergence of new aspects of reality is not a matter of depth but of seeing what actually exists, but is consigned to the background. As Latour argues:

> I call this background *plasma*, namely that which is not yet formatted, not yet measured, not yet socialized, not yet engaged in metrological chains, and not yet covered, surveyed, mobilized, or subjectified. How big is it? Take a map of London and imagine that the social world visited so far occupies no more room than the subway. The plasma would be the rest of London, all its buildings, inhabitants, climates, plants, cats, palaces, horse guards … [Sociologists] were right to look for 'something hidden behind', but it's neither behind nor especially hidden. It's *in between* and not made of social stuff. It is not hidden, simply *unknown*. It resembles a vast hinterland providing the resources for every single course of action to be fulfilled, much like the countryside for the urban dweller, much like the missing masses for a cosmologist trying to balance out the weight of the universe. (emphasis in original)[49]

In ANT, as an alternative science of relationality, what is missing in terms of governmental understanding is not relational depth but relationality on the surface: the presence of actual relations which give entities and systems their coherence or weight in the present moment. Thus, for ANT, modernist understandings of the world, whether those of natural or of social science, give too much credence to entities as if they have fixed essences rather than shifting relations to other actants:

> The world is not a solid continent of facts sprinkled by a few lakes of uncertainties, but a vast ocean of uncertainties speckled by a few islands of calibrated and stabilized forms ... Do we really know that little? We know even less. Paradoxically, this 'astronomical' ignorance explains a lot of things. Why do fierce armies disappear in a week? Why do whole empires like the Soviet one vanish in a few months? Why do companies who cover the world go bankrupt after their quarterly report?[50]

In February 2008, Latour and Harman participated in a public seminar at the LSE, in which the differences between what are heuristically described here as the ontopolitical assumptions behind Mapping and Sensing as modes of governance were brought to the surface. Noortje Marres made some useful interventions regarding the importance of ANT for the discovery of new ways of seeing agency in the world on the pragmatic basis of 'effect' rather than a concern for emergent causation:

> because pragmatists are not contemplative metaphysicians, because they say 'we will not decide in advance what the world is made up of', this is why they go with this weak signal of the effect. Because that is the only way to get to a new object, an object that is not yet met nor defined.[51]

Marres argued that taking 'as our starting point stuff that is happening' was a way of 'suspending' or of 'undoing' ontology, in order to study change.[52] This aspect is vital to Sensing as a mode of governance, as this inversing of Mapping enables a focus upon the surface appearances of change, which is not considered so important in an ontology of non-linear causality and assemblages:

> It's about saying that we have a world where continuously new entities are added to the range of existing entities, everything continually changes and yet in this modern technological world everything stays the same. We have stabilized regimes ... But if we engage in studying specific objects, we do not find this singularized thing that is well put-together, as an object. We do not find it at the foundation but we find it as an emergent effect.[53]

Surface appearances of things are continually changing as their relationships do, not through an ontology of depth but through networks and interactions on the surface: in plain sight. As Latour states, regarding the 'plasma' or the 'missing masses' of ANT: 'it's not the unformatted that's the difficulty here. It's what is in between the formatting. Maybe this is not a very good metaphor. But it's a very, very different landscape, once the background and foreground have been reversed.'[54]

Thus, my argument here is that the ontopolitical assumptions of Sensing as a mode of governance can be usefully grasped in terms of actor network theory in that the concern is not the nature of systems or substances but ways in which change can be detected through seeing processes of emergence as relational. Relational processes without a conception of depth are co-relational rather than causal as the processes of relation may be contingent and separate conjunctions. The fact that all forms of being are co-relational means that new opportunities arise to see with and through these relations and co-dependencies: whether it is the co-relation of pines and matsutake mushrooms (mobilised by Anna Tsing)[55] or the co-relation between sunny weather and purchases of barbecue equipment or the co-relation between Google search terms and flu outbreaks.[56] These are relations of 'effects' rather than of causation, when some entities or processes have an effect on others they can be seen as 'networked' or 'assembled' but they have no relation of immanent or non-linear causation which can be mapped and reproduced or intervened in.

The co-relational rather than causal aspect of actor network theory distinguishes it from assemblage theory or the neo-institutional or ecosystem approaches with their ontology of depth, which enable an adaptive mode of governance of indirect intervention into structured processes of emergence. Actor network approaches therefore lack the temporal and spatial boundedness of assemblages or of nested adaptive systems and have no assumptions of iterative interactions producing state changes to higher levels of complex ordering.[57] They say nothing of 'ontology' or of the essences of things, merely focusing on the transmission of effects at particular moments; thus they can draw together 'litanies' of actors and actants − the plasma, or 'missing masses' − crucial for describing or understanding how change occurs in systems or states. Suspending or 'undoing' ontology, opens ANT approaches to the world of interaction in the actual, or brings the open-ended processual understanding of the virtual into the actual. New actors or agencies are those brought into being or into relation to explain 'effects' and to see processes of emergence through 'co-relation'. In this respect, new technological advances, driving algorithmic machine learning, Big Data capabilities and the Internet of Things, seem perfectly timed to enable Sensing as a mode of governance.

The rise of the correlational machine

Human-nonhuman assemblages of sensors enable new forms of responsivity but the advancements are not to do with causal knowledge but with the capacities to see through the breaking down of processes via the development of 'correlational machines'. I use the term 'correlational machines' to distinguish the governance mode of Sensing as a very distinct paradigm in contra distinction to Mapping with its ontology of depth and immanence. The development of correlational machines is not new to the Anthropocene, but is part-and-parcel of the extension of human agency through the use of artificial prostheses to enable sensing the environment. Perhaps the classic example, provided by Merleau-Ponty's work on the phenomenology of perception, would be the walking stick, which enables a blind person to sense the obstacles around them, through the resistance to touch and the sounds made, etc.[58] Another example would be the deployment of canaries as sensors for carbon monoxide in mineshafts.

Human, nonhuman and technological aids thus have long histories in enabling the extension of human responsivity to effects, through the power of co-relation or correlation. It is important to illustrate why this is correlation and not causation, as this is key to the governance mode of Sensing. Sensing relies on causal laws or regularities but the key aspect is that they are secondary to correlation rather than primary. As Latour would argue, the key concerns are not ontological but relational: the causal becomes background to the relational foreground. Take the example of the canary in the mineshaft. The precondition for the canary signalling the existence of carbon monoxide is the causal regularity of poisonous gas killing the canary before mine workers are aware of its existence and prone to its effects. However, the problem of carbon monoxide is not addressed at the level of causation (predicting it or preventing it from appearing or solving the problem afterwards) but through developing a method of signalling the existence of poisonous fumes and of increasing human sense-ability through the power of correlation. The canary is a nonhuman correlational machine for signalling the existence of carbon monoxide. The canary enables the unseen to be seen: it brings the 'missing masses', which exist in the mineshaft, into perception. The addition of the canary into the situational context reveals the existence of other actants, the poisonous gases, which were there but previously operated unseen.

Two everyday examples, which draw out more clearly the 'machinic' nature of artificial prosthetics for Sensing, are the development of the thermometer and the compass. Both the thermometer and the compass enable the extension of human sensitivity and agency. The prosthetic support they provide is correlational although based upon causal laws or regularities. The compass, based originally on the magnetic qualities of the naturally occurring mineral magnetite or lodestone, can enable a magnetised needle to point a course in relation to the geomagnetic north pole. Thus mariners could see or sense their direction through the power of the compass as a 'correlational machine', enabling new 'actants' (magnetic fields of attraction) to be enrolled in navigation through their correlational effects.[59]

The story of the thermometer is similar; it relies on causal relations, the thermal expansion of solids or liquids, such as water, alcohol and mercury, with the increase in temperatures. These thermal properties of expansion were known to the ancient Greeks and applied or 'machinised' in the 18th century with the Fahrenheit scale.[60] A thermometer is an artificially constructed correlational machine that enables the seeing or sensing of atmospheric changes that would otherwise be unseen. New 'correlational machines' are being developed all the time, enabled by a variety of new technologies, for example, more accurate quantum thermometers, measuring thermal changes at the quantum level. New actants, in this case, intrinsic quantum motions, can be enrolled to create new machinic prostheses for seeing changes in temperature at ever more precise levels.[61]

While chains of non-linear causation, formed through interactive assemblages, extend beyond the modernist or linear understanding of causation as a set of fixed relations or properties, they remain fixed at the level of responsivity: at the level of phenomenological openness to the 'great outdoors'. Correlational machines operate to get beyond the phenomenological limits discussed in relation to Mapping as a mode of governance through indirect intervention. Often these new assemblages involve the extensive use of new sensing technologies, often termed 'the Internet of Things', where sensors can be connected to the internet and provide real time detection of changes in air and water quality, earth tremors or parking capacity etc. The potential use of sensing technologies is extensive. At the MIT Senseable City Lab, for example, researchers informed me of work being carried out using robotic sensors in sewers tracking minute quantities of bio-chemical material. Potentially, local authorities could receive real time information on localised health profiles and illegal drug use.[62] If sewers can be turned into key information generators for bio-sensing and drug and health profiling, it is clear that Sensing could provide a whole range of new avenues for governance monitoring and regulatory policing.[63] Thus new assemblages are being artificially constructed that enable new actants to be enrolled in Sensing, including nonhuman and non-living actants, and in doing so, changes can be seen or sensed and therefore responded to, often revealing new threats or dangers or expanding human sensitivity to existing ones.

While these 'more-than-human' machinic assemblages are constructed on the basis of causal laws and regularities their purpose is a correlational one: seeing what exists in the present, in the actual, but is unknown or unseen. To take one contemporary example, Elizabeth Johnson has done insightful work on Sensing as a more-than-human form of governance in her analysis of the work of commercial biosensing and the use of organic life to monitor fresh and marine water sources for pollution.[64] Here an array of animal species, small fish, worms, molluscs, crustaceans and micro-organisms are monitored intensively to discover their norms of functionality and to develop ways of measuring changes in these indicators. They are then ready for use as 'correlational machines':

> [The company] monitors a suite of 'behavioral fingerprints' as these organisms are exposed to different systems. Locomotor activity, reproductive rates, and embryonic developments are measured together to indicate the severity of hazardous anthropogenic chemicals as well as biologically produced toxins, such as blue-green algae. In this way the company boasts, it can make 'pollution measurable.'[65]

As Johnson notes, the governance mode of Sensing is less about causation than seeing the unseen: 'making imperceptible harms perceptible'.[66] This approach sees through correlation, which enables new problems and possibilities to be detected. For example, changes in the bodily indicators of the animal organs can alert human agents to identify potential problems even if the sources are unknown. Thus the company concerned argues that problems can be detected 'in due time before pollution irreversibly spreads in the environment or even harms human health'.[67] In a technological extension of the nonhuman prosthesis of the canary down a coalmine, 'biosensing enables a way of seeing with nonhuman life'.[68]

Just as for the thermometer to work as a correlational machine the properties of mercury needed to be understood for its enrolment, for biosensing technologies, green florescent protein (GFP) has been a widely used tool to enable organic life to be modified into correlational machines, potentially signalling a wide range of changes in acidity and alkalinity as well as the presence of pathogens, toxins and cancer-causing agents.[69] Sensing, on the basis of developing new forms of correlational sight, enables a fundamental shift from governance on the basis of 'problem-solving' and analysis of 'root causes' to the governance of effects. In this mode of governance, distinctions between scientific disciplines and individual entities tend to disappear as these historically depended upon organic conceptions of causation. In contrast, the ontopolitics informing Sensing as a mode of governance is not concerned with entities or with causation, enabling 'more-than-human' assemblages of responsivity to become the new governmental norm.[70]

From Mapping to Sensing

This book is organised on the basis of drawing out Mapping, Sensing and Hacking as three distinct modes of governance, grounded in the ontopolitical assumptions of the Anthropocene. It goes without saying that in policy experimentation on the ground there is much less clarity over the distinctiveness of these modes and their inner logics and consequences. Nevertheless, it is argued here that there is a general, though uneven, shift towards a greater affirmation of the Anthropocene, which can be charted as a continuum from Mapping, through Sensing and towards Hacking. A good example of how this shift occurs, in this case, from Mapping towards Sensing, as a mode of governance, is that of the experimental deployment of new technologies for counter-insurgency and policing.

Traditional surveillance techniques, in the Mapping paradigm, would gain information about suspected insurgent groups and sympathisers – mapping these relations and speculating with regard to the path-dependencies of actor motivations and modes of operation, potentially enabling attacks to be prevented or predicted. This information would be intentionally gathered, usually covertly. Increasingly, however, an alternative mode of intelligence gathering is developing, based on open source data rather than covert surveillance and derived from untargeted sources. The first approach works on the basis of a clear ontology of causal connections in a relational assemblage, while the second works in a much broader or open ontology, seeking to see patterns and correlations across a range of data. This shift can be illustrated by a consideration of the methodologies of two US government data-mining programmes in Afghanistan, deployed in 2009, seeking to use new digital technologies to develop qualitative insights and to see effects in their emergence.[71]

The first case is a data-mining programme based on the latest predictive analysis work being done in the commercial sector, but using NSA intercepts of media communications and military data from Afghanistan. The prominent university computer scientist in charge, Peter Lee, explained: 'For example, we were trying to understand if the price of potatoes at local markets was correlated with subsequent Taliban activity, insurgent activity, in the same way that Amazon might want to know if certain kinds of click behaviors on Amazon.com would correlate to higher sales of clothing versus handbags versus computers.'[72] Sensing, unlike Mapping, seeks to isolate patterns and correlations not non-linear lines of causation. Thus the US counterinsurgency Big Data team could be seen as transitional between Mapping and Sensing, on one level trying to predict as if non-linear causal relations could be gleamed from the material, but on another level, trying to see or to 'sense' on the basis of patterns of correlation. The team:

> was particularly interested in using patterns of daily life, including the costs of transportation and exotic vegetables, to make predictions about insurgencies in Afghanistan. 'We were really using the latest research in quasi-experimental design, in machine learning, and data mining literally on hundreds of intelligence feeds to make inferences about what would happen next.'[73]

In this example, it could be argued that there is a thin line between Sensing (seeing what is already in existence through greater correlational clarity) and Mapping (seeing non-linear assemblages of emergent interaction). However, the conceptual distinctions are increasingly clear, highlighted by the fact that the shift towards Sensing enables the assimilation of much greater varieties of information. Firstly, this is required for the benefits of correlation, for example, the potential correlation with 'the costs of transportation and exotic vegetables'. Secondly, this is possible because 'Sensing', as a mode of governance, is not looking for causal lines, this means that the information required does not have to be reduced or homogenised. Qualitative information can be processed just as easily as quantitative information, which is not properly regularised (and thus of little use for causal analysis).

The shift towards Sensing becomes clearer in the second data-mining programme, the US-developed crowdsourced programme called 'More

Eyes'. This was carried out under the guise of humanitarian mapping aid, where Afghan participants, often drawn from the humanitarian and development communities, were provided with GPS-enabled phones and instructed to mark the location of buildings and streets.[74] It is useful to quote the *Foreign Policy* article to get a better flavour of the ontopolitical assumptions at play, both in terms of the use of data and the role of crowdsourced data gathering:

> Paterson said More Eyes worked directly with the Defense Intelligence Agency on a project called 'Afghanistan Atmospherics,' which involved using 'selected local persons to passively observe and report on things they see and hear in the course of everyday activities.' ... Paterson described More Eyes as a way 'to catalyze the local population to generate "white" data useful for assessing stability at multiple levels (regional, provincial, district and village).' The advantage of this white data, as opposed to the black world of intelligence, is that it is 'generated spontaneously by the local population ... untainted by influence of outsiders.' In other words, More Eyes was recruiting unwitting spies.[75]

'More Eyes' deploys Afghan informers passively reporting in much the same way as nonhuman sensors might do. Placing the gathering of 'white data', surface and everyday information, at the heart of this project would seem to follow Noortje Marres' methodological insights into ANT (cited above), taking 'stuff that is happening' as the starting point as a way of 'suspending' or 'undoing' ontological assumptions.

The US military intelligence gathering operation in Afghanistan may have been talked up as 'literally being able to predict the future'[76] but this form of boosting the shift towards Sensing is mistaken at a number of levels. Empirically, the shift towards Sensing could be seen as a recognition of defeat or at least as a product of a lack of clarity and direction, rather than as a totalising aspiration for full knowledge and control. This would seem to be supported by the fact that the application of Sensing to counter-insurgency was short lived in this case; not least because the project over-estimated the ability of Afghans to access the internet and the reach of mobile phone services in Afghanistan.[77] Methodologically, as is reflected in the idea of 'Afghanistan Atmospherics', Sensing is not really about building up a store of causal knowledge to trace causal processes and thereby 'predict' the future. Sensing is instead about seeing what is happening in the present; this form of seeing is through correlations or real time signs or indicators, which enable the modulation of processes.

An alternative illustration of the shift from Mapping towards Sensing can be seen in discussions of 'predictive' policing. Crime, like insurgency, is amenable to formulations which see it as an emergent effect of contingent connections, which can be increasingly perceived – usually through breaking down types of criminality and correlating the times and locations for patterns to emerge.[78] This type of mapping does not have an ontology of depth or of causal interconnection, but enables correlations to operate as the basis for the reallocation of resources.[79] There is no attempt to intervene to adapt or change causal outcomes but rather to enable a better allocation of policing resources on the assumption that the pattern can provide correlational insights and enable greater responsivity. This shift to Sensing goes furthest in the development of crime apps, like CityCop, which are not intended for police use but for use by crowdsourcing citizen-sensors. City-Cop relies on the depth and detail of crowdsourced information, according to co-founder and CEO Nadim Curi:

> So, if CityCop is able to generate enough users to report crime – be it a bike theft or vandalism or a fight – we'd all have a better understanding of the recent history of the neighborhoods we live in and walk through on the way to a friend's place, a bar or wherever.[80]

Crimes are reported on the app – which would not necessarily be reported to the authorities, such as broken windows, rubbish dumped, vandalism etc. – not so the police can pursue them as crimes to be solved but so that citizens are aware of their surroundings and can take care to avoid or respond to crime reported by others.

The shift from Mapping to Sensing is never straightforward but the implications of moving away from causality to correlation are quite radical. In a causal paradigm, the police are on the lookout for known or suspected criminals, to be cautioned or arrested, thus stopping the proximate cause of crime. In a Sensing paradigm, seeing crime in real time is held to enable people to avoid criminal hotspots or police to focus upon them to minimise any potential disruption to the status quo. Crime is not a problem to be 'solved' but a fact of the world to be modulated, sensed and responded to: awareness of crime becomes the means as well as the end.

Sensing is less concerned with adaptive change (to prevent problems before they occur or with transformation afterwards) than with responsiveness to problems understood as emergent effects. Responsiveness, in resilience discourses, is increasingly seen as a real time necessity: living with and being sensitive to problems and threats is understood to be the best way of ameliorating their impact.[81] Sensing as a mode of governance thus appears to have a lot in common with Deleuze's conceptualisation of a 'control society', where time is held constant: instead of a before (prevention) or an after (reaction) there is the continual modulation of responsiveness, an 'endless postponement' of a problem.[82] The essence of entities, be they systems, societies or individuals, becomes much less important than the emergent appearance of surface 'effects', which are to be modulated and responded to.

Perhaps this is best highlighted in Stephanie Wakefield and Bruce Braun's work on the deployment of 'green infrastructure', relying on the agency of nonhuman actors, such as the deployment of oysters as seawall infrastructure, enabling Sensing, grounded on the ontopolitics of responsivity rather than adaptation.[83] Thus nonhuman life is managed as a way of securing human life. The 'oystertecture' approach fits excellently with the Anthropocene ontopolitics laid out here as it seeks to respond to rather than adapt to climate change. The responsive approach does not concern causation but correlation in terms of changing in response to sea level rises. Most importantly, Wakefield and Braun highlight the distinctiveness of this mode of governance, in that rather than seeking to adapt in an autopoietic way, oriented towards the future, Sensing seeks to *'ward it off'*, attempting to keep everything as it is by 'cancelling out or absorbing events' (emphasis in original).[84] Rather than seeking to reform or adapt existing modes of infrastructure, as suggested in the governance mode of Mapping, Sensing seeks to maintain existing forms of infrastructure but to add other forms of sensing and responsivity. While Mapping has a hierarchy of centralised reporting and adaptation – based on non-linear causal links and connections and adaptive intervention from authorities at a higher level – Sensing has a much flatter ontology of self-generated responses, whether at the level of society, community or the quantified self.

Conclusion

While Mapping as a mode of governance can be seen as a response to the limitations of modernist or liberal universal approaches to knowledge and causal relations, the mode of Sensing can be understood as a response to the limitations of Mapping as an autopoietic process of adaptive learning to 'bounce back' better from disruptions. The mapping of internal relations to enable adaptive interventions thus gives way to the responsive mode of Sensing: being aware of changing relations between things that can indicate the emergence of effects. With Sensing, there is no longer a 'line' of causality but a 'plane' of relationality – this shift is fundamental in terms of governance, which, as analysed above, no longer needs to assume a normative horizon or normative goals external to the actuality of the world. As Agamben has highlighted, the governance of effects can thereby be seen to be thoroughly depoliticising, as the tasks of governance are discursively derived 'empirically' from the world, rather than from human actors as subjects. The posthuman aspects of Sensing as a mode of governance will be drawn out further in the next chapter.

As will be considered in Chapter 5, key to the growing technological attempts to develop Sensing as a mode of governance has been the application of new technologies for data analysis. These have been developed across contemporary society from the technologies of the quantified self, to the application of data analysis in schools and businesses, to the development of new sensing capacities through international collaborative initiatives. The latter include the United Nations' Global Pulse, established by the UN Secretary-General to research and coordinate the use of Big Data for development,[85] the World Bank's Open Data for Resilience initiative (OpenDRI), seeking to see the emergence of natural hazards and the impacts of climate change in real time,[86] and the PopTech and Rockefeller Foundation initiatives on Big Data and community resilience.[87] Big Data approaches develop the themes raised in this chapter, particularly the need for new 'correlational machines' to see processes of emergence, and highlight the development of new post-epistemological approaches, which view correlation as a more reliable and more objective 'empirical' method than the extrapolations and predictions of causal analysis.

Notes

1 Harman, 2010: p.180; see also 2009: p.127.
2 Bhaskar, 1998: pp.7–8.
3 See, for example, Ramalingam et al., 2008; Ramalingam, 2013.
4 Department for International Development et al., 2011.
5 Agamben, 2014a.
6 Ibid.
7 See further, Chandler, 2014b; 2014c.
8 Robert Cox prepared the ground, famously differentiating approaches that saw problems from a narrow status-quo perspective from those that sought to critically rethink the bigger picture (1981).

9 Beck, 1992.
10 On the importance of the normalising effects of insurance see, for example, Ewald, 1991; Defert, 1991; Dillon, 2008.
11 He argued: 'If we anticipate catastrophes whose destructive potential threatens everybody, then the risk calculation based on experience and rationality breaks down. Now all possible, to a greater or lesser degree improbable, scenarios must be taken into consideration; to knowledge drawn from experience and science we must add imagination, suspicion, fiction and fear.' (Beck, 2009a: p.53)
12 For the critics of the principle, which has been taken up in a number of ways in international policy documents, the problem was the paralysing aspects of 'possibilistic' thinking (see, for example, Sunstein, 2002).
13 Latour, 2011: p.27.
14 Beck, 2015: p.79.
15 Ibid.: p.76.
16 Ibid.: p.80.
17 See also the analysis of Hurricane Katrina in Protevi, 2009: pp.163–83.
18 See also Beck, 2016.
19 Beck, 2015: p.78.
20 Beck, 2016: p.104.
21 Beck, 2015: p.78.
22 He died of a heart attack in January 2015.
23 See, for example, Latour, 1993a; 2004a.
24 Latour, 2011: p.25.
25 Ibid.
26 Ibid.: p.27.
27 Exemplified in the example of Frankenstein's failure to care for his creation, which then turned into a tragic monster, Latour, 2011.
28 See, for example, Clark, 2010; or Klein, 2014: pp.1–3, which opens with the ironies of anthropogenic feedback loops, for example, when extreme hot weather, caused by the profligate burning of fossil fuels, melted the tarmac and grounded aircraft at Washington DC in the summer of 2012.
29 Latour, 2013b: pp.94–5; see also, Connolly, 2013; Bennett, 2010. Latour (2013b: p.112) echoes Connolly and Bennett on the cultivation of sensitivity: 'To become sensitive, that is to feel responsible, and thus to make the loops feedback on our own action, we need, by a set of totally artificial operations, to place ourselves *as if we were* at the End of Time.' (emphasis in original.)
30 See, for example, Haraway, 2015; Tsing, 2015: pp.37–43; Gillings, 2015.
31 Latour, 2013b: p.96.
32 Ibid.: p.135.
33 Ibid.
34 As Gilles Deleuze and Felix Guattari (2014: pp.11–22) note, tracing causal chains could only be a 'selective', 'artificial' and 'restrictive' procedure, 'overcoding' and reproducing its starting assumptions in a transcendent manner.
35 Deleuze (1988: p.128) nicely captures the difference between transcendent and immanent approaches in his suggestion that transcendent approaches introduce a 'dimension supplementary to the dimensions of the given'; i.e. ideas of goals, direction and causal connections, which separate the human subject from the object of governance. Whereas, on the plane of immanence: 'There is no longer

a subject, but only individuating affective states of an anonymous force. Here [governance] is concerned only with motions and rests, with dynamic affective charges. It will be perceived with that which it makes perceptible to us, as we proceed.'

36 Latour, 2013b: p.126.
37 Ibid.: p.26.
38 Ibid.: p.49.
39 Haraway, 1988.
40 See further, Venturini and Latour, 2010.
41 Latour, 2013b: p.126.
42 Beck, 2015: p.83.
43 See, for example, Mayer-Schönberger and Cukier, 2013; Kitchin, 2014a.
44 See Latour et al., 2011.
45 Harman 2009: p.17.
46 Ibid.: p.28
47 Harman, 2010: p.176.
48 Latour et al., 2011: p.95.
49 Latour, 2005: p.244.
50 Ibid.: p.245.
51 Latour et al., 2011: p.62.
52 Ibid.: p.89.
53 Ibid.: pp.90–1
54 Ibid.: p.84.
55 Tsing, 2015: p.176.
56 Madrigal, 2014.
57 Harman calls this 'occasionalism' and argues that Latour provides the first known example of 'secular occasionalism' (2009: p.228) where there is no fixed way of explaining causation or the continuity of events. In ANT, nothing follows from anything else: 'Nothing is by itself either reducible or irreducible to anything else' (Latour, 1993b: p.169). The work of composing relations begins again 'every morning' (Latour et al., 2011: p.76). Regarding complexity theory, see Chandler, 2014a.
58 Merleau-Ponty, 1989.
59 Dill, 2003.
60 Radford, 2003.
61 NIST, 2016.
62 As Charlotte Heath-Kelly (2016) notes, big data ontologies of complexity lead to universal rather than targeted surveillance parameters.
63 Researcher, Senseable City Lab, Massachusetts Institute of Technology, 30 March 2017.
64 Johnson, 2017.
65 Ibid.: p.284.
66 Ibid.
67 Ibid.
68 Ibid.: p.286.
69 Ibid.: p.285.
70 This form of governance through the modulation of effects can be usefully grasped in terms of Deleuze and Guattari's concept of 'machinic enslavement',

derived from cybernetics, where responses are automated to manage or govern on the basis of maintaining equilibrium. In this process there is no distinction between using a machine and being part of the informational input to the machinic process: the process itself is more important than distinctions between entities or individuals. See Deleuze and Guattari, 2014: pp.531–6; Lazzarato, 2014: pp.23–34.

71 Weinberger, 2017.
72 Ibid.
73 Lee, cited in ibid.
74 Weinberger, 2017.
75 Ibid.
76 Ibid.
77 Ibid.
78 See, for example, Perry et al., 2013.
79 Aradau and Blanke frame this process of the correlation of different factors, or their 'between-ness', as taking place in an algorithmically constructed 'feature space' (2017: p.382).
80 Wistrom, 2017.
81 Evans and Reid, 2014.
82 Deleuze, 1995: p.179.
83 Wakefield and Braun, 2018.
84 Ibid.
85 United Nations Global Pulse initiative website can be accessed at: www.ungloba lpulse.org/.
86 The World Bank's OpenDRI webpages can be accessed at: www.gfdrr.org/op endri.
87 For information on the Data-Pop Alliance see: www.datapopalliance.org/; and for the Rockefeller Foundation: www.rockefellerfoundation.org/our-work/cur rent-work/resilience.

5

BIG DATA SENSING

Introduction

The governance mode of Sensing deploys new technologies in a very different way to that of Mapping on the assumption that the key to governing is the capacity to respond to effects rather than to act instrumentally upon the basis of causal chains of interconnection. While the focus shifts from an ontology of depth to that of the surface of appearances, Sensing is nevertheless dependent on a high level of technological regulation and analysis. In fact, the problem of infinitude, raised in Chapter 3, can be understood to be reposed through the Sensing paradigm as a problem of seeing the world of entangled interaction in its real-time emergence. In effect, the problem space of governance shifts from the depths to the surface and becomes a concern of time rather than space. In the language of speculative realism, the 'great outdoors' comes ever closer and becomes much more tangible. However, in coming nearer, the world of exploration becomes less full of alternative possibilities: while the paradigm of Mapping was autopoietic, with the subject or entity adapting through encountering problems, that of Sensing is homeostatic: rapid responsivity to effects enables the world to remain as it is.

Sensing, as a mode of governance, is driven by what is increasingly seen as the emergence of a correlational alternative to modernist forms of causal knowledge. This alternative is often viewed as a fortuitous by-product of new digital technologies enabled by a 'data deluge', as highlighted by the *Economist* in 2010,[1] and it is increasingly alleged that data-driven knowledge – or Big Data – is capable of changing the ways in which knowledge of the world is produced and thus the ways in which it can be governed. In the area of international relations, Big Data discussions have largely been based on excitement with regard to the possibilities of applying the knowledge generated by technological and computational advances, particularly in the possible alleviation of – and speedy responses to – disaster, conflict, health and environmental problems.[2] However, the potential uses of the knowledge gleamed from Big Data have been focused upon rather than its contribution to the transformation of what it means to 'know' and to 'govern' in the Anthropocene.

This chapter analyses the rise of Big Data as a key attribute of Sensing as a mode of governance and focuses upon the impact of this in key areas of concern for policy-making in international relations. It foregrounds an analysis of Big Data's epistemological claims and ontopolitical assumptions,[3] rather than engaging with Big Data from already well-established critical positions, largely developed in the fields of politics and sociology. For many critical theorists, epistemological and ontopolitical claims are secondary to concerns raised with regard to civil liberties, privacy, ownership and access issues.[4] Alternatively, when concerns with issues of knowledge production are raised, critics can tend to quickly dismiss the claims of Big Data advocates on the basis that practical limits, regarding both the quantity and quality of the data available, mean that these claims cannot be satisfied.[5]

While not denying the salience of these critiques, this chapter seeks to open up an alternative critical space for discussion through highlighting the broader ontopolitical assumptions (often obscured behind the discussion of technological advances in data generation) – substantiating new modes of governance in the Anthropocene.[6] Thus it suggests that the attractiveness of Sensing as a mode of governance lies less in the serendipitous development of technological possibilities than in the growing dominance of post-epistemological or 'actualist' trends in the social sciences;[7] trends that are increasingly influential in the policy and practice of international relations. In conclusion, it highlights that in bringing contingency to the surface of governance, the possibilities of the world being other than it is then disappear. The 'what-is' of the world is thereby reified in discussions of Sensing as a mode of governance and of Big Data as a technique of knowledge production, profoundly constraining the possibilities for politics: reducing governance to an ongoing and technical process of responsiveness, accepting the world as it is.

This chapter is organised in four sections. The following section introduces the concept of Big Data, highlighting the process of 'datafication' as key to Sensing as a mode of governance on the basis of responding to emergent effects. The next section then engages with how Sensing can be seen as a non-modern epistemology, considering how Big Data analysts and policy advocates share a common methodological approach with actor network theory, which similarly focuses on the level of appearances or effects. The third section uses a range of policy examples to analyse the connection between Big Data approaches and understandings of distributed agency, suggesting that the extension of Sensing as a mode of governance redistributes policy responsibility to individuals and self-governing communities, imagined as becoming resilient through the self-quantification of their corelations. The final section analyses how this understanding of self-government is very different from a modernist conception of governmental agency and is closely analogous to classical neoliberal approaches of self-responsibility.

Big Data

While there is no fixed definition of Big Data, analysts often mention the 3 'Vs' which characterise it: volume, velocity and variety.[8] Big Data includes information from a multitude of sources, including social media, smart phones and mapping, visualising and recording equipment[9] and the number of data-sharing devices is growing exponentially. This hardware, collectively known as the 'Internet of Things', includes machine sensors and consumer-oriented devices such as connected thermostats, light bulbs, refrigerators and wearable health monitors.[10] Data is thus being produced and used in increasingly diverse and innovative ways. The term 'Big Data' is capitalised to distinguish it (as a set of ideas and practices discursively cohered around a certain approach to knowledge production) from its use as a merely descriptive term for a large amount of data. Big Data thus is not used with reference to discussions about the volume of data per se; however, many authors argue that volume is relevant in terms of an analytical 'tipping point' or 'data threshold' where data gathering is no longer based upon selection and sampling with limited parameters but aspires to be exhaustive or becomes a closed data set, no longer requiring generative rules.[11] Thus Big Data discursively refers to a qualitative shift in the meaning of data, in not just the amount of data (approaching exhaustiveness) but also its quality (approaching a dynamic, fine-grained relational richness).

This data is very far from the abstract and reductionist constructions of data of the past[12] and is increasingly understood as approaching 'reality' itself. This understanding of data as giving an insight into the 'actual', rather than working at a level of representation or abstraction, provides a fundamental ontopolitical grounding for Sensing as a mode of governance. Sensing relies on an 'actualist' or surface view of emergence, rather than focusing on causal relations, where continuities over time are crucial to establishing lines of linear and non-linear causation.[13] Thus, Big Data transforms our everyday reality and our immediate relation to the things around us. It does this through seeing the unseen but existing processes and effects through 'datafication'. As analysed in the previous chapter, Sensing as a mode of governance relies on the development of 'correlational machines', which sense indirectly: Big Data sensing, via the mediation of algorithmic computation, is the most important of these machines. The process of sensing or of datafication is straightforward in theory, although work on perfecting the correlations required is more complicated. For example, if search terms put into Google correlated with processes in the world, for example shopping intentions, flu outbreaks or increases in conflict tensions, then these processes in the world could be 'datafied' i.e. they could be seen indirectly through the algorithmic detection and analysis of these terms via Google. This would work in the same way as the canary in the coalmine, as a real-time indicator based on correlation and enabling responses on this basis.

This 'datafication' of everyday life is at the heart of Big Data: a way of accessing reality through bringing interactions and relationships to the surface and making them visible, readable and thereby governable, rather than seeking to understand hidden laws of causality.[14] Sensing as a mode of governance thus relies upon increasing the field of vision through the power of correlation. As alluded to at the end of the previous chapter, the ability to 'sense' better through datafication is imagined to allow the modulation or regulation of processes and thereby to perpetually 'ward off', 'cancel out' or 'absorb' crises or breakdowns.[15] In the world of perfect 'actual' knowledge, where effects could be seen in their real-time emergence, it would be as if time slowed down, making a shock or crisis impossible.

Perhaps a useful analogy would be the different perceptual 'temporality' of the fly versus the person attempting to swat it with a newspaper. For the person, the action of swatting is quick and instinctive, for the fly the action is slow and the ability to 'datafy' or to sense the changes in the air means that the fly 'senses' the movement and can respond long before the danger or the event actually has a damaging impact. Thus, understanding Big Data as a technical sensing prosthesis enables 'events' to be not 'prevented' but, in François Laruelle's terminology, 'cancelled' or submerged into being itself.[16] The 'crisis' is suspended in time so much so that responses enable life to go on, in fact, life would be a world of the status quo where events 'merely happen' at a mundane level in which they have no important effects.[17]

Hopefully the analogy enables us to see that datafication is not about problem solving through chains of causality but about sensing changes, which would otherwise go unseen. So, while data can be understood as digital – in terms of binary code – the world itself becomes more analogue or less differentiated in terms of distinctive properties or essences of objects. Big Data is concerned with the surface of the 'actual' not the ontological nature of being or the processes of emergence in complex causal interactions. The 'knowledge' generated is thereby not something fixed or that can be stored and reused, but is about 'seeing' the flux or flow of change through mechanisms of correlation (the 'correlational machines' introduced in the previous chapter). In the governance mode of Sensing, Big Data is thereby generally understood to generate a different type of 'knowledge': more akin to the translation or interpretation of signs rather than that of understanding chains of causation.[18]

In science and computer sciences, this increase in data gathering possibilities and development of computational capacity has enabled analysts to talk of a 'fourth paradigm' of knowledge production (beyond theory, experiment and simulation).[19] Thus Big Data appears to lack certain attributes of the modernist 'production process' of knowledge and appears as less mediated through subject-centred conceptual apparatuses. As Rob Kitchin highlights, Big Data is unique in that its construction is often not part of a conscious process of knowledge production: the data is often already there, in social media or other electronic processes of data capture, and it is the discovery of correlations which is the key aspect.[20] It is understood as generated from complex life or reality itself, for example, in the data trails left from our digital footprints as we go about our everyday lives.[21] Big Data is thus the mirror image, methodologically, of other large data gathering exercises, such as national censuses based upon 30 or 40 questions, designed to elicit comparative and analytical data for policy-making. The data is not generated through having a specific question or purpose in mind and is mostly a by-product or side-effect of activities undertaken in fields with technologically generated and stored records.[22] The analysis comes after the data is collected and stored, not prior to this. However, the fact that the data is not consciously generated, through the desire to test theories or models, is seen as an asset rather than a problem: 'Big Data analytics enables an entirely new epistemological approach for making sense of the world; rather than testing a theory by analysing relevant data, new data analytics seek to gain correlational insights "born from the data".'[23]

Wolfgang Pietsch usefully outlines how Big Data approaches differ methodologically from computer simulations, which rely (as does much of social science) on the deductive method: a sequence of theory-model-treatment-solver-results, derived from a general theory.[24] All computer simulations have in common a reliance on elaborate modelling assumptions that originate outside the computer, in terms of dynamic equations or rules of evolution, then specific values are assigned to the parameters and boundary conditions and translated into an algorithm to yield results. Rather than starting with the human and then going out to the world, the promise of Big Data is that the human comes into the picture relatively late in the process (if at all).[25] Instead of beginning deductively with an hypothesis or theory, which is then tested through experimentation and modelling, as with causal analysis, Big Data seeks to be more inductive and thereby to preserve more of the 'reality' left out by abstract and sometimes reductionist causal assumptions. The promise is that, with high levels of data generation and developments in computational analysis, the world (coded through datafication) can begin to speak for itself without its (more than) fallible human interpreter.[26] The most important thing is that, in bypassing the construction of theories to be tested, Big Data approaches appear to remove the need for a causal imaginary. This very radical distinction from modernist approaches and assumptions is rarely commented upon as important by critical commentators but is, of course, key to the ontopolitical assumptions deployed here, legitimating new modes of governing and their distinctive epistemological stakes.

Sensing and correlation

In the Anthropocene, as considered in the introductory chapter, it is held that causal imaginaries are part of the problem rather than the solution. Thus Big Data approaches appear to have emerged at an opportune moment as the more our interrelations become datafied and become transparent and readable the more we can understand the coming together of contingent, complex and emergent effects which previously were invisible.

The newfound visibility of the complex world removes the need for causal theory and for top-down forms of governance on the basis of cause-and-effect. As the researchers at the Senseable City Lab at MIT, argue, the datafication of everyday life, through new sensing mechanisms based on algorithmic correlations for seeing and recording space and its usage, for example, road traffic and parking usage, can enable 'hidden patterns' to emerge – the 'circadian rhythms' of city life – which then can lead to more efficient forms of organisation.[27] Traffic and parking can be modulated in real-time without formal or informal governance interventions, such as infrastructure innovations, legal restrictions or financial incentives.

The new machinic more-than-human assemblages of Sensing that enable new forms of awareness in a datafied world blur the distinction between human and nonhuman and subject and object. There is an infinite recursivity as the use of Big Data or sensing technologies itself becomes data for the further use of these technologies by others or even the users themselves. Using these technologies and techniques serves the technologies in developing their databases or enabling their capacities to learn, or more precisely to correlate, with greater accuracy. Big Data thereby articulates a properly more-than-human ontology of self-governing, homeostatic assemblages of the technological and the social. Whereas the 'human' of modernist construction sought to govern through unravelling the mysteries of causation, the more-than-human or 'posthuman' of our present world seeks to govern through enabling the relational reality of the world to become transparent, thus enabling responsivity to emergent effects. Nigel Thrift, for example, has clearly highlighted the intimate connections between Sensing as a mode of governance and Big Data approaches:

> human beings can no longer be considered as the only actors. Rather than acting as simple relays, what might be called the world of things (within which I include the material surfaces made possible by Big Data) comes to occupy a central place, confirming the tenets of speculative realism but no longer in abstracto.[28]

Here, Big Data materially changes the way the world is seen and how it is understood and governed. For Thrift, new technologies 'make this kind of relationality easier to initiate and conjugate'; they are enfolded within emergent interactions and essentially turn abstract constructions of relational ontologies into a perceivable social reality.[29] Bruno Latour's work (discussed in the last chapter) can also be read in a similar vein, where he suggests that

Big Data enables access to a much 'flatter' reality, where the modernist divisions between quantitative and qualitative methods no longer needs to apply and that the 'statistical shortcuts' that constituted the 'fictive division' between the two levels of micro-interactions and macro-structures are no longer necessary. This two-level or dualist approach, which has traditionally dominated social theorising, works well, according to Latour, to describe emerged phenomena but not for grasping phenomena in their emergence, in real-time. The need for abstractions at the higher level of the 'general', 'collective' or the 'social' disappear as the real-time interactions and connections can be assembled to enable the study of the concrete and the individual to encompass ever larger collectivities or assemblages (both human and nonhuman).[30]

It should be increasingly clear to the reader that Big Data does not work on the basis of extrapolating from limited or selected data on the basis of rules or regularities which emerge (the basis of Ian Hacking's critique of the power of statistical probabilities)[31] but works the other way around, not 'up' to general laws but correlates with increasing accuracy 'down' to the contextualisation of the concrete relations, thereby promising personalised or individualised health care, political campaigning or product purchasing information.[32] Big Data adds the relations to the entity or individual (as was analysed in the last chapter, it is the relations not the entities that are key to Sensing) rather than fitting the individual into a set of deterministic or causal understandings based on selecting a small number of social or cultural attributes. Big Data is thereby representative of other shifts both in social theory and in computational analysis, which tend to focus on the enrichment of smaller or micro-level descriptive analysis rather than macro-level theory-building.

Even traditional modelling techniques are shifting from equation or parametric modelling, based on a limited number of parameters dependent on linear relationships, to non-parametric modelling based on data-driven computational power. The knowledge generated is therefore highly context dependent and not intended to be integrated into broader theoretical understandings or for government levers of macro-policy intervention. In fact, as will be discussed below, correlational understandings specifically work to substitute for intervention or to make it unnecessary, while causal understandings work to enable it. Both correlational and causal frameworks work through processes of self-amplification; they have their own combinatorial logic and both build up their own worlds of understanding.[33] Correlations become smarter and more accurate – just think of correlational algorithms for face recognition or for language translation – just as causal frameworks become richer through testing, experimentation and practical application. This is why it would be a major mistake to think that Big Data, the Internet of Things and Sensing as a mode of governance are somehow fads or only a marginal concern for governance discourses.

Big Data's appeal appears to be exactly that it promises to overcome the limits of theorising and modelling: the gap between abstract theory and (concrete) reality. Big Data or data-intensive science clearly focuses more on the materiality of the world than the subjective constructions of this reality in theories or models, which tend to assume linear causal chains of connection. Big Data analytics, for these reasons, has been described as 'horizontal' rather than vertical or hierarchical.[34] It consciously presupposes a flatter ontology of agency and causality and therefore does not intend to make causal claims in the manner of modernist understandings of linearity and universality. This would seem to precisely fit Bruno Latour's perspective (following Tarde) regarding an actor network approach:

> In the tired old debate pitting a naturalistic versus an interpretative social science, a strange idea appears: that if we stick to the individual, the local, the situated, you will detect only qualities, while if we move towards the structural and towards the distant, we will begin to gather quantities. For Tarde the situation is almost exactly the opposite: the more we get into the intimacy of the individual, the more discrete quantities we'll find; and if we move away from the individual towards the aggregate we might begin to lose quantities, more and more, along the way because we lack the instruments to collect enough of their quantitative evaluations.[35]

As considered in the previous chapter, the world of the actual is presumed to be much (in fact, infinitely) richer than is imagined in modernist thought which tends to reduce the world to entities rather than see the rich relational dynamics that make entities what they actually are: irreducibly distinct. This process of seeing relationality, and grasping this as a dynamic process which composes the world as it actually exists, is key to Sensing as a mode of governance. Thus, the point about Big Data is that no data should be excluded. There is no need for data reduction; in fact the more data there is, the less need there is for models and theories to bridge the gap between the particular and the general at the risk of subsuming the concrete under the abstract.

The radical inversion at play in the shift from theories and rules to letting the correlational data do the work, to have the agency, and thus to blur or make meaningless the subject/object divide of modernist knowledge production can be highlighted simply in the case of language translation. The rules-based approach models the complex hierarchy of grammatical rules for both languages and translates using a conventional dictionary. The data-driven approach ignores grammatical structure and rules and instead works on the basis of correlations in terms of regularly repeated word frequency and location over a large number of texts. The Google algorithms developed for this task seek to develop and refine their correlational abilities through the processing of vast amounts of data; they do not use this data to derive causal interconnections or rules and regularities that could be grasped by a language expert. As Anderson has stated:

> That's why Google can translate languages without actually "knowing" them (given equal corpus data, Google can translate Klingon into Farsi as easily as it can translate French into German). And why it can match ads to content without any knowledge or assumptions about the ads or the content.[36]

Data-driven approaches thus no longer rely on specialist knowledge and expertise: correlational algorithms based on mass data sets take the 'knowledge' out of knowledge production, whether this concerns language translation, political election information or sales and marketing. The implication is that Big Data, through deriving richer correlations, can datify relational emergence, providing a new form of access to the real, multiple and complex world. Given enough data and computing power, the reductionist categorisations upon which causal decision-making was made – for example, in election campaign targeting, upon traditional variables of race, gender, class and location – disappear from the picture. The promise of Big Data is that of actor network theory: the 'externalities', which Bruno Latour has argued are left out of modernist thinking, are 'brought back in' on the basis of the analysis of relations rather than of entities.[37] According to a much-cited article by former *Wired* editor, Chris Anderson, Big Data promises a world without the need for abstract theoretical models: 'Correlation supersedes causation, and science can advance even without coherent models, unified theories, or really any mechanistic explanation at all'.[38]

The possibility of data-intensive knowledge production informing policy developments has been broadly welcomed in international relations, especially in the fields of disaster risk reduction, disease and health concerns, peacebuilding and resilience. In these areas, it is hoped that correlational approaches can enable new innovative, and cheaper, responses to problems at the level of the community facing them. The epistemological shift towards the 'data' and away from causal theory is therefore intimately connected to the rise of Sensing as a mode of governance and the retreat from policy interventions based on causal approaches of 'problem-solving'. The shift from depth to surface relations and from causation to correlation, discussed in terms of the approach of actor network theory, is paralleled in both the business and policy understandings of Big Data approaches and their conceptual framings. Reading the views of Google research scientists, Alon Halevy, Peter Norvig and Fernando Pereira, on the methodology of Big Data, it is difficult not to bring to mind the work of Bruno Latour:

> So, follow the data. Choose a representation that can use unsupervised learning on unlabelled data, which is so much more plentiful than labelled data. Represent all the data with a nonparametric model rather than trying to summarize it with a parametric model, because with very large data sources, the data holds a lot of detail ... See how far you can go by tying together the words that are already there, rather than by inventing new concepts with clusters of words. Now go out and gather some data, and see what it can do.[39]

Or, to take another example, it is worth considering the striking similarity in the epistemological claims made in ANT theorist John Law's influential book *After Method: Mess in Social Science Research*, first published in 2004,[40] and those made ten years later by Big Data experts Kenneth Cukier and Viktor Mayer-Schönberger, in the prestigious US foreign policy journal *Foreign Affairs*, who argue that:

> [Big Data] requires three profound changes in how we approach data. The first is to collect and use a lot of data rather than settle for small amounts or samples, as statisticians have done for well over a century. The second is to shed our preference for highly curated and pristine data and instead accept messiness: in an increasing number of situations, a bit of inaccuracy can be tolerated, because the benefits of using vastly more data of variable quality outweigh the costs of using smaller amounts of very exact data. Third, in many instances, we will need to give up our quest to discover the cause of things, in return for accepting correlations.[41]

In epistemological and ontological terms the desire to grasp the messiness of the world and to understand governance on the basis of seeing and being sensitive to more-than-human relations and co-relations rather than the essence of fixed entities means that Big Data approaches discursively turn the critical ontopolitical alternatives of the Anthropocene into mainstream governance agendas. Big Data welcomes the irreducible and infinite heterogeneity and multiplicity of the world, as datafication enables more and more attributes and social practices, including body movements and pulse rates, to become part of the complex micro-picture. Perhaps, most importantly, Big Data ontopolitically affirms that the fact that the world is unknowable through modernist reason, not bound by generic laws and rules but by emergent effects and changes through contingent and complex relational processes, is not a problem but instead a positive opportunity for discovering (and governing) it anew.

Distributed agency

This section is concerned with the claims made for Big Data in international relations as a tool for Sensing as a mode of governance, concerned less with top-down regulation or with community development and empowerment as an adaptive autopoietic process than with the redistribution of governing agency as a project of self-regulation, self-monitoring and self-policing. This is not how Big Data approaches are often understood within the discipline and it is understandable that international relations theorists share a lot of ground with colleagues in cognate disciplines, in warning of the potential dangers of Big Data if misused by centralised authorities. It would not be difficult to scale up the Big Brother concerns to the global level.[42] However, Big Data discourses suggest the outsourcing or redistribution of governmental agency rather than its centralisation. As Kate Crawford points out, it is 'the anxieties of Big Data' that seem most revealing:[43] there is a concern that data gathering is never going to be enough if governments govern in traditional ways (as considered in Chapter 3). The discourse of Big Data seems to be inexorably drawn to reproducing its own methodological dynamic, data which cannot be used to govern from above, 'serendipitously' becomes a mechanism to enable governance through the modulation of effects at the level and location of their appearance. Thus Sensing is not a mode of governing 'from below', as articulated through the assemblage approach of Mapping; in contra position, the space of governance is redistributed to the surface of appearance, beyond the top/down binaries of debates on international intervention considered earlier.

Not surprisingly, the rise of Big Data as a real-life policy solution (away from the commercial hype of modernist imaginaries of deterministic predictions and total knowledge) is intimately linked not with the increase in modernist governing responsibilities, based on centralised digital technologies of knowledge production and use, but the opposite: the conceived need to enable communities to govern themselves through Sensing. The failure of centralised and bureaucratised forms of international intervention and external attempts to address international questions of peace, conflict, rights and development has led to the imagination of Big Data as both an effective and an ethical substitute for traditional forms of international intervention, which are seen as too slow, too unwieldy and too reductionist to adequately engage with the concrete contextual realities of the world (as discussed in Chapter 3).[44] Big Data thus emerges not as a tool of international interveners equipped with the non-linear causal knowledge of Mapping and able to redirect paths to development and peace but rather as a tool of local communities and 'civil societies', expected to generate their own Sensing 'knowledge' of emergent effects and to act upon it accordingly.

In this discourse, the questions of privacy and intentionality lead not to an argument against the gathering of Big Data but to careful and strategic considerations of its use: 'to help build community resilience in the face of a range of stresses – environmental, political, social and economic.'[45] Thus, not only does Big Data ethically need to be owned and used by its producers, it is also argued that the producers of Big Data, in their concrete and relational interaction, are also in the best place to make use of Big Data findings: 'Large data collection and analysis may support communities by providing them with timely feedback loops on their immediate environment.'[46] The context-specific nature of Big Data enable it to facilitate local communities as proactive agents in their own governance, for example, in the ability to measure energy consumption, even located down to the energy consumption (from multiple sources of consumption) of individuals and households,[47] or in the local measurement of environmental attributes such as pollution, river levels and land use changes. Big Data is thus held to enable empowerment in new ways at the most micro levels due to the digitalisation or 'datafication' of life.[48]

Rather than centralising data produced through everyday interactions and applying algorithms that produce linear and reductive understandings, the aspiration of Big Data is that multiple data sources can enable individuals, households and societies to practise responsive self-management in ways which were considered impossible before. In fields such as disaster risk reduction and disaster management the shift is particularly apparent (as will be discussed below). Big Data derives correlational or Sensing knowledge often to enable the people themselves rather than for them to provide knowledge to others. Thus it is hoped Big Data can potentially empower precisely those that are most marginal and vulnerable at the moments of highest risk. It is regularly argued that open information flows contribute to the building of resilience by making communities aware of the risks and hazards they may encounter so that they can mobilise to protect themselves.[49]

Disasters, conflicts and other problems thus easily become reinterpreted as problems of knowledge and of communication breakdowns within communities, with policy-makers arguing that at-risk communities need information as much as water, food and medicine, or shelter, and thereby that 'disaster is first of all seen as a crisis in communicating within a community – that is, as a difficulty for someone to get informed and to inform others'.[50] Thus, it is increasingly argued that Big Data should not merely be used by communities in response to disasters but could play a more 'pre-eventive' or 'cancelling' role. However, the 'pre-eventive' role of Big Data should not be confused with the linear predictions of reductionist models based on cause-and-effect theorising. It is this lack of the need for causal depth that enables Big Data to be context dependent on local knowledge and correlations or factual information generated in real-time. As Robert Narvaez notes, international agencies are increasingly promoting a 'proactive stance towards the use of crowdsourcing, noting that crowdsourcing could be used extensively as a way to reduce the likelihoods of disasters taking place'.[51]

A good example of this is the understanding of natural disasters. While disasters were traditionally perceived as sudden and short lived events, there is now a tendency to look upon disasters as continuous processes of gradual deterioration and growing vulnerability.[52] This shift towards understanding disasters as emergent effects is particularly important with regard to the Sensing role of Big Data.[53] As the UNDP Coordinator of the Disaster Risk Reduction and Recovery Team states:

> Disaster risk can often be anticipated and contingencies developed. Recent large-scale natural disasters, such as the floods in Pakistan, earthquake in Haiti and drought in the Horn of Africa remind us that we need to put resilience to crises at the heart of development.[54]

It is important to emphasise that the role of Big Data is not that of understanding and predicting disasters so as to prevent them but to enable communities to cope with them, through a better understanding of their co-relation to emergent effects. This process of correlational knowledge of the 'actual' replacing causal or ontological knowledge is captured well by Patrick Meier:

> Thanks to ICTs, social media and Big Data, we now have the opportunity to better characterize in real-time the social, economic and political processes ... this doesn't mean that we have a perfect picture of the road to collapse; simply that our picture is clearer than ever before in human history. In other words, we can better measure our own resilience. Think of it as the Quantified Self movement applied to an entirely different scale, that of societies and cities. The point is that Big Data can provide us with more real-time feedback loops than ever before. And as scholars of complex systems know, feedback loops are critical for adaptation and change.[55]

Big Data aims not at instrumental or causal knowledge but at the revealing of co-relational or emergent effects in real-time, enabling unexpected effects to be better and more reflexively managed. Disaster risk reduction thus becomes a way of making communities more responsively aware so that the unintended consequences of social interaction do not undermine coping capacities. Meier highlights that this process of Sensing as monitoring and co-relational awareness is the essence of some of the UN's Global Pulse projects, for example, using Big Data for real-time awareness of food price changes for famine prevention. Big Data thus enables analysis of social media to access the digital 'nervous system' of social interaction, capturing 'the pulse of our social systems'.[56]

Work on Big Data in relation to conflict risk reduction follows in the footsteps of work on disaster risk reduction. One example, highlighted in the US journal *Foreign Policy*, is the establishment of a web of Kenyan NGOs proactively engaging to prevent violence breaking out in the 2013 Kenyan elections (after over one thousand people died in conflict during the 2007 elections). Here the real-time monitoring and responsiveness essentially involved open-source data collection and the mapping of social media with donor-sponsoring of text messaging, calling for peace to be maintained when tensions arose.[57] Big Data – in terms of social media monitoring and responsiveness – was being used to ensure that communities policed themselves through real-time feedbacks. In fact, as John Karlsrud notes, this redistribution of agency in knowledge production is well captured in the term 'crowd-sourcing', literally out-sourcing agency and responsibility to the many rather than an individual or expert.[58]

The logic of this understanding of conflict is important in highlighting Sensing as the modulation of effects on the basis of correlational mechanisms. Conflict is 'sensed' through picking up the earliest signs or signals from social media search or from direct notifications, with the aim of responding to 'pre-event' its escalation. It should be noted that Sensing as a mode of governance has fundamental implications for the discipline of conflict and peace studies as this form of governing is as distinct from conflict prevention as it is from post-conflict reactive intervention. For Sensing, it does not make sense to think in traditional disciplinary terms of pre-conflict or post-conflict as conflict is a state of the world, ever present but needing to be seen and recognised as such to enable responsivity and care towards its management. This is what it means to see conflict as a relational process rather than as an entity or a state of being which then either exists or it does not. Conflict is no longer excluded as somehow an aberration or an exception; the modernist binary of peace and conflict thus no longer appears useful for seeing the world, in fact, it becomes a barrier to seeing the world as it actually is in reality. Through this process of grasping conflict through Sensing, conflict becomes normalised as an aspect of life that requires modulation, preferably through the development of community self-responsivity or, more precisely, through community 'resilience'. Resilience then becomes not the 'solution' to conflict but the way of managing it in the mode of governance of Sensing.

Of course, it is not only the vulnerable and marginalised that Big Data is held to enable to be self-aware and reflexive. Another high profile example of Big Data, as a methodology for Sensing and responsivity rather than for intervention into causal processes, is the centrality of Big Data to policy and academic discussion of urban governance and urban planning: in discourses of 'smart', 'intelligent', 'resilient' or 'sentient' cities.[59] The increasingly popular imaginary of cities that monitor, regulate and govern themselves is driven by the technological possibilities of Big Data, where cities are understood as industrial and social hubs of complex interconnections, which through datafication can produce real-time knowledge of emergent effects. This reflexive awareness of cities' own 'vitality' – their own 'pulse' – then enables a second order of responsivity or of artificial intelligent 'life':

Perhaps one way in which we might consider this question is precisely through looking at how vitality develops when computational things are explicitly included in the contours of experience. Then it becomes clear that it has only gradually arisen, line by line, algorithm by algorithm, programme by programme. Cities are full of a whole new layer of emergent entities which, because they are underpinned by code using data as fuel, might be thought of as akin to sentient beings, in that they are able to produce some level of transference through correlation and measurement.[60]

The role of 'correlational machines' is thus key to the Big Data imaginary of self-governing individuals, communities and cities, able to see their relational embeddedness and to respond to fluctuations and changes on this basis, enabling 21st century problems of urban governance, disasters and conflict to be managed and regulated. Thus, it would be more useful to see Big Data as responsive knowledge rather than as causal knowledge. Big Data cannot help explain global warming but it can enable individuals and households to measure their own energy consumption through the datafication of household objects and complex production and supply chains.

In Chapter 2, the birth of the ontopolitics of the Anthropocene was analysed with the development of Mapping in response to the problem of the 'natural' operation of the market and the development of neoliberal constructions of limits. It seems possible that the development and the imaginary of Big Data could be seen as a return to the knowledge scepticism of classical neoliberal discourse, except with Big Data enabling the sensing of a wide range of processes of emergent effects rather than merely market prices. Whereas, for Hayek, the market served as an information processor, enabling real-time responsivity to changes in relations between prices, Nathaniel Tkacz argues that the signal-ontology of Sensing has become increasingly generalised through new modes of datafication:

> Data signals share price signals' capacity to register or 'sense' individual distributed activities. These could relate to economic exchanges – which generate transactional data – but any number of other activities can be encoded. A body at rest, a surgical procedure, movements of a river, available car parking spaces in a city, applying for a driving licence, the 'sentiment' of social media comments – the empirical sources of data signals are degrees above that of prices. Indeed, the entirety of price signals is now a mere subset of data signals.[61]

Sensing, as a mode of governance understood as modulation around the status quo, can thereby be understood as a retreat from 'actually existing neoliberalism' as a discourse of adaptive intervention.[62] It therefore appears that the aspiration of Sensing is that of intensifying the discourse of responsivity from the sphere of the market to the governance of life as a whole. Sensing, in retreating from Mapping discourses of intervention, establishes a much more distributed framework of governmental agency, from the individual quantified self up to self-governing 'resilient' communities at different scales. If, through Big Data, it was possible to detect and manage individual biorhythms and sense the effects of poor eating or a lack of exercise, people could monitor their own health and not need costly medical interventions. Equally, if vulnerable and marginal communities could 'datafy' their own modes of being and relationships to their environments they would be able to augment their coping capacities and resilience without disasters or crises occurring.

While Sensing avoids the problem of Mapping, of 'drilling down' into processes of causation, through focusing on the governance of effects, the distinctions are not always so clear in practice as both approaches work on the basis of relations rather than the ontology of entities.[63] Work on the datafication of the self in its co-relational embeddedness can appear to be little different than Mapping, despite the fact that Sensing does not have an ontology of depth or of structures working through time. Examples of the crossover between Sensing and Mapping were provided in the final section of the previous chapter and can also be seen in disaster discourses, where resilience thinking can present disasters as 'transformative'. In Mapping, disasters can be transformative in that they reveal the unintended consequences of, for example, faulty policy planning which played a role in the assemblage of emergent causation. In Sensing as a mode of governance, disasters (as with any effect) can be understood as correlational signs or signals, which indicate the need to develop better awareness and responsiveness. Disasters themselves can thus become a form of 'datafication', revealing correlations that were not previously taken in to account.[64]

Sensing change, preventing change

Big Data thereby datafies or materialises an individual or community's co-relational being in the world. Thus, the governance mode of Sensing works to construct a pluralised and multiple world of emergent effects which can be registered, modulated and responded to. The imaginary of Big Data is that the producers and consumers of knowledge and of governance would be indistinguishable; where both knowing and governing exist without external mediation, constituting a perfect harmonious and self-adapting system: the ubiquitous world of 'community resilience'. In this discourse, increasingly articulated by governments and policy-makers, knowledge of causal connections is no longer relevant as communities respond to the real-time appearances of the world, without necessarily understanding them. As Meier states:

> Connection technologies such as mobile phones allow individual[s] ... to make necessary connections and decisions to self-organize and rapidly recover from disasters. With appropriate incentives, prepared-ness measures and policies, these local decisions can render a complex system more resilient. At the core here is behaviour change and thus the importance of understanding behaviour change models.[65]

In these instances, Big Data goes from being an accidental by-product of digitalised exchanges and becomes a technique of governing through the inculcation of Sensing as co-relational knowledge and the requisite beha-viour changes to make this a necessary mode of responsible and responsive life. As Evgeny Morozov argues, Big Data approaches aspire to remove the need for governance on the basis of rules and laws, displacing this with real-time feedback mechanisms based on new forms of (datafied) relational awareness:

> If so much of our everyday behaviour is already captured, analysed and nudged, why stick with unempirical approaches to regulation? Why rely on laws when one has sensors and feedback mechanisms? If policy interventions are to be – to use the buzzwords of the day – 'evidence-based' and 'results-oriented', technology is here to help ... suddenly, there's no need to develop procedures for governing every contingency, for – or so one hopes – algorithms and real-time, immediate feedback can do a better job than inflexible rules out of touch with reality.[66]

In this way, Big Data enables the governance mode of Sensing to increas-ingly be applied to any problem where the resources to deal with causes appear to be lacking because of inadequate health facilities for disease out-breaks, inadequate infrastructure for environmental catastrophes, or inade-quate state resources for mediating conflict. The advocates of Sensing thereby see Big Data not just as reflecting reality but as transforming it through enabling community co-relational awareness: 'building the capacity of vulnerable groups to be resilient by making themselves aware or inform themselves of the various surrounding risks and hazards, and in so doing be able to organise the proper formal and informal interventions'.[67]

It is important to note that in this perspective of Big Data as empowerment, the 'power' which Big Data Sensing promises local communities, in terms of capacity-building, co-relational awareness and resilience, is not the same type of power which governments claimed for themselves in the modernist era of linear cause-and-effect understandings. It is not the power to direct and shape societies based on the accumulation of causal knowledge. Unfortunately, it could be argued that what works for Google does not work so well for marginal and vulnerable people and communities that desperately need to transform their circumstances. The modernist 'transformation' of the world depended upon the positing of causal connections and possibilities, tested through trial and error. As Pietsch insightfully argues:

> A mere correlation cannot tell how to effectively intervene in the world, e.g. the birth rate cannot be changed by increasing the population of storks, even though studies consistently show a significant correlation between both quantities. By contrast, headaches can be cured by taking acetylsalicylic acid because there is a direct causal connection.[68]

The offer of new technologies of Big Data, at the heart of development, sustainability and resilience programmes of aid and support, to enable Sensing as a mode of governance which can be internationally exported, does not seem to be very empowering for those who most need social change. Big Data can assist with the management of what exists, for example, redesigning transport or energy networks to meet peak demands or adapt to system breakdowns but it cannot provide more than technical assistance based upon knowing more about what exists in the here and now. The problem is that without causal assumptions it is not possible to formulate transformative strategies and responses to problems of social, economic and environmental threats. Big Data does not empower people to change their circumstances but merely to be more aware of them in order to respond more rapidly to changes in them.[69]

The imagined end of causality and its displacement by the governance of effects through the governance mode of Sensing can be understood as moving beyond or, more accurately, inversing the modernist conception of politics. Politics becomes based upon the subject responding to and being sensitive to the world and its environment, rather than acting to change it.

The promised outcomes might appear to be similar, perhaps a reduction in crime, improvements in health and security or even a cleaner environment, but the understanding of the problems and the means of addressing them are very different. As Morozov states:

> [T]his belief that algorithmic regulation is based on 'a deep understanding of the desired outcome' … disconnects the means of doing politics from its ends. But the 'how' of politics is as important as the 'what' of politics – in fact, the former often shapes the latter. Everybody agrees that education, health, and security are all 'desired outcomes', but how do we achieve them? In the past, when we faced the stark political choice of delivering them through the market or the state, the lines of the ideological debate were clear. Today, when the presumed choice is between the digital and the analog or between the dynamic feedback and the static law, that ideological clarity is gone – as if the very choice of how to achieve those 'desired outcomes' was apolitical and didn't force us to choose between different and often incompatible visions of communal living.[70]

As Morozov argues, the default solution to these problems is increasingly a technical one, not the application of technological solutions to address problems at a causal level but the governance mode of Sensing through the development of individual or communal responsivities via apps and sensors. For Morozov (as for Agamben, discussed in the previous chapter) the governance mode of Sensing through Big Data and the Internet of Things reduces politics to the regulation of the interactions and choices of the private and social sphere, where individuals are increasingly 'responsibilised' for social, economic and environmental problems, rather than a mode of governance and politics aimed at addressing the causes of these 'effects':

> For what else could possibly explain their health problems but their personal failings? It's certainly not the power of food companies or class-based differences or various political and economic injustices. One can wear a dozen powerful sensors, own a smart mattress and even do a close daily reading of one's poop – as some self-tracking aficionados are wont to do – but those injustices would still be nowhere to be seen, for they are not the kind of stuff that can be measured with a sensor. The devil doesn't wear data. Social injustices are much harder to track than the everyday lives of the individuals whose lives they affect.[71]

For Morozov:

> algorithmic regulation offers us a good-old technocratic utopia of politics without politics. Disagreement and conflict, under this model, are seen as unfortunate byproducts of the analog era – to be solved through data collection – and not as inevitable results of economic or ideological conflicts.[72]

The view of Big Data as empowering and capacity-building relies upon the reconstruction of societies as self-governing but these societies are no longer constructed as autopoietic (as in the Mapping discourse). Big Data does not so much enable learning and growth as stability and the reproduction of the status quo; in this respect, Sensing as a mode of governance is homeostatic rather than autopoietic. Any disruptions to the fixed or 'natural' order of life are seen as problematic, in the very apt words of Levi Bryant, in this mode of governing the Anthropocene: 'Gaia, it turns out, is either a fascist or a totalitarian.'[73]

This approach to 'self-government' appears to be very different to top-down linear modernist approaches to governance or non-linear Mapping approaches of 'bottom-up' governance, both of which were based on cause-and-effect understandings of policy interventions. In the Sensing framework, in which Big Data methodologies and understandings are central, the power of self-governance and autonomy does not stem from a development of liberal or modern forms of power and knowledge but from their rejection. 'Smart', 'resilient' or 'sentient' cities, for example, are not successful because of a development of cause-and-effect understandings, which can then be operated upon by centralised authorities. The 'conscious' or 'cognitive' self-awareness of the 'sentient' city is understood to be very different from that of human cognition or self-awareness.[74] Thus the concerns that algorithmic forms of rule are 'dehumanising'[75] are doubly true, in that Deleuze and Guattari's fears of 'machinic enslavement', the subordination of the human to the technological means of modulation and regulation, seem well founded on an empirical level,[76] while at the ontopolitical level this 'de-centring of the subject' is affirmed as a recognition that greater responsivity and sensitivity to our 'more-than-human' relational embeddedness is a necessity in the Anthropocene epoch.

Conclusion

This chapter's concern was not to survey the range of meanings implied in the understanding of Big Data as a method or approach – Big Data is clearly a messy and emerging concept, sometimes used to intimate the extension of causal understandings and reductionist knowledge claims and at other times to question these; sometimes conflated with technological innovation or the development of social media and sometimes clearly concerned with the epistemological implications of sensing and correlation.[77] Instead, the object has been to highlight the growing consensus driving Sensing as a mode of governance: that modernist forms of knowledge production are increasingly inadequate, reflected both in academic discussion and in the critical conceptual approaches to the technologically driven possibilities of letting the data 'speak for itself'. Thus Sensing as a mode of governance does not seek to add to a universal store of understanding or to derive rules of causation, which can enable instrumental or means-ends policy practices, which were the essence of the politics of the Holocene.

This emerging consensus appears to confirm the hegemony of Anthropocene ontopolitical approaches: policy and conceptual understandings which focus upon embedded relationality and reject understandings of objective and universal knowledge from a 'God's eye view'.[78] Modernist approaches to knowledge, and the linear, reductionist and universalist assumptions upon which they are based, have been roundly rejected by critical, feminist, post-colonial, post-structuralist, pragmatist, speculative realist, actor network and new materialist approaches, which are increasingly influential throughout the social sciences. Big Data approaches thereby confirm or reinforce Anthropocene ontopolitical assumptions rather than necessarily being constitutive of them. Big Data discursively enables the alternative ontological and epistemological framings of the Anthropocene to make sense as governmental approaches: enabling them to make the transition from the critical margin to become central to government thinking and the transformation of policy-making and understanding. Thus, the rise of Big Data should not be seen as merely about the possibilities of increased computing power and the crossing of the data 'threshold', alleged to enable real-time feedback and responsive co-relational awareness to replace 'top-down' forms of governance based on causal and linear understandings.

It would therefore seem that the rapid rise of Big Data approaches to policy-making and of Sensing as a mode of governance cannot be deterministically explained as a technological phenomenon: technological advances could easily have been used to expand causal understandings (as they have throughout modernity). It would also suggest that Big Data should not necessarily be understood as a revolution in epistemological or ontological understanding. As Nigel Thrift, Bruno Latour and others have noted, Big Data approaches share the methodological and ontological assumptions of currently fashionable social science understandings, which have similarly rejected the search for causal connections and the development of social theory.[79] At the level of ontopolitical assumptions, Big Data offers a broader variety of research techniques, reliant on computer generated data and analytics, but is essentially indistinguishable from other empirically driven approaches, particularly actor network ones, which prioritise co-relations over causal imaginaries of fixed entities.

Notes

1 Economist, 2010.
2 See, for example, Poulin, 2014; Karlsrud, 2014; Allouche, 2014; Bays, n.d.
3 Bruno Latour argues that, despite the deficiencies and constraints of data collection and its imbrication within power relations, Big Data nevertheless opens up a powerful methodological alternative for 'flatter' forms of social theorising (see, Latour et al., 2012; Venturini and Latour, 2010).
4 Zwitter and Hadfield, 2014; boyd and Crawford, 2012; Crawford et al., 2013. Some international relations academics are involved, for example, in the large European Union Framework 7 Programme, 'Increasing Resilience in Surveillance Societies' (IRISS) which focuses on the counterproductive aspects of intrusive state data gathering and new forms of resistance and evasion. See also the work of the engine room academic collective: www.theengineroom.org/ responsible-data-a-conceptual-framework/.
5 See, for example, Kitchin, 2014b; boyd and Crawford, 2012.
6 These assumptions are highlighted in contemporary theoretical approaches, particularly process-oriented ontologies of becoming, in which the human subject is much more 'attached' or relationally-embedded in the materiality of the world. This perspective is linked closely to speculative realism, to new materialist approaches and to actor network theory; see, for example, Millennium, 2013; Cudworth and Hobden, 2011; Braidotti, 2013; Harman, 2010; Latour, 2005.
7 As suggested in Chapter 4, Sensing, as a mode of governance, and Big Data approaches, within this, can be distinguished from other 'process-oriented' ontologies on account of their 'actualist' underpinnings.
8 Kitchin, 2014a: p.68.
9 Google's Eric Schmidt claims that every two days we now create as much information as we did from the dawn of civilisation up until 2003; see Siegler, 2010.
10 Bertolucci, 2014. As Evgeny Morozov notes (2014): 'Thanks to sensors and internet connectivity, the most banal everyday objects have acquired tremendous power to regulate behaviour'.
11 Halevy et al., 2009.
12 See, for an excellent examination of the birth of statistical analysis, Hacking, 1990.
13 See the discussion in Chapter 4.
14 Anderson, 2008; Cukier and Mayer-Schönberger, 2013.

15 Wakefield and Braun, 2018.
16 See the excellent analysis in Galloway, 2014: pp.72–89.
17 Ibid.: p.86.
18 Elena Esposito (2013) makes the useful analogy with pre-modern forms of prophetic or divinatory knowledge where surface phenomena are interpreted as signs rather than as causal effects.
19 See Jim Gray's classic statement (cited in Pietsch, 2013: p.2).
20 Kitchin, 2014b: p.2.
21 As Alexander Galloway (2012: p.137) notes, in the digitalised world, 'a body has no choice but to speak. A body speaks whether it wants to or not… and somewhere an algorithm listens.'
22 See also Cukier and Mayer-Schönberger, 2013: 'Today, when we gather all the data, we do not need to know beforehand what we plan to use it for. Of course, it might not always be possible to collect all the data, but it is getting much more feasible to capture vastly more of a phenomenon than simply a sample and to aim for all of it. Big data is a matter not just of creating somewhat larger samples but of harnessing as much of the existing data as possible about what is being studied.'
23 Kitchin, 2014b: p.2.
24 Pietsch, 2013.
25 As Aysadi (a Big Data computing firm working with the US Office of the Director of National Intelligence, amongst others) CEO, Gurjeet Singh states: '[C]ustomers can finally learn the answers to questions that they didn't know to ask in the first place. Simply stated… [it] is "digital serendipity".' Cited in Clark, 2013.
26 Steadman, 2013.
27 Researcher, Massachusetts Institute of Technology, 30 March 2017.
28 Thrift, 2014: p.7.
29 Ibid.
30 For example, Latour et al., 2012; Venturini and Latour, 2010.
31 See, Hacking, 1990.
32 Williams, 2014.
33 See, for example, Fuller and Goffey, 2012: pp.116–17.
34 See, Pietsch, 2013.
35 Latour, 2010b: p.149.
36 Anderson, 2008.
37 Latour, 2003.
38 Anderson, 2008.
39 Halevy et al., 2009: p.12. For a comparison, see Latour, 2005.
40 Law, 2004.
41 Cukier and Mayer-Schönberger, 2013.
42 This is captured well in the 2014 Marvel Studios film *Captain America: The Winter Soldier*, in which World War II fascist ideologues infiltrate and take over the earth's future global security governance with the aim of securing complete control through high-tech patrolling gunships informed by a data-mining algorithm that can identify and wipe-out all individuals who might become future threats. See also, Himelfarb, 2014; Karlsrud, 2014.
43 Crawford, 2014.

44 See, for example, Ramalingam, 2013.
45 Crawford et al., 2013: p.1.
46 Ibid.
47 See Skoglund, 2014.
48 See, for example, Marres, 2012.
49 Ahrens and Rudolph, 2006: p.217.
50 Coyle and Meier, 2009: p.17.
51 Narvaez, 2012: p.47.
52 As Manuel Perlo Cohen (2000) states: '… a "natural" disaster is inevitable only insofar as the social conditions allow it. Disaster is the culmination of a process and continuum of a disconnect between human beings and their interrelations with the environment.'
53 Meier, 2013.
54 Scheuer, 2012.
55 Meier, 2013.
56 Ibid.
57 Himelfarb, 2014.
58 Karlsrud, 2014.
59 Thrift, 2014: p.8.
60 Ibid.: p.10.
61 Tkacz, 2018.
62 See also Brenner and Theodore, 2002.
63 As Latour notes, digital technology enables the flat ontology of actualist approaches to become a viable project of knowledge production: 'levelling' both the micro-interactions of individuals and the consequences of these interactions through the tracing of the (previously unknowable) networks and interconnections; see, for example, Latour et al., 2012: p.599.
64 See, for example, ó Súilleabháin, 2014.
65 Meier, 2013.
66 Morozov, 2014.
67 Narvaez, 2012: p.52.
68 Pietsch, 2013.
69 See further, the critical work on resilience as adaptative responsivity, for example, Joseph, 2013; Evans and Reid, 2014; Chandler, 2013.
70 Morozov, 2014.
71 Ibid.
72 Ibid.
73 Bryant, 2011: p.277.
74 In fact, there has been a reaction against the loss of vision and political possibilities involved in the 'smart city' imaginary. See, for example, Greenfield, 2014; Pagh and Freudendal-Pedersen, 2014.
75 For example, O'Connor, 2016; Perrotta, 2016; Mazenec, 2017.
76 Deleuze and Guattari, 2014: pp.531–6.
77 See, for example, Annemarie Mol (2002), on the multiple uses and meanings associated with phenomenon, which enables an assemblage of meanings to take a coherent shape.
78 Haraway, 1988; Haraway, 1991: pp.188–96; see also Epstein, 2014.
79 For further on the critical rejection of social theory, see Koddenbrock, 2015.

PART IV
Hacking

6

FROM SENSING TO HACKING

Introduction

Whereas the governance mode of Sensing aspires to manage, modulate and respond to emergent effects on the basis of homeostatic regulation, the mode of Hacking seeks to develop a more open and future-oriented framework of governance. As analysed here, and in the following chapter, Hacking develops in reaction to the perceived limitations of the rigidities of Sensing and its Big Data frameworks of automated responsivity. Hacking is much more open and experimental and, in this way, can be seen to offer a distinct mode of governance in the Anthropocene. Hacking does not have the fixed separations of earlier modes and therefore cannot really be grasped as either autopoietic (there is no adaptive process, no telos towards problem-solving) or homeostatic (there is no aspiration to maintain the status quo, rather an ontology of interactive fluidity). In the analytic framing proposed in this book, Hacking is best grasped as sympoietic: in the ontopolitics of Hacking there is little distinction of fixity of subject and object, involving a much flatter relational ontology. Hacking could be understood as a relational and interactive process which itself constitutes subjects and objects in ever changing ways. Thus Hacking reveals new capacities and attributes or enables the recomposing or repurposing of aspects and relations as the basis for further incremental changes and possibilities.

One way of articulating the emergence of Hacking as a distinctive mode of governance is as an extension of the mode of Sensing. Where Sensing could be understood as closing down possibilities of alternative worlds coming into being, Hacking takes the non-modern or post-epistemological framings of Sensing and turns them into a more affirmative and open governing paradigm. This mode of governance is much more celebratory of the possibilities which the Anthropocene is held to provide. The first two modes sought to negotiate or manage the end of modernist knowledge assumptions, gradually enabling governance to cohere new approaches and technologies without linear causal assumptions. As we have seen, the first mode, Mapping, sought to govern through understanding causation as non-linear and path-dependent, constructing life as a complex set of relational interactions which could be mapped for the purpose of governance as a framework of indirect intervention to shape outcomes. Governing actors were thus constructed not as modern subjects, initiating policy programmes, but rather as adaptive or reactive, always 'in the middle' of processes of interaction, which could be reflected upon and influenced. Sensing, as a mode of governance, sheds Anthropocene ontopolitics of its interventionist and goal-directed aspirations, seen as too hubristic and subject-centred; instead, seeking to be sensitive and responsive to the 'what-is' of the world in the fluidity of its emergence.

Hacking maintains the sensitivities of Sensing but seeks to return the human subject to the world, not as the controlling, goal-directed subject of modern forms of governance, but as an experimenting, compositional or playful subject, fully aware of its lack of causal knowledge and confident and at home with contingency and the unexpected. This may seem counterintuitive as, in traditional approaches to governance and policy-making, the figure of the hacker is a problematic and disruptive one, posing a threat to computerised networks and high tech infrastructures essential to the smooth, fixed and linear, running of modern economies.[1] However, the concept of 'hacking' is ambiguous.[2] In the fluid and less linear ontology of the Anthropocene, Hacking – as a form of political and ethical practice – takes on a much more positive relationship to governance and security discourses, and is used in this book to outline the development of a distinct policy methodology or approach, sensitive to contexts and inter-relationships and critical of the Mapping or Sensing approaches to governance, laid out in the previous chapters. This will be illustrated here using, as a case study, policy experiments in Jakarta, Indonesia.

Key to the analysis being made here is that Hacking, as a mode of governing, calls into being a new approach to international policy practice, where awareness of embedded relationships enables the empowerment of communities, not merely to respond to emergent effects through Sensing, in order to homeostatically maintain the status quo, but to creatively engage with emergence itself; thus turning problems or threats into new opportunities. This approach is often methodologically counter positioned to a failed or failing modernist discourse of governance, which assumes that risks or problems can be 'solved', 'prevented' or 'removed' through technological or engineering approaches. Hacking as a mode of governance thus becomes less dependent on its etymological roots in computing technology and becomes a transformative process of building engaged communities through experimentation and grasping momentary and fluid connections and inter-relations. Governance policy interventions, on this basis, thus no longer seek to 'solve' problems or to address them through adaptation (Mapping) but neither do they see responsivity as something that can be automatic and organised around maintaining the status quo (Sensing).[3] Instead, the problems themselves are reinterpreted as enabling and creative opportunities.

It is important to emphasise that the conception of Hacking as a mode of governance is heuristically developed and outlined here (and further in the following chapter) as a result of my reflections on the epistemological and ontological framings being worked through and negotiated in policy practices. The international policy activists interviewed in different projects in Jakarta, and cited below, do not necessarily see their work in these terms and have differing understandings of how new policy approaches can be developed as well as the potential political and philosophical stakes involved in their deployment. It is the process of policy experimentation itself that this chapter wishes to focus upon. Of particular interest, in the field work undertaken in Jakarta, was the attempt to see how new digital technologies have been deployed in ways which enact or performatively stage this broader shift in governance policy understandings towards the presentation of emergent effects in terms of Hacking rather than Sensing: as enabling or revealing new forms of agency and community capacity, previously unrecognised.

The interview material that forms the bulk of the following sections is taken from fieldwork undertaken in Jakarta in February 2016. This fieldwork was hosted by a flood awareness NGO, PetaJakarta, and included extended interviews with representatives from PetaJakarta, the Jakarta Open Street Map Project and the United Nations Global Pulse, Jakarta Pulse

Lab.[4] The interview material is deployed as a backdrop to how new digital technologies are appropriated to enable Hacking, as a mode of governance thinking, to emerge through the Anthropocene problematic. Jakarta seemed to be one of the best places to undertake this research as these concerns motivate the work of many international agencies in the city and it is not unusual to come across references to Jakarta as 'the city of the Anthropocene' in both policy and academic research.[5]

Indonesia has been a leading actor in mainstreaming disaster risk reduction approaches since the 2004 Aceh tsunami.[6] However, it is its capital city, Jakarta, which has been at the centre of climate change and disaster risk concerns: on one hand, it is symbolic of an ever-expanding megacity, on the other hand, it is rapidly approaching ecological catastrophe.[7] The problem of securing the city against rising water levels (the threat from rainfall, river turbulence and rising sea-levels) throws into relief the limits of structural engineering projects and has increasingly called forth new approaches that no longer assume modernist, or linear, accounts of progress.[8] This is the context in which digital policy activists have sought to re-envision ways of living with the emergent effects of climate change and of using new technologies to engage with and transform citizen awareness.

The rest of this chapter draws out this argument step by step. The next section provides an introduction to the concept of Hacking as a mode of governance and its articulation through a close relationship to but also a problematisation of both Mapping and Sensing approaches. The second section focuses on the key distinctive attribute of Hacking: the transformation of problems into opportunities, highlighted in the conceptualisation of 'becoming with' rather than of progress being made through struggling against or 'pre-eventing' processes of emergence. The following section analyses the empirical research findings regarding Hacking as a paradigm enabling and giving coherence to international policy intervention for disaster or crisis response in Jakarta. The chapter concludes by suggesting potential limits to the displacement of modernist discourses of policy intervention by a process of governance through Hacking as a mode of policy engagement.

Hacking in the Anthropocene

As has been analysed in the previous chapters, the question of how to engage with the present with more creative and imaginative insight is key to the new modes of governance in the Anthropocene. In other words, the methodological concern in adaptive Mapping or responsive Sensing is for contextual meaningfulness rather than for the extraction of causal laws or theories of causation, which can be taken and applied elsewhere. This 'new empiricism'[9] has sought a less abstract, representational or conceptually mediated access to the world[10] and is more concerned with relations in their immediate context, rather than attempting to extract knowledge of the inner essences of discrete entities by abstracting from their context. The focus on empirical immediacy, essential for effective policy responses, is often highlighted in the contradistinction between analogue views of sensing, affect, relations and correlations,[11] as opposed to modernist homogenising or 'digital' forms of representation and ideas of causation which reduce reality to homogenous units based on binary distinctions.[12] A world understood as a fluid set of inter-relations is not amenable to statistical regulation or to causal lines of prediction and implementation. Knowledge has to be fine-grained and real time rather than abstract or universal.[13]

In the previous chapter, the attraction of what are called 'Big Data' approaches was seen to stem from the promise that new computer technologies, high-speed algorithms and machine-learning can provide relational insights through correlation and pattern recognition, without the need for causal theory.[14] The question of governing in the Anthropocene is thus increasingly less one of understanding and manipulating relations and feedback processes than of being sensitive and responsive to the 'great outdoors': the liveliness and potential of a world sidelined by reductionist or linear approaches. This is why radical theorists are drawn, often, to approaches that start with the external world, by 'following the actors'[15] or 'following the data', rather than with human-centred questions and theoretical constructions and models.[16] It is held that this openness to the world, this new empiricism or pragmatism, needs to be vectored via social and technological means of mediation, which provide access to a relational reality obscured or hidden by the modern episteme.

McKenzie Wark, at the New School, has long highlighted the links between hacking and the sensibilities of the Anthropocene, and his *Hacker Manifesto* gestures to the logic of Hacking as the development of new approaches and possibilities from what already exists, through information enabling new relations to be seen and actualised.[17] Wark argues, in the *Manifesto*, that:

> The hack produces a production of a new kind, which has as its result a singular and unique product, and a singular and unique producer ...

Production takes place on the basis of a prior hack which gives to production its formal, social, repeatable and reproducible form. Every production is a hack formalised and repeated on the basis of its representation. To produce is to repeat; to hack, to differentiate.[18]

Hacking is an iterative, gradual approach to policy interventions, where each hack uses and constructs new inter-relationships creating new possibilities for thinking and acting. However, as soon as a hack is reproduced (turned into 'production' on the basis of representation) it loses its creative capabilities. A hack is a form of intervention, which seeks to reveal and to construct new relations and interconnections: it does not seek to construct new forms (structured or technologicial solutions addressing causes and solutions) but neither does it passively accept the world as it is. 'Instead, adaptation is the act of polities making-worlds by repurposing and reengineering infrastructure not as a heroic or redemptive activity, but as a strategic force of selection, affirmation, and affinity.'[19] As the Invisible Committee state:

> The figure of the hacker contrasts point by point with the figure of the engineer, whatever the artistic, police-directed, or entrepreneurial efforts to neutralize him may be. Whereas the engineer would capture everything that functions, in such a way that everything functions better in service to the system, the hacker asks himself 'How does that work?' in order to find its flaws, but also to invent other uses, to experiment. Experimenting then means exploring what such and such a technique implies ethically. The hacker *pulls techniques out of the technological system in order to free them.* (emphasis added)[20]

'Pulling techniques out of the technological system in order to free them' from the grand designs of social engineers and technocratic planners captures well the aspirations of digital policy activists in Jakarta. The following sections illustrate how Hacking approaches have been pursued in practice and the discourses and understandings associated with Hacking as an emerging mode of governance, here demonstrated in terms of experimentation taking the form of both ontological and epistemological performativity. Of particular importance is the articulation of Hacking through a critique of 'Big Data' Sensing approaches and the argument for active participatory engagement in the facilitation of processes of emergence. The following section emphasises the distinctive logic of Hacking as 'becoming with' and analyses how Hacking reworks problems as opportunities; the final section highlights the impact and importance of Hacking as a mode of governance and raises some potential limits to this approach, further analysed in the following chapter.

The limits of Sensing

One thing that international digital activists are clear about is that they are hostile to approaches they term as 'Big Data'. In their understanding, Big Data merely replicates current thinking, providing mundane reflections on the world.[21] For example, Big Data analysts might undertake a field study on the fear of volcanoes and work out that people are anxious or do data-mining of social media to discover that people prefer to lie-in on a Sunday morning. For advocates of Hacking, often the best that Big Data can come up with is the mundane reality, and often it fails to even achieve this as it is not easy to train a computer to read and understand Tweets, or a drone to recognise the difference between a barracks and a hospital or between a terrorist suspect and a civilian.[22] At worst, Big Data is seen as problematically reproducing dominant understandings of the world and as serving the needs of commercial companies and producing problematic linear and securitised forms of knowledge.[23] As well as providing less access to 'reality', activists argue that passively data-mined information does little to change the circumstances of people, bypassing communities and privatising data to aid governments and corporations. Even the active generation of data can be problematic when the information is never the responsibility of the community itself.

An organiser of the Jakarta Open Street Map project sees an entirely different relation between mapping and the citizen. Rather than mapping being the province of 'armchair' mappers with drone cameras, mapping was necessarily a local project as the information mapped was only 'real' while it was in the context in which it was generated. This was firstly because local people could identify objects and sites in fine-grained ways, which would be impossible for 'armchair' outsiders; secondly, because the categories used to describe or to classify sites and objects were not readily transferable (the use of road or street classification in Western Europe would be of little use to a street mapper in many parts of Africa, for example);[24] and, thirdly, because mapping could not be a one-off project, but was necessarily an on-going and participatory process:

> Even a global fine-grained map would not be adequate. Things keep changing and changing: a sub-village could disappear and become a

shopping mall, a hospital might close down. The map has to be continually updated, even in a matter of days. Really, really updated. The
main challenge is to ingrain that kind of motivation/attitude in people
responsible for updating the area.[25]

The challenge was, in effect, to engage enough people to construct live
maps as a better, crowdsourced, 'living' representation of the world. Other
approaches to real time mapping, however, take a more mixed[26] or less modern
ontology to heart in the design of digital policy projects. A leading example of
this new empiricist methodology is that being developed by the academics
and practitioners of the PetaJakarta project, based on facilitating geo-social
forms of collective intelligence.[27] As one of the PetaJakarta project coordi-
nators stated, 'Data cannot be "mined", it is not a resource to be used by
others. It is not about taking something out of one place and giving it to
someone else, it is about feedbacks, not "mining"'.[28] It is about using data in a
system of 'intimate sensing' to enable contextual seeing and understanding.[29]

From PetaJakarta's perspective, the population of the major city are a
resource still in need of mobilisation: they are already extensively networked through social media and could make great citizen sensors, especially once information offered can be verified through geo-spatial tagging
of the precise time and location of the information (this enables others to
check and compare the information from multiple sources and makes ver-
ification much easier). Social media can be reconfigured with humanitarian
apps to activate these civic citizenship elements. Different problems then
can be used to construct engaged and active communities able to play a role
in addressing them as a form of 'civic co-management'.[30] Rather than passively reproducing a pale imitation of reality, the development of civic
communication technologies could enable a more dynamic reality to
unfold, amplifying the collective networked social intelligence of the city.
At present, new civic technologies are being bankrolled and tested in relation to disasters and emergencies, but the hope is that this could be the
beginning of new forms of geo-social networked systems enabling much
more distributed and democratic forms of real time governance.

Radical and tech-savvy academics and activists are keen to see the possibilities
for human citizen-sensor-led initiatives, in which citizen knowledge and
ownership is seen as vital for the development of civic apps. Where Big Data
approaches of data-mining are seen to be passive, and led by the desire to
monetise civil networked capacities, citizen-led approaches are seen to be active
and transformative.[31] More importantly, they are seen to be self-transformative

initiatives, not just generating information to be used by others but a different politics: 'Recognising a problem is not the same as resolving a problem. The momentum of "intimate sensing" is to enable people to think differently and thus to feel differently.'[32] For these radical advocates of governance as Hacking, it is clear that 'Big Data and Twitter won't save you, won't stop the floods. To be successful the key point is to be able to see what's beyond the interface ... the relationships of care'.[33]

Seeing the unseen relationships was also the objective of representatives of the UN Global Pulse Jakarta Pulse Lab project, who very much bought into the policy methodologies of Hacking, being developed elsewhere, by PetaJakarta and others. Again they were not in favour of 'Big Data' approaches, which relied on the passive data-mining of social media and other sources, instead emphasising the importance of 'thick data': the use of Big Data but also of fine-grained ethnographic research. The Pulse Lab is involved with a large number of projects but one emphasised in particular was a study of the impact of El Niño, in conjunction with the World Food Programme. This project relied on recruited (paid) volunteers, i.e. on active rather than passive data collectors, who used a humanitarian app to record a range of market prices, taking a photo of the particular item and entering its quality and price. This information was then geo-located and time-stamped to build up a fine-grained and real-time picture of market fluctuations. Like PetaJakarta, the Pulse Lab found that passive data-mining of social media was not fine-grained enough to provide reliable information.[34]

This actively generated market price data was then matched against other data streams, such as household resilience surveys and local weather data to map the effects of changes in community sustainability. Importantly, for the points made here, the project was based on locating outlier communities: those that seemed to do either better or worse than the average. Thus, the purpose was not so much to provide a complete picture but to see the as yet unseen: to find the communities that were in trouble (reaching their tipping points or threshold levels) and requiring intervention by the World Food Programme (this approach thereby has aspects of both Sensing and of Mapping) but also, crucially, to initiate research projects to learn from the resilience capacities of communities which did better than average.

This provides a useful performative demonstration of Hacking as a mode of governance, in that the UN Global Pulse and World Food Programme wanted to use new data technologies not in a Mapping way (to see unfolding relations and interactions that could be intervened in) nor in a Sensing way (to respond in real time with sensitivity to minor changes in relationships), but in a distinct Hacking framing: to locate the exceptions, the surprises and the unexpected aspects and elements, the intimation being that certain communities have 'tricks up their sleeve', the ability to 'hack': i.e. ways of thinking or organising that enable them to engage differently with certain contingencies. The reality that is being looked for is not something that can be neatly fitted into categories and charts but the reality of the sign that provides the possibility for analogic reasoning to reveal relations and connections whose importance may have been ignored. Long gone is the idea that international development organisations already possessed ways of knowing or technological solutions that could be generalised and exported through training or project grants.[35] If there are solutions to problems of climate change and poverty then these are held to be context specific and generated through communities themselves, but the ways in which these creative solutions emerge can be learnt from and provide possible opportunities for others in the region.[36]

Becoming 'with' not 'against'

Citizen-sensors are not just more attuned to reality, in mobilising or inculcating the power of the geo-socially networked citizen. The immanent capacities of geo-social networks are used to enhance awareness of problems and issues in new ways. At present, many social, economic and ecological questions are not posed or are ignored. A good example, in Jakarta, is the city's relationship to the river system, which often floods in the monsoon season. The city is currently undertaking a massive project of 'normalisation', tearing down informal settlements on the river banks and concreting the walls of the river; in some areas the river itself is being concreted over. For many middle-class citizens, this 'beautification' of the river is a good thing and they support the river being pushed underground and out of sight. For Western policy activists, 'They are turning their backs on the reality of the city. The river is an ugly monster that no one wants around.'[37] Thus, the attitude of covering over the problem *is the problem*, preventing ways of rethinking the city's relationship to the river system and, even more importantly, this approach is seen to be counterproductive: increasing the rigidity of a river system which is constantly in flux, and therefore storing up more problems for the future.

Despite the constant and worsening flooding, it seems that the message is not getting through to either the city or its inhabitants:

When you get sick, it's the body's way of saying that something is wrong. Flooding is a sign that something is wrong with the city. PetaJakarta is like a thermometer. It enables us to see, it alerts us to the facts. You can't see a fever. PetaJakarta is a quantification of the problem.[38]

In my own understanding, this is not really a 'quantification' of the problem; this would intimate that it was building up a representative store of knowledge. It is, as analysed in the previous chapters, a 'datafication' of the problem, bringing to light a set of relationships and interdependencies rather than just measuring something on a universalisable basis.

This process of datafication as enabling the seeing of relations in the actual or concrete context is not just crucial to the governance mode of Sensing (considered in the previous two chapters), the concrete context of interaction is also important to Hacking approaches of governance. Hacking as a discourse of 'becoming with' is necessarily grounded in the concrete specificity of relationships. As Maddy Harland argues, from the perspective of the permaculture movement, the key principle is 'working with not against natural forces' like the wind, sun, water, the forces of succession, animals and other 'natural' energies.[39] Thus, the data generated by PetaJakarta is not a passive representation nor is the purpose merely that of responsiveness to maintain a homeostatic status quo. The project uses machinic or technological enhancement to construct a more dynamic, relational, version of reality. It is this digitally enabled vision that enables a community to be able to see the unseen and thereby responsively care for its now enhanced and extended relational self.[40]

At PetaJakarta there is an understanding that a new methodology is emerging with the work being undertaken and that its full outline is still in process. Key is the desire to visualise relational infrastructures, networks and interdependencies, and new technologies are seen as central to this process:

What are data? Data are signs that can be assembled as a relational structure but can only be read mathematically. Signs produced can be read/organised by mathematics not by language. For example 'Banjir' [flood] is not linguistic, it is a code that is machine readable.[41]

A PetaJakarta coordinator continued later:

We want to develop a post-intentionality platform. The role of CogniCity [the open source software programme][42] is not to generate greater intentionality but machine solidarities. Big Data is problematic [with its predictive assumptions] it identifies volition/will in systems without them ... Big Data traces, it only provides the evidence of the Anthropocene's existence rather than augmenting its unfolding.[43]

While the articulation may not be immediately clear, the aspiration is to use technology to see 'posthumanly', which means not to impose linear cause-and-effect assumptions (intentionality, will or volition) but to see things for how they really are, open to contingent connections and relations. This is why it is argued that emergent effects can only be seen 'mathematically', through data-fication and machine recognition. The assumption is that, through seeing contingent and fleeting interconnections and relations, the unfolding of the Anthropocene can be 'enhanced', through interaction and innovation. Rather than using Sensing technology for responsive adaptation, the aspiration is to shift from Sensing to Hacking, enabling change to unfold inter-actively through an iterative process of working 'with' rather than 'against' the river. For this reason, the project team opposes attempts to generalise and take information or data out of their context in order to instantiate major projects of social or technological engineering (which would hold back, or work against, the development of 'Anthropocene' approaches).

As one member of the PetaJakarta team told me: 'Understanding the river as a line is the first problem. It doesn't move in one constant direction or with a constant thickness.'[44] Paradoxically, the application of modernist approaches to solve the problem of the river system is seen to create the unintended consequence of making the problem worse: sporadic con-cretisation of the river is held to make the river even more turbulent. This is not just an ontological problem; it also highlights the paradox of the modernist episteme itself.

> The denial of the river as the enabler of life in the city stems from the Dutch linear view of the river, which is still prevalent since the 17th Century. This means that planners are not addressing the reality: the river cannot be forced into a box.[45]

The more that modernist approaches are applied with inherited under-standings of scientific approaches to hydrological engineering (working on the same basis of equations which have not changed in a hundred years), the less the city's inhabitants are able to see the shifting relations and possibilities of their environment or to understand the river itself:

The 'normalisation' of the river has made it much more turbulent and less predictable. Before, local people knew the behaviour of the river when the gates were lifted upstream. People living informally on the banks of the river had a syncopated rhythm of daily life, living with the river. They would be prepared for flooding and move their stuff upstairs and they would know when the river was receding and quickly move out the (toxic) mud before it dries. Now they can't predict how long it will take for the water to flow. All the ways through which the city learned to live and adapt to the river have become irrelevant.[46]

It is viewed that responding to the challenge of governing the Anthropocene through modernist forms makes the problems worse rather than better, at the level both of ontological reality and of epistemic possibilities of thinking about approaches to these problems.[47] This negative approach is summed up by the Great Garuda sea wall initiative.[48] A huge planned extension of the city into the sea; the image of the Great Garuda – a warrior bird, facing out to the ocean, as if it is defending Jakarta against climate change – is seen as particularly unfortunate.[49] 'Promoting the idea that climate change is something *out there* and we can just stop it; not let it in.'[50]

The PetaJakarta project activists are against the city's 'normalisation' approach but that does not mean that they want to just let the flooding take its course. As several of the international researchers argue, 'resilience can only be built through community not form'.[51] The general understanding of the Great Garuda and normalisation initiatives, which seek to formalise the river, to control it, is that: 'We will be more resilient because we will be in control.'[52] For PetaJakarta, this is the wrong approach to take to the problem. The PetaJakarta project is therefore very different: 'It's not trying to solve flooding, it's trying to give a voice to the flooding: to give a voice to the river.'[53] The alternative to 'form' is 'community': 'Communicating smarter about the environment and helping people to get through flood events.'[54]

'Community' starts from a very different set of ontological and epistemological assumptions, rethinking the city from a relational perspective in which the city and river are fundamentally interconnected, in a process of 'becoming with'. 'We need to put the river at the centre of the city, the river comes first and secondly there is the human development on top. By blocking off the river we are making the main character less visible.'[55] The Twitter feedback from the project participants helps in the process of remapping the city, making it more dynamic, or lively, than the reality of the river on the map. 'This enables thinking differently. The river is not a line but a body ever present across the city.'[56] Here, mapping is used as a technology for sensitising perceptions and for being open to the possibilities of collaborative 'becoming with': for increasing openness and flexibility, not for intervening in non-linear causal relations or responding through automatic and unthinking forms of Sensing and adaptation.

'Community' is not the geo-social networked intelligence of the citizens alone but the use of the geo-social networked technology to re-envision what the city is and what it means to be a citizen of it. It is a mechanism for opening possibilities for 'becoming with' rather than closing them down. For PetaJakarta researchers:

> We need to visualise the city as a set of relations that cannot be pinned down. We need to move beyond binaries. Information is the commodity of change ... Architects and engineers need to take this on board. There are no technical solutions. Planners, architects and engineers need a whole new level of thinking about the medium we are working with.[57]

This view, that in the Anthropocene there are 'no technical solutions', highlights the fundamental shift involved in the emergence of Hacking as a policy methodology for governance under conditions of uncertainty. It also poses the fundamental question of what role planners, architects and engineers are to play in this new framework:

> What are we trying to design? A better functioning image of today? Shouldn't we be designing for the system to live better, to live smarter? Maybe it doesn't have to look different. It's hard to say. When you talk about resilience through form it's difficult to take it away from capitalist investors. It's difficult to take it away from who it's meant to work for.[58]

The PetaJakarta project very much works on the basis that things do not necessarily have to look very differently for radical change to take place. There is already a socially networked citizenship through social media and the technology is already available for geo-spatial mapping of communication (the project sends out automated responses with a video telling people how to enable the Global Positioning System (GPS) location). The project seeks to 'hack' this already existing geo-social technological infrastructure to reconfigure it and to activate elements not at the fore, thus, taking the existing capacities and transforming them to remap problems and issues, through taking apps developed as open source software and making them capable of mobilising and re-envisioning community relations in open-ended and experimental directions. What could perhaps be seen as the extension of emergency or disaster risk reduction to the politics of everyday life is here reread as a hack to enable an empowering network able to amplify the power of self-organising community intelligence.

The Anthropocene of slums[59]

It's not just the river that activists in Jakarta seek to re-envision through bringing to the fore agencies previously held to have been ignored, problematised and unseen. The governance mode of Hacking has much broader resonances and synergies, which it both feeds off and into. Important here is the policy debate over the future of the informal/slum dwellings or kampongs, with the activist movement centred on kampongs opposing the tearing down of informal housing and the relocation of people to social housing.[60] Rather than removing the problem or relocating it, people argue that informal/slum housing could be done better through looking at what works and what doesn't work and working with the resources and capabilities that are available. In fact, for some, the kampongs are the best example of how to live in the Anthropocene: building community through Hacking understood as an open-ended system of collective experimentation.[61] International activists argue that while kampong dwellers have responded to flooding in innovative ways of coping and communicative interaction, the modern city dwellers fail to appreciate these capabilities.[62] Symptomatic of the approach to the river system is that those who are best placed to develop innovative ways of 'becoming with' the river through strategies of Hacking have been ignored or marginalised in policy discussions.

Jakarta is the 'City of the Anthropocene', in that the nexus of epistemological and ontological shifts, which ground the new governance modes of the Anthropocene, are at the forefront of policy discussions and reflect broader international changes. Since the early 1990s, there has been a major policy shift from earlier slum removal to slum improvement, slum-rehabilitation and slum development programmes.[63] Slum dwellings are increasingly high on international policy agendas, enabling the merging of governance concerns of poverty, climate change and urban growth to be renegotiated through the lens of resilience.[64] In these developing approaches, resilience is something that can be generated through engagement with urban slums and often through the application of new technologies for community engagement and local leadership. Slums are becoming much more part of the solution to governing in the Anthropocene than part of the problem.[65] As an international academic researcher, working with a Jakarta NGO, stated:

> What is a kampong? A mediator between the river and the city: a safety-net for the city. A flood is an opportunity for them; they pick up the slack, see the opportunity and work as a unit; what we see as an obstacle, they see as an opportunity. They live in rhythm with the water unlike the city. This bridges the gap, away from the 'monster' image of the river that we want to punish.[66]

The key point is that the link between poverty and vulnerability, central to disaster risk reduction in the 2000s, has been increasingly replaced by perspectives which focus on capacities for Hacking as an experimental form of innovation through reimagining relations both inside the community and with the external environment:

> Though there are shared characteristics, 'poverty' and 'vulnerability' are not the same thing. While poverty reflects a lack of economic and social assets, vulnerability additionally implies a lack of capacity, security, and exposure to risks. Though the overlap is significant, not all poor are vulnerable and not all who are vulnerable are necessarily poor. This has important implications for policy – as does understanding the assets and capabilities even very poor populations possess in their resilience and response to either slow-onset climate change or disasters. Much can often be built from communities, especially once assumptions regarding their capacities are put aside.[67]

There is increasingly a shift in attitude to slum dwellers which flags up the new approach to governing as Hacking in the Anthropocene: seeing slum dwellers as both vulnerable through poverty but also as having creative capacities for organisation and resilience which need to be inculcated and developed. If new forms of seeing relationally are the model for policy intervention then slum dwellers and the urban poor are the most proficient in organically developing solutions based on seeing the unseen. As the *Economist* notes:

In a way, slums are areas of high sustainability – they use less water and electricity, for example. There is also a stronger sense of community and solidarity than in big cities in general, which are much more anonymous. Slum dwellers are particularly entrepreneurial, with families converting their ground floor into a soup kitchen or a school. Policymakers in developed cities should learn to listen to citizens rather than adopt a top-down approach to planning – a core component of the 'slum upgrading' method.[68]

As indicated by Global Pulse, data gathering and visualisation projects are a fast growing area for international institutions engaged in developing resilience to climate change, particularly those focusing on urban poverty.[69] Here, the approach is very different to the liberal grand schemes of social engineering and slum clearances or the neoliberal assumption that slum dwellers are, in some way, lacking capacities and in need of external agencies to provide them with resilience (still noticeable in some of the World Bank material until recently).[70]

Conclusion: life hacks of the Anthropocene

The PetaJakarta approach promises both an epistemological and ontological transformation in how cities and citizens and the problems of the Anthropocene are imagined. However, underneath this radical gloss is a sense of making do with what we have, not by doing nothing but by re-envisioning the problem, the river, the drought, the kampong etc. and then being able to 'hack' into existing resources and capabilities to make the most of opportunities and interconnections. These forms of micropolitics – empowering people based on their own relational capabilities – depend on an intimate knowledge of communities and attention to shifting possibilities and is very different from traditional framings of intervention or non-intervention.

This ethos of governing the Anthropocene through attention to repurposing and re-envisioning, attempting to enable existing potential interconnections is, I think, highlighted in the idea of Public Service Jams or Civic Hackathons where Smart City Labs, the UN Development Programme or other donors invite ideas and proposals to deconstruct problems and try out prototype solutions with volunteer hackers, technologists and designers immersing themselves in the problem. These ad hoc forums are lauded as mechanisms for reaching out to citizens to develop new ideas, exposing governing authorities and international institutions to new tools and skill sets and for re-envisioning problems, seeing issues in a different light.[71] When it comes to governing the Anthropocene, it seems that traditional forms of social research and policy analysis are barriers to this form of creative engagement, condemned to repeat the mistakes of the past and reproduce problems and forms of social and economic exclusion.

What this misses though is the temporary and short-term nature of these new community approaches. This is exactly the idea of a 'Life-Hack' as a short-term solution for a 'problem hair day', for example.[72] When the World Food Programme organises with the UN Global Pulse to develop a dashboard of information on drought, food prices and household resilience this is not because they have an ambitious programme of transformative initiatives for development but precisely because they have no such programme and, in its absence, they are seeking to design a system in which communities can develop their own resources to cope at the edge of poverty. The same can be said of the other short-term project-based initiatives, within the governance mode of Hacking, enabled by data-based re-envisioning, community engagement and empowerment.

The world of digitally enhanced geo-social intelligence and real time empirics seems more dynamic and lively than the world of traditional governance discourses. But, I would suggest that its dynamic appearance does not come so much from the power of open source data gathering and of geo-spatial mapping but rather from the breaking up of reality into short-term and momentary quick fixes. This approach is neither the interventionism of Mapping, as an attempt to socially and technically engineer choice-making through indirect forms of intervention, nor the non-intervention of Sensing, of community self-responsibility for its own responsive awareness; but its engaging and transformative ethos remains perpetually stuck in the 'Life-Hack' mode for fear of doing either too little or too much.

Governance in the Anthropocene, it seems, cannot be done by attempts to socially or technologically engineer the world but it can be done by applying technological applications to citizens recast as a geo-socially networked community of sensors, attuned to the 'unfolding' of the Anthropocene as a human-nonhuman assemblage of open-ended inter-relations. This is what gives the correlated or datafied worlds of Sensing and Hacking their hyper-reality.[73] The lack of temporality of the emergent assemblages of the Anthropocene mean the 'what-is' of the world[74] is enhanced by seeing it only as a momentary event, liable to momentary interventions, rather than in terms of long-term problems that need long-term solutions.

Discourses of Hacking, governing the Anthropocene through an ontology of interdependency, imply open-ended forms of engagement and intervening that seem, at first sight, to be radical, creative and empowering. However, the following chapter engages Hacking less empirically or performatively and more in terms of the radical frameworks of contemporary social theory, which focus on the innovative and creative aspects of this form of governance. It suggests that Hacking, as a radical affirmation of the Anthropocene, is possibly the most important governance paradigm to critically engage with and outlines that – while the ontopolitical assumptions which ground Hacking posit a more experimental and agential world than the automated responses of Sensing – underneath this radical gloss is a similarly humble approach to the world, which also tends to enshrine the status quo as ontological necessity.

Notes

1 Abrahamsen and Williams, 2011; McClure et al., 2001.
2 See McCormick, 2013.
3 See Duffield, 2013.
4 Further information about the work of PetaJakarta can be accessed here: https://petaja karta.org/banjir/en/; the Jakarta Open Street Map Project here: www.gfdrr.org/sites/ gfdrr/files/publication/Pillar_1_Using_Participatory_Mapping_for_Disaster_Prepa redness_in_Jakarta_OSM.pdf; and the United Nations Global Pulse, Jakarta Pulse Lab, here: www.unglobalpulse.org/jakarta.
5 See, for example, Turpin et al., 2013.
6 See, for example, BNPB, 2014; GFDRR, 2015.
7 Rukmana, 2014; Holderness and Turpin, 2016.
8 Sukardjo, 2013; Leigh Geros, 2015.
9 Clough, 2009; see also Latour et al., 2012; Venturini and Latour, 2010.
10 This non-representational reality is engaged with by a number of theorists, using a variety of conceptual terms to capture this shift; see, for example, Thrift, 2008; Massumi, 2002; Protevi, 2009.
11 Several authors locate the historical emergence of this policy approach in the discussions around cybernetics in the post World War II period; see for example, Halpern, 2014; Invisible Committee, 2014: pp.35–44; Pickering, 2010; Hayles, 1999.
12 See Galloway, 2014. In the 'non-philosophical' method of Laruelle, information or data that is relevant bears no necessary relation to the essence of the problem or threat but is a direct form, trace or sign of its appearance. This 'clone' world does not provide representational knowledge of the problem or threat in-itself but enables us to orientate ourselves towards it: to pay attention to it.
13 These sensibilities also shape a lot of the conceptual arts, as avant-garde 'uncreative writer' Kenneth Goldsmith puts it 'context is the new content'; see Wilkinson, 2015.

14 Anderson, 2008; Aradau and Blanke, 2015.
15 For example, Law and Hassard, 1999; Latour, 2005.
16 Chandler, 2015.
17 Wark, 2004; see also Chardronet, 2015.
18 Wark, 2004: sections 8 & 9.
19 Turpin, 2015.
20 Invisible Committee, 2014: p.43.
21 PetaJakarta coordinator, Jakarata, 17 February 2016.
22 See Grothoff and Porup, 2016; Robbins, 2016; MSF, 2015.
23 This framing is dominant in the critical academic literature. As Read et al. note (2016: p.13): 'Ultimately we conclude that the new aspiration towards hubristic big data processing is just another step in the same modernist process of the production of statistical truth.'
24 On problems of classification, see, for example, Bowker, 2000.
25 Jakarta Open Street Map coordinator, Jakarta, 19 February 2016.
26 For a good history of cybernetic or relational approaches that exceed the subjective desires of the scientific researchers that initiated them see Pickering, 2010. Mixed ontologies therefore are not uncommon in the more 'hands on' world of scientific and policy experimentation, which is one of the reasons this chapter seeks to draw on real world engagements rather than sticking to the purely conceptual realm.
27 PetaJakarta is a research project focused on the use of social media for the real time mapping of flooding in Jakarta (led by the SMART Infrastructure Facility, University of Wollongong in collaboration with the Jakarta Emergency Management Agency (BPBD DKI Jakarta) and Twitter Inc.), see Holderness and Turpin, 2015 for an assessment of the Joint Pilot Study for the project, operationally active from December 2014 to March 2015.
28 PetaJakarta coordinator, Jakarata, 19 February 2016.
29 Ibid.
30 PetaJakarta coordinator, Jakarta, 17 February 2016.
31 See also McQuillan, 2014; Read et al., 2016; Kitchen, 2014b.
32 PetaJakarta coordinator, Jakarta, 19 February 2016.
33 Ibid.
34 For example, apparently there are a lot of Indonesian words for prostitute (including chicken and chillies) thereby undermining the veracity of market pricing, using only passive data from social media. Jakarta Pulse Lab coordinator, Jakarta, 18 February 2016.
35 See, for example Haldrup and Rosén, 2013.
36 The attempt to use digitally enhanced framings, varieties of mapping techniques, etc. to find the exceptions or outliers – framed as abilities to creatively use existing but non-visible relational connections – is still in its infancy. Discursively, this approach can appear similar to attempts to develop universal metrics of resilience, which attempt to locate thresholds at which communities risk tipping into unsustainability. These (more traditional or modernist) approaches seek to use new technologies to develop more responsive, real-time 'early warnings' of crisis, triggering external intervention and do not seek to develop new approaches based on revealing innovative Hacking capacities for contextual insight; see, for example, Concern Worldwide, 2015a; 2015b.

37 International visiting researcher, Jakarta, 17 February 2016.
38 Ibid.
39 Harland, 2013.
40 As Bruno Latour might state, the community has enlarged its 'common world' by recognising its interdependency with previously ignored agencies, 'bringing nonhumans and the demos into the expanded collective' (2004a: p.215).
41 PetaJakarta coordinator, Jakarta, 19 February 2016.
42 CogniCity information can be accessed here: http://cognicity.info/cognicity/.
43 PetaJakarta coordinator, Jakarta, 19 February 2016.
44 International visiting researcher, Jakarta, 17 February 2016.
45 Ibid.
46 Ibid.
47 The building of floodwalls and levees is quite possibly the least viable option in the epoch of the Anthropocene. Kathleen Tierney, for example, quotes Gerald Galloway, chair of the presidential committee report on the 1993 Mississippi River floods as stating 'there are only two kinds of levees: those that have failed and those that will fail' (2014: p.59). It is a classic example of what the Stockholm Resilience Centre (2014) term 'coercive resilience', tackling symptoms rather than the problem and therefore storing up greater problems for the future.
48 Koch, 2015.
49 Mezzi, 2016.
50 International visiting researcher, Jakarta, 17 February 2016.
51 PetaJakarta international researcher, Jakarta, 17 February 2016.
52 Ibid.
53 Ibid.
54 Ibid.
55 Ibid.
56 Ibid.
57 Ibid.
58 Ibid.
59 Sub-Saharan Africa today has a slum population of 199.5 million representing 61.7 per cent of its urban population. This is followed by South Asia with 190.7 million in slums making up 35 per cent of urban residents, East Asia with 189.6 million (28.2 per cent), Latin America and the Caribbean with 110.7 million (23.5 per cent), Southeast Asia with 88.9 million (31 per cent), West Asia with 35 million (24.6 per cent), North Africa with 11.8 million (13.3 per cent), and Oceania with six million who constitute 24.1 per cent of the urban population (UN, n.d.).
60 Jakarta Post, 2015.
61 These radical sentiments have an increasingly broad appeal across the political spectrum. Prince Charles has praised slum architecture for its 'underlying, intuitive grammar of design' and 'the timeless quality and resilience of vernacular settlements', even predicting that: 'In a few years' time such communities will be perceived as best equipped to face the challenges that confront us because they have built-in resilience and genuinely durable ways of living' (Tuhus-Dubrow, 2009).
62 Sihombing, 2004; Burhaini, 2011.
63 Davis, 2006.

64 For example, the Participatory Slum Upgrading Programme (PSUP), a joint effort of the African, Caribbean and Pacific (ACP) Group of States, the European Commission (EC) and UN-Habitat, launched in 2008 (http://unhabitat.org/urban-initiatives/initiatives-programmes/participatory-slum-upgrading/); see also Sticzay and Koch, 2015.

65 Castroni, 2009; Ogunlesi, 2016.

66 PetaJakarta international researcher, Jakarta, 19 February 2016.

67 UN-Habitat, 2014: p.15.

68 Brillembourg, 2015.

69 Santa Fe Institute, 2016.

70 For example, a chapter titled 'Building Resilience for the Urban Poor' (World Bank, 2011).

71 See, for example, Anggakara et al., 2016.

72 See, for example, LifeHack.org: www.lifehack.org/articles/lifestyle/100-life-hacks-that-make-life-easier.html.

73 Jean Baudrillard (1994) argues the 'hyperreal' exists independently when signs and signals no longer need to be related to (a modernist representation of) reality.

74 Latour, 2013b: p.126.

7

HACKING AS SYMPOIESIS

Introduction

For the first two modes of governance in the Anthropocene the task is that of managing or preventing the unfolding of the Anthropocene. For Mapping approaches, governance problems are to be addressed through the reactive or adaptive governance of path-dependencies and feedback loops on the assumption that the interconnections between human actions and their recursive effects can be seen, understood and acted upon. For the sciences of Sensing, these responsivities are focused not on non-linear causal chains of interconnection but on correlations, which enable the datafication of the world, so that effects can be seen in their emergence. For the imaginary of these governance modes based on the ontopolitical assumptions of the Anthropocene, complexity does just enough to problematise modernist understandings of universal knowledge and linear causality while still retaining the human subject able to guide and manipulate processes, if not govern them directly, though techniques and technologies of tracing, mapping and sensing.

New modes of governance, thus far, have focused on generating new forms of knowledge, engaging with epistemological problems of perception and projection, and sought to resolve the problems of governance through the emphasis on a growing awareness of empirical entanglements. However this very process of critiquing and seeking to surpass modernist or rationalist approaches has been seen as reinforcing and reifying modernist assumptions of instrumental reason, thereby prioritising and preserving existing modes of existence.[1] Claire Colebrook skilfully argues that these ontopolitical approaches, often considered to be 'posthuman', because of their critique of modernist epistemological assumptions, in fact, extend the calculative reasoning of Enlightenment approaches.[2] She correctly highlights, for example, that the Gaia hypothesis, of non-modernist theorists, such as Latour, reflects the extension of humanism so

> man can project his organic being onto life as a whole … it is man who will read the conditions of this system, discern its proper order, break free from merely instrumental attitudes and arrive at a proper mode of self-regulation.[3]

From the perspective of Hacking as a mode of governance, Mapping and Sensing are no less anthropocentric than the transcendental problem-solving of modernist promises of progress. As long as modes of governance view the Anthropocene condition as a problem to be mitigated, adapted to, managed, controlled or 'solved' in some way, then the end of the modernist assumptions about the world is constituted as a problem to be faced in the future rather than our present condition. As Colebrook states:

> Insofar as it is imagined as a globe or living whole with its own order and proper potentiality that might be restored, the earth will continue to be sacrificed to the blindness of an organic thinking that can only insist upon its own self-evident value.[4]

Rather than rethinking what it means to live in the Anthropocene, Mapping and Sensing seek to preserve current ways of being through adapting a non-modern ontology in order to enable a 'happy ending' by securing the present against a threatening future.[5]

Hacking is distinctive as a mode of governance in that it seeks to emphasise the creative and innovative possibilities and potentials of 'life in the ruins': life after the end of the modernist construction of the world.[6] Rather than seek to solve existing problems, Hacking seeks to expand the potential for openness and experimentation. For Hacking, therefore, the means and the ends are the process itself, in its unfolding: there are no fixed goals external to the process and no community separate to it. As Laurent Berlant suggests, Hacking does not work within the formal sphere of politics as governance from above or over life but through the attempt to form 'new idioms of the political, and of belonging itself'.[7] As highlighted at the end of the last chapter, in embracing the potentiality of the 'stretched-out' or intensified present, Hacking is a long way from modernist discourses of futurity. Like the governance mode of Sensing, Hacking works in the actuality of the moment rather than in a linear temporal framing. Transformative potential comes from interaction in the actual moment: repurposing and rearranging what exists already, rather than through the potential of drawing out autopoietic capabilities which exist within entities or systems.

The 'life hack' analogy used at the end of the last chapter captures the process well in that it repurposes and rearranges everyday entities and relations as a temporary step in an ongoing process. There is no fixity or direction from within a system or assemblage but the creation of a new set of relations: a new object or entity or assemblage comes into being through 'becoming with' differently, i.e. there is no immanence to the process. Thus, the paradigm of Hacking retains a more critical or open-ended approach to governance than the modes of Mapping and Sensing and tends to be more closely aligned to activist and experimental perspectives. Hacking is exploratory through being world- or reality-oriented; not in seeking non-linear trails of causation or fixed correlations but the surprises: the outliers; the exceptions; the gaps of possibility; the new avenues or connections. Hacking is the science of the possible and, in being so, makes new possibilities available in the present. As Jairus Grove states: 'Reality is not path dependent. Precisely what makes catastrophe possible is also what makes creative evolution possible, or the capacity to effect change that is unprecedented, novel, and therefore unpredictable.'[8]

Alexander Galloway nicely intimates how Hacking, as the discourse of unfolding the Anthropocene, captures the ethos of computer hacking, not as a form of resistance to new non-modernist modes of governance, but as their driving force.[9] He suggests that key to this is the fact that coding is never abstract or representative, but rather '*hyper*linguistic': '*code is the only language that is executable*' (emphasis in original), it has a materialist logic in that code effects material change.[10] Hacking thus engages with existing material code in order to discover how it works and to experiment with changing or altering what exists to create new material possibilities, thus, for Galloway, the hacker has a '*unique connection* to the realm of the possible' (emphasis added).[11] The possible already exists but not in a hidden potential within an entity or system (as a virtual potential) but in the actual moment of co-becoming or of material inter-relation (as an actual potential).

This 'unique connection' is examined further below. The chapter is divided into three sections, the first section considers Hacking as a mode of governance which intensifies relationality, breaking down the time and space of the Anthropocene into a fluid set of combinations, recombinations and potentialities. In this respect, Hacking lacks the securing aspects of governance of Mapping or Sensing. The second section draws out more this aspect of dissolving distinctions into the flux of generalised becoming or 'becoming-with', specifically in terms of sympoiesis. Sympoiesis is an important conceptual framing for Hacking, highlighting the dynamic and creative aspects of inter-relations in recomposing or repurposing what already exists. The final section considers different approaches through which theorists articulate the work that needs to be done to enable governance through Hacking as a regime of experimentation open to the unfolding of contingent processes of emergence.

Hacking: intensifying relationality in the Anthropocene

As noted above, initial experiments with new modes of governance, perhaps inevitably, approached co-relations and entanglements, as enabling new forms of management and regulation. The governance mode of Sensing, relying on the extensive use and development of new digital technologies and new developments in biosensing and bioengineering, has been seen to be particularly problematic, in that it assumes that 'more-than-human' assemblages of sensing and responsivity can 'pre-event' problems and crises, enabling the maintenance or modulation of the status quo in a homeostatic manner. Here the 'posthuman' world of entangled interaction seems to be surprisingly like the modernist world, and the 'de-centring of the subject' seems to make little difference to the confidence of global governance agencies. As Elizabeth Povinelli notes, these framings can be seen as extending the sphere of being at home in the world, enabling 'late liberal governmentality' to 'saturate Being with familiar and reassuring qualities'.[12]

Povinelli cautions against the view of relationality as making the world more meaningful rather than stranger for us: 'The generosity of *extending* our form of semiosis to [non-human forms of being] forecloses the possibility of them provincializing us.'[13] In seeking to 'hear' what the melting icebergs or extreme weather events etc. are 'saying' to us, we return humans to the centre of a world, as if it was made with us in mind.[14] Povinelli argues that objects do not speak to us or act on our behalf to point the way to knowledge and understanding, because relationality is much too intense: 'And objects do not stay one thing but become other things because of these forces of shaping and shifting and assemblage.'[15] In attempting to reduce emergent effects to signals for us to read-off and automatically respond to, the actual world is never really 'given its due', never appreciated in all its multiplicity and potentiality but instead flattened and reduced to networked relations. It is argued that non-rationalist or non-representational approaches – such as actor network theory, vitalist materialism and post-humanism – tend to work on the basis of a new set of binaries of what 'man is not', enabling man to then enrol these entities into ever more complete and real time understandings.[16]

In contrast, proponents of Hacking do not seek to argue that 'everything is related' or that life itself can be datafied to provide signals and indicators to be responded to in automatic ways. Things, entities, systems etc. are not seen as already in a relation that must be responded to as a dictat but rather as offering an invitation to creatively join. Thus, there is not a set of signs and relations handily available for use in alternative or 'posthuman' forms of regulatory climate-friendly governance for the Anthropocene. The work has not already been magically undertaken for us by Gaia or some other complex self-adaptive system of self-organisation, working external to human consciousness. As Donna Haraway famously notes, there is no choice but to 'stay with the trouble'.[17] 'Nothing is connected to everything; [but] everything is connected to something.'[18] Relations are concrete and fluid sets of shifting and contingent interconnections, not amenable to easy intervention or datafication. Relational entanglements and interconnections are not a ready-made or 'natural' solution: they do not provide new forms of problem-solving, or an additional prop for acquiring more modernist ways of knowing. As seen in the previous chapter, for the governance mode of Hacking, entanglements are an invitation to explore alternative possibilities rather than to resolve problems of governance to maintain the existing modes of being. Viewed from this perspective, the tensions within Mapping and Sensing as governance approaches are not due to the fact that they emphasise the contingency of relations and interaction rather than rationalism, but the opposite, that they are seen as not taking relationality and contingency far enough.

For example, discussions of resilience are increasingly destabilised through emphasising that rather than seeing resilience as a governing practice – which stabilises and extends the present condition and wards of the crisis of climate change through adopting the techniques of Mapping or Sensing – it would be better to accept that the crisis has already occurred. As Stephanie Wakefield, for example, has forcibly argued, this approach, which foregrounds the fact that we are already living in the Anthropocene, calls for an entirely different set of understandings and practices.[19] Assuming that the crisis or disruption of the Anthropocene epoch has already occurred would mean (taking C. S. Holling's concept of the 'adaptive cycle', discussed in Chapter 2) that we are today living in the 'back loop', i.e. in a period of flux and reorganisation, in contrast to the 'front loop' of stability and gradual progress,[20] associated with the Holocene. This would enable seeing the present as a period of reorganisation, repurposing and repositioning, where everything is in play and nothing can be taken for granted. Rather than trying to hold everything together as it is, Hacking as a mode of governance sees the Anthropocene as a time when everything is in flux and new possibilities continually become available.

This chapter suggests that the work of Wakefield and others is important in analysing the fundamental shift in approach to governance that the Anthropocene appears to call forth. As Donna Haraway states, the Anthropocene (or Terrapolis):

> exists in a web of always-too-much connection, where response-ability must be cobbled together, not in the existentialist and bond-less, lonely, Man-making gap theorized by Heidegger and his followers. Terrapolis is rich in world, inoculated against posthumanism but rich in com-post, inoculated against human exceptionalism but rich in humus, ripe for multispecies story-telling.[21]

This entangled relationality has been captured well by Beth Dempster, particularly in her understanding of complex interaction on the basis of sympoiesis, in distinction to autopoietic approaches (which are dominant in the Mapping paradigm of governance). Sympoiesis is crucial to understanding the distinctiveness of Hacking and will be dealt with further below. The key aspect I wish to introduce at this point is the emphasis on unbounded relationality. As Dempster argues: 'The concept [of sympoiesis] emphasises linkages, feedback, cooperation, and synergistic behaviour rather than boundaries.'[22] Synergistic relations invert the ethico-political framing of Mapping. For Levi Bryant, for example, key to Mapping is the ethical prescription that objects, entities and systems cannot be reduced to their relations.[23] Actual relations are merely the existing actualisations or 'local manifestations' of their being, while other potential effects, capacities, properties and affordances are necessarily concealed.[24] Hacking, instead, focuses precisely on these 'local manifestations' of the actual, and sees these effects as the raw materiality of the world, capable of being repurposed or reassembled in multiple ways, through interaction.

This intensification of relationality and of interaction illustrates a highly agential perspective of the unfolding of the Anthropocene, as Joanna Zylinksa argues: 'Seeing things across different times and scales is more than an attempt to represent the universe: it actively produces entities and relations.'[25] Being, in the governance mode of Hacking, is therefore inseparable from and 'already a "doing"'.[26] Zylinska's 'minimal ethics' for the Anthropocene thereby 'needs to involve a material working out of the relations between entities and of their varying forces' in the 'recognition of the entangled positioning of the human in, or rather with, the universe'.[27] Zylinska draws upon the work of Karen Barad on intra-active agency to highlight that it is this process of interaction that comes before the existence of stabilised entities, subjects and objects, in which interactive or rather 'intra-active' agency constitutes the world.[28]

In a world of liveliness, flux and change, Hacking appreciates the entangled potentials, which the previous paradigms of governance are held to close off from us. Anna Tsing captures the process well:

> Making worlds is not limited to humans. We know that beavers reshape streams as they make dams, canals and lodges; in fact, all organisms make ecological living places, altering earth, air, and water ... In the process, each organism changes everyone's world. Bacteria made our oxygen atmosphere, and plants help maintain it. Plants live on land because fungi made soil by digesting rocks. As these examples suggest, world-making projects can overlap, allowing room for more than one species.[29]

Hacking is a form of participation in the collective becoming of life without the organisational closure and phenomenological limits of the Mapping paradigm with its entity and system boundaries. It is the intensification of relationality rather than its reduction that enables this shift.

Anna Tsing calls this open-ended process, of collective and connective experimentation, 'ways of being', understood as 'emergent effects of encounters': the possibilities inherent in fluid assemblages with others.[30] Tsing's work on the matsutake mushroom is illustrative of Hacking as the unfolding or evolving of entangled life, suggesting even that evolution may be driven more by species relationality and 'symbiopoiesis'.[31] In life after modernist dreams of progress, disturbances and peturbations are not threats to the status quo but are interactive invitations to creativity, seen as positive opportunities to make 'life in capitalist ruins'. Tsing, for example, tells the story of woodland revitalisation groups: 'who hope that small-scale disturbances might draw both people and forests out of alienation, building a world of overlapping lifeways in which mutualistic transformation, the mode of mycorrhiza, might yet be possible.'[32] She states: 'They hope their actions might stimulate a latent commons, that is, an eruption of shared assembly, even as they know they can't actually *make* a commons' (emphasis in original).[33] Here, we can see Hacking as a set of techniques not really 'making' something but rather acting as a stimulus, exploring, probing, facilitating, repurposing what already exists but can only come into being 'with': the new potentialities thus do not lie latent within a pre-existing entity but lie in the creation of a new 'commons'.

Donna Haraway powerfully reinforces the importance of this approach, arguing that ongoing processes cannot be grasped through autopoietic frameworks, which assume too many separations between entities, i.e. that relations are structured and limited rather than too rich too grasp. As she states:

> The earth ... is sympoietic, not autopoietic. Mortal worlds ... do not make themselves, no matter how complex and multileveled the systems ... Autopoietic systems are hugely interesting – witness the history of cybernetics and information sciences; but they are not good models for living and dying worlds ... Poesis is symchthonic, sympoietic, always partnered all the way down, with no starting and subsequently interacting 'units'.[34]

Instead of focusing on preventing and slowing climate change, preserving the status quo through the application of non-traditional epistemological forms of reason, the recognition that we are already in the Anthropocene leads to a different set of, much more positive, assumptions and practices: those of Hacking as a mode of governance. In this framing, new possibilities are not hidden but, on the contrary, surround us such that we could understand ourselves as immersed within the 'great outdoors' of potentiality. As Timothy Morton notes, the withdrawnness of objects is not ontological, in terms of time or space, but rather the opposite; in his 'weird essentialism' objects are 'too close' to focus upon, too full, too present for us.[35] Their distance from us is a product of the richness of the relationality of the world.

This richness provides the basis for the creativity of Hacking as a mode of governance. As William Connolly argues:

> It seems to me that real creativity arises in part because the world is marked by heterogeneous connections of numerous sorts. The idea here, at any rate, is to curtail both the themes of *cultural internalism* and *cultural incommensurability* by amplifying those *heterogeneous connections* between entities and processes of manifold sorts. (emphasis in original)[36]

Connolly's formulation here is useful in that he emphasises precisely the key points of Hacking as a distinctive governing mode. Unlike Mapping, Hacking does not seek to play up the centrality of internal processes, as in assemblage theory, nor does it seek to problematise the withdrawn nature of objects and impossibility of knowing as object-oriented theorists initially tended to. Unknowability is not a problem but an asset, an invitation to limitless possibilities. Hacking posits a much more affirmative and future-oriented perspective of creative interactivity through the discovery of interconnections which enable processes of 'becoming with' to rearticulate and repurpose elements which already exist. Levi Bryant, for example, highlights the importance of recompositioning through the use of the bio-logical concept of 'exaptation', where something takes on a different function from the one that it originally played.[37]

For Hasana Sharp, this ontopolitical framing is crucial to the project of 'renaturalizing politics', and in 'underscoring a notion of freedom as nontranscendence'.[38] She is worth quoting at length:

> The freedom yielded by the politics of renaturalization depends upon the lived, critical understanding that our conditions of activity are not entirely given but constructed, made out of the materials at hand. *Freedom is a recomposition and reappropriation of what is given* by the shared reality of historical, social and natural life. Recomposition represents not just a perspectival shift but a rearrangement of constituent corporeal relations and activities ... thinking otherwise entails being otherwise, relating to ourselves, bodies and ambient beings in new ways ... (emphasis added)[39]

Stephanie Wakefield and Bruce Braun have highlighted a very similar political ontology in Georgio Agamben's understanding of 'destituent' rather than 'constituent' power.[40] Drawing on Foucault's understanding of apparatus or dispositif they argue that 'the governmental aspect of things is not inherent to the things in question; rather, it obtains from the relations into which they are drawn'.[41] Governing power depends on the elements of the apparatus being withdrawn from common use and articulated as a regime of control or regulation; thus, destituent power seeks to disrupt this apparatus and to 'detourn' or 'profane' these elements, releasing them to the 'open' or to common use and revealing other potential dimensions to them, outside their governing function.

Thus destituent power can be read to affirm Hacking as a mode of governance, destituting the elements of power and regulation and repurposing them as open potentials for worlding in other ways.[42] All elements, entities, relationships and objects can be removed from assemblages and repurposed or enabled to reveal new potentialities through becoming placed in other contexts or relationships. Rather than seeking to shore up assemblages or make them more resilient, as in the governance modes of Mapping and Sensing, Hacking requires experimentation to free elements from their imagined or engineered relations. The Invisible Committee state, in their advocacy of the resistance of destitutive power:[43]

> The world doesn't environ us, it passes through us. What we inhabit inhabits us. What surround us constitutes us. We don't belong to ourselves. We are always-already spread through whatever we attach ourselves to. It's ... a question of ... learning to better inhabit what is there, which implies perceiving it ... Perceiving a world peopled not with things but with forces, not with subjects but with powers, not with bodies but with bonds ... It's by virtue of their plenitude that forms of life will complete the destitution.[44]

As Sharp argues, this is 'an affective politics that seeks enabling relationships, wherever they can be found', rather than a struggle for recognition or for a collective identity; instead, as a mode of governance, Hacking is experimental in its attempt to enable 'powers, linkages and transformation'.[45] The object of liberation, or emancipation, is not so much the human subject but the process of becoming itself. As Braun and Wakefield assert, the goal is 'thus to affirm the world not to escape it':[46]

> This implies less of a revolutionary act that 'overturns', than a pragmatic, experimental practice that depends upon the groups practicing it and the places where they do so. To make the radical import of

Agamben's 'politics of use' explicit, we could say that 'use' is a method or even an orientation, rather than a program or a solution. With this concept Agamben's goal is to free us from the static spaces and times of classical politics – with its telos of constituted power and its efforts to foreclose the exploration of possible worlds – and to sketch a political method that begins from the middle of the worlds we inhabit, in order to see what we can build and do from there.[47]

Hacking as sympoiesis

Thus Hacking is neither autopoietic nor homeostatic but sympoietic; it is no longer a politics of subjecthood, but rather a politics of the undoing of the subject conceived as an individual or collective that is somehow separate or distinct. Connolly draws upon evolutionary theorist Lynn Margulis's concept of 'symbiogenesis', which has radicalised evolutionary theory through emphasising the importance of interspecies interaction and interpenetration to form new composite organisms, through the exchange of DNA.[48] Hacking's centrality to contemporary modes of understanding is no better highlighted than in its naturalisation to becoming a theory of life itself. As Connolly notes, following Deleuze, it now appears to be increasingly scientifically accepted that 'evolution is more like a rhizomatic than an arboreal process'.[49] Life is a contingent and fluid process of interaction and experimentation, not the immanent unfolding of fixed essences as portrayed in the branching hierarchy of development in the evolutionary metaphors of the 'tree of life'.[50]

As Bryant argues: 'Evolution is a *bricoleur*, always building on *pre-existent* biological structures that served different functions in the past (exaptation) and that don't perfectly serve the new functions for which they've been enlisted' (emphasis in original).[51] Elizabeth Grosz similarly reads Darwin to argue that life is experimental, far from the unfolding of fixed essences or responsive adaptation:

> [Darwin] makes life itself, not a rational strategy for survival, not a form of adaptation, but the infinite elaboration of excess, the conversion of the excesses of bodies, of natural objects and forms, into both new forms of body and new forms of culture, new modes of social organization, new arts, new species.[52]

The Anthropocene, construed through the governance mode of Hacking, posits creativity and change as ontological. There is not merely unpredictability because modernist science has not fully progressed to discover all that there is to know about the laws of nature, but because real creativity is in the world. The world is lively because of the richness of relational interaction:

> These are thus conditioned modes of creativity that proceed from interacting, striving organisms operating within certain constraints. It is not creation ex nihilo, since every creative process is constrained and enabled by its preconditions of initiation. These intersections are teleodynamic in the sense that they are irreducible either to simple processes of mutation, information, and replication or to a fundamental bent of the world already there.[53]

Perhaps the clearest and most influential work, which could be read to ground Hacking as a mode of governance, may be Donna Haraway's contributions which specifically highlight sympoiesis and interspecies forms of being and engage with the present in ways which are creative rather than merely responsive:

> Staying with the trouble does not require such a relationship to times called the future. In fact, staying with the trouble requires learning to be truly present, not as a vanishing pivot between awful and edenic pasts and apocalyptic or salvific futures, but as mortal critters entwined in myriad unfinished configurations of places, times, matters, meanings.[54]

Haraway argues that there are three aspects to her methodological approach of 'SF', which she names variously as 'speculative fabulation', 'string figures', 'speculative feminism' or 'science fact'. The first step is following or tracing the interconnected threads to become sensitive to tangles and patterns (taking up from where the mode of Mapping ends). Secondly, she suggests that the key is not the tracing itself, 'not the tracking, but rather the actual thing, the pattern and assembly that solicits response, the thing that is not oneself but with which one must go on'.[55] This responsiveness to the thing itself is however not the fixed or automatic, homeostatic response of Sensing: 'Third, string figuring is passing on and receiving, making and unmaking, picking up threads and dropping them. SF is practice and process; it is becoming-with each other in surprising relays; it is a figure for ongoingness in the Chthulucene.'[56]

Haraway articulates the ontological assumptions grounding Hacking as a mode of governance with great clarity, highlighting that while it is future-oriented it is not the future of a liberal or modern telos of progress, it is a future drawn from the repurposing or recompositioning (or 'composting') of the present: 'staying with the trouble': 'Staying with the trouble requires making oddkin; that is, we require each other in unexpected collaborations and combinations, in hot compost piles. We become-with each other or not at all.'[57] Rather than seeking to respond or be sensitive to signs and signals she seeks

> real stories that are also speculative fabulations and speculative realisms. These are stories in which multispecies players, who are enmeshed in partial and flawed translations across difference, redo ways of living and dying attuned to still possible finite flourishing, still possible recuperation.[58]

Like Connolly, Haraway draws inspiration from Lynn Margulis' work on evolutionary biology, using the terminology of 'holoents' or 'holobionts' to understand the forms of symbiotic being of complex processes of 'becoming-with'. She borrows the definition of sympoiesis from environmental studies as a term for 'collectively-producing systems that do not have self-defined spatial or temporal boundaries. Information and control are distributed among components. The systems are evolutionary and have the potential for surprising change.' This contrasts with autopoietic systems, as articulated through assemblage theory, which are autonomous and 'self-reproducing', 'with defined spatial or temporal boundaries that tend to be centrally controlled, homeostatic and predictable.'[59] Thus the ontopolitical basis for Hacking is the problematisation of the modernist legacies and separations that enable the governance modes of Mapping and Sensing. As Haraway states: 'The more ubiquitous symbiogenesis seems to be in living beings' dynamic organizing processes, the more looped, braided, outreaching, involuted, and sympoietic is terrain worlding.'[60]

Sympoiesis is increasingly accepted, not just as a framework for the evolution of life itself but also as an approach to understand the development of the specifically human aspects of life: arts and culture. Modernist understandings of the development of the cultural and creative realm were very much subject-centred, making a clear co-constitutive distinction between culture and nature. This perspective was famously articulated by Marx in Volume One of *Capital*:

Labour is, in the first place, a process in which both man and Nature participate, and in which man of his own accord starts, regulates, and controls the material reactions between himself and Nature. He opposes himself to Nature ... in order to appropriate Nature's productions in a form adapted to his own wants ... We pre-suppose labour in a form that stamps it as exclusively human. A spider conducts operations that resemble those of a weaver, and a bee puts to shame many an architect in the construction of her cells. But what distinguishes the worst architect from the best of bees is this, that the architect raises his structure in imagination before he erects it in reality. At the end of every labour-process, we get a result that already existed in the imagination of the labourer at its commencement.[61]

The model or the plan is already conceived in the mind of the artisan or architect and then imposed upon nature, forcing nature to adapt to man's needs and desires. This perspective is often seen as a 'hylomorphic' account of creativity, where designs or plans have their origin inside the human head and are then imposed upon the passive materiality of the world.[62]

This approach is challenged by contemporary sympoietic understandings of the historical development of arts and culture. For Tim Ingold, for example, 'we really need a new word, something like "anthropo-ontogenetic" ... neither making nor growing'.[63] Humans do not make their own worlds through adaptation (autopoiesis) but neither do they passively respond to the world (homeostasis). There is an active agential process of sympoiesis: becoming with. As Levi Bryant argues, the process of the artistic or cultural production of artifacts 'is much closer to negotiation than the simple imposition of a form upon a passive matter'.[64] Matter and even the tools that are used impose themselves upon the artisan, shaping and altering the capacities and affordances of their body. Design can thereby be seen as more a matter of sympoiesis than as the autopoietic product of man's self-directed engagement with nature. Human bodies and cognitive processes are shaped and moulded by their environments and engagement with technologies in ways that are not intended, planned or necessarily understood; the same goes for all entities.

Hacking as a mode of governance should therefore be seen as seeking to enable the process of creative flux rather than as carving out a specifically human sphere of politics or culture over or against nature. Thus, artists can be understood to be Hacking when they feel that their material or medium of work is directing them, or novelists or philosophers when they feel that their characters or ideas seem to take on a life of their own.[65] Timothy Morton goes further, in terms of his analysis of the music of John Cage and others, attuned to the essence of the piano, where the composer seeks not to impose their will but to become the operator, servant or technician in the service of the object itself.[66] Here, Morton argues, the pianist can become the medium for the piano, enabling approaches of Hacking as 'a *tuning* to the object':[67]

> Art becomes a collaboration between humans and nonhumans ... art becomes an attunement to the demonic. The more we know about an object, the stranger it becomes. Conversely the more we know about an object, the more we realize that what we call *subject* is not a special thing different from what we call *object*. (emphasis in original)[68]

As will be analysed in the following section, Hacking appears to be the most politically transformative of the governance modes of the Anthropocene as it is the most agential. The implication of this is that openness to experimentation and engagement becomes a political task. While some of the necessary skills for creativity in 'becoming with' have been long practised and developed in the fields of arts and culture, advocates of Hacking as a mode of governance seek to inculcate these skills more generally as directly political capacities for unfolding the potential of the Anthropocene.

Work on the self

Work to unfold the Anthropocene rather than to prevent it would seem to largely involve work on the self not as in Mapping, to enable more optimal or rational responses of adaptation, or as in Sensing to be more responsive to the signs and signals of the environment,[69] but to enable a more externalised perspective of experimentation. This work on the self is not a matter of learning how to think abstractly but of learning how to practise and to experiment. For Stengers, this process is one of composing with Gaia, working through processes in context and collectively in a milieu that is open and working 'in real time, with real questions, not in protected experimental places' where shortcuts may be possible and assumptions left unchallenged.[70] She describes this process as 'relaying', unlike Mapping or Sensing:

> relaying is never 'reflecting on' but always 'adding to.' It demands consenting to an ongoing process, accepting that what is added can

make a difference to the process, and becoming accountable for the manner of that difference ... This is no blind pragmatism but an adventurous, response-able one ... what matters is not to define or evaluate but to address the question that may transform the researcher into a relayer.[71]

The openness of Hacking is crucial for Stengers as it provides a creative alternative between the hubris of intentionality and the arbitrariness of chance:

It is not a matter of allowing chance to decide, but of having recourse to a procedure that, between us and what we do, makes what is not ours exist, opening up a situation in relation to which we do not have a claim to be up to it.[72]

Hacking is thereby enabled by artifices, which sensitise us to the world, rendering it possible to pay attention to scarcely perceptible signs and opening up new ways of experimenting.

For Connolly: 'A tactic of the self ... is an experimental strategy to touch and work on entangled microperceptual or micro-intentional tendencies flowing beneath direct conscious awareness and regulation.'[73] However, the task is not to draw out new capacities from within, either to initiate new actions or to respond to external directions, but to be creatively open to the processes that one is already immersed within:

the creative element in human agency is closer to something we participate in than to something we intend from the start or control through autonomous agency. It depends on clashes between creative impulses that insinuate an element of chance into the emergent result rather than to chance as entirely responsible for that which deviates from efficient causality.[74]

Human freedom is thus 'precariously tied to an aesthetic of conditioned creativity', where we participate in creative processes, which exceed our abilities to understand or control. Thereby the goal of creative processes is not the achievement of a goal but to potentially 'amplify our attachment to this world' and to appreciate 'the complexity of freedom'.[75] For Connolly, 'creativity is an uncanny process within which we are embedded rather than the effect of an agent; it is tinged by an aura of mystery.'[76]

Donna Haraway is particularly sensitive to Hacking as a practical mode of politics, which she articulates in terms of string figures as a metaphor for 'thinking as well as making practices, pedagogical practices and cosmological performances'.[77] She argues that 'the arts for living on a damaged planet demand sympoietic thinking and action'.[78] Importantly, Haraway empha- sises that 'response-abilities' are contextually situated, not abstract or auto- matically given by path-dependencies or by adaptive sensing. One way in which these arts can be encouraged, she argues, is 'learning how to play'.[79] By this Haraway suggests that the cultivation of the practice of curiosity is vital, challenging assumptions 'that beings have pre-established natures and abilities' and instead 'holding open the possibility that surprises are in store, that something interesting is about to happen, but only if one cultivates the virtue of letting' those being encountered 'intra-actively shape what occurs'.[80] Thus Hacking can be understood to be a 'subject- and object- making dance', a process of 'learning to engage that changes everybody in unforeseeable ways'.[81] This is a process of experimentation 'with, rather than on', a working together on the basis of attentiveness: 'thinking from' not 'of' or 'about' the other.[82]

In order to free alternative possibilities and to see the world without the assumptions of essence and fixity of modernity, play is thereby essential to the sympoietic politics of Hacking. Play is 'the most powerful and diverse activity for rearranging old things and proposing new things, new patterns of feeling and action, and for crafting safe enough ways to tangle with each other in conflict and collaboration.'[83] Perhaps the most interesting exploration, into the ontopolitical assumptions informing Hacking as a mode of politics, comes from a professor of interactive computing and leading object-oriented theorist, Ian Bogost, in his book *Play Anything* (2016). Bogost's work is important as it articulates Hacking as a form not only of work on the self but specifically as a mode of politics of 'becoming- with' on the basis of affirmation, acceptance and even joyfulness. For Bogost, the Anthropocene is not a problematic condition but a liberating or emancipatory one. Key to his analysis is the overturning of the modernist idea of limits.

For Bogost, limits are not problems or barriers but the precondition for games, of for play: 'Games aren't appealing because they are fun, but because they are *limited*. Because they erect boundaries' (emphasis in origi- nal).[84] It is these limits that make play fun and limits can be found all around us if we choose to see our environment rather than take it for granted. Play, as experimentation with objects and entities around us, opens us to our world by making it strange or challenging in new ways. Play, as a form of Hacking, enables us to see the 'great outdoors', not as somewhere outside to be explored but as where we are already:

> What if we treated everything the way we treat soccer and Tetris – as valuable and virtuous for being exactly what they are, rather than for what would be convenient, or for what we wish they were instead, or for what we fear they are not? Walks and meadows, aunts and grand-fathers, zoning boards of appeals meetings and business trips. Everything. Our lives would be better, bigger, more meaningful, and less selfish … That's what it means to play. To take something – anything – on its own terms, to treat it as if its existence were reasonable.[85]

The point about constraints and boundaries is that play is a sympoietic process; play introduces us to Hacking as a mode of being:

> We think that in play we do what we want, that we release ourselves from external duty and obligation and finally yield to our clearest, innermost desires. We think we know what we want, and we believe that we are in control of our fates. But all of these beliefs are mistaken.[86]

Play is thus often mistakenly understood as an escape from our daily con-straints into a realm of freedom; in fact, it enables us to develop our capa-cities for freedom through the 'opportunity to explore the implications of inherited or invented limitations'.[87] Play as work on the self, in the analysis of Bogost, enables us to 'engage fully and intensely with life and its con-tents' and in the process encourages a greater attention, care and respect for 'things, people and situations around us'.[88]

The universe may be indifferent to us but we can make new lives 'in the ruins' by learning how to find meaning and how to thrive and flourish by not just making do with what is but engaging creatively and experimentally to constantly be surprised by the wonder and potential of the world. Creative and open-ended engagement with the world – Hacking – works not by imposing our will on something or attempting to change or direct it but by 'treating something as it actually is' and thus enabling, through sympoiesis, the release of 'secrets we might otherwise miss'.[89] Bogost con-trasts the approach of play, of being open to the world, as the development of 'worldfulness' as opposed to the emphasis on 'mindfulness': rather than thinking about what other entities can do for us we accept other entities for what they are.[90] We first 'pay close, foolish, even absurd attention to things' as a way of allowing them to shape our experience of them.[91] In other words, enabling us to work with or 'become with' things, on their terms, rather than against them, on the basis of our preconceptions.[92] Play therefore works through decentring the human subject and allowing more of the world to be present for us and enabling the appreciation of the potentiality already contained in the world. Play can be understood as agential capacity released through the politics of Hacking as sympoiesis.

As noted by Timothy Morton, the problem of complex relationality is that we are too close to multiplicities of entanglements rather than too far away.[93] In the governance mode of Hacking, what is necessary is a way of seeing things close to us, or considered to be mundane, in new or imaginative ways. Bogost therefore uses the concept of 'play' to enable 'us to see the hidden potential in ordinary things so that we can put them to new uses'.[94] This is where the close connections appear between the recompositioning or repurposing of Hacking and the conceptual approach of object-oriented ontology, read as an affirmative aspect of the limits of knowability or access to a world of meaning. Bogost draws on, fellow object-oriented theorist, Graham Harman's work to emphasise the importance of the withdrawn nature of objects and entities: that 'things are always *more* than our perceptions or uses of them reveal' (emphasis in original).[95] Play is therefore a way of understanding the potentiality that exists in every thing, entity or context. The starting position for Hacking is that the open-ended possibilities of the world develop sympoietically, not through immanent or innate processes or through acts of innovation or creation. The possibilities for recompositioning or repurposing exist by virtue of the fact that: 'Everything has greater potential than we initially suspect – or than we can ever fully know.'[96]

Conclusion

All three modes of governance, examined in this book on the basis of their grounding in the ontopolitical assumptions of the Anthropocene, could be read as seeking to reveal or to bring into view that which was previously unseen. Mapping seeks to reveal the unseen interconnections of non-linear path-dependencies that enable differences to make a difference. Sensing seeks to see changes in relations that signal the processes of emergence enabling real time responsivities. Hacking seeks to see the unseen potentials which exist in recomposing relations through 'imagining and deploying new actions on and with that thing'.[97] This attentionality enables sympoie-tic processes because 'rather than distancing ourselves from things, in play we draw them close and meld with them. We give ourselves over to them, even, subordinating our own agency to a larger system.'[98] This aspect of openness to the world is crucial for the governance mode of Hacking. Braun and Wakefield take this approach to its logical conclusion, in their critique of the residual humanism in Agamben's framework of deactivating power through destitution:

> it is only when the human 'deactivates' its world that it achieves the same status of the animal, for the animal does not imagine or believe in a transcendent order that stands apart from or above factical existence, but only factical conditions that exist as potentiality and without telos. For the animal, unlike the human, nothing needs to be 'profaned', everything is already and continuously returned to common use.[99]

For Hacking as a mode of governance, the Anthropocene is to be affirmed as after 'the end of the world' of modernity and after the end of the pre-sumption of a knowing, controlling and directing subject. This is very much the 'minimal ethics' advocated by Joanna Zylinska, which 'gives up on any desire to forge systems, ontologies or worlds and makes itself content with minor, even if abundant, interventions into material and conceptual unfoldings'.[100] Thus the 'great outdoors' is all around us if we can see it and every moment can be one of experimentation, play and wonder, where everything can be other than how it seems. As will be considered in the following chapter, Hacking transvalues critique through grasping the Anthropocene condition as an opportunity rather than as a problem. As Connolly argues:

> Incompleteness, the insufficiency of argument and explanation, and time out of joint now lose their standing as mere lacks or deficits. They become ambiguous conditions of risk and possibility. To affirm *belief* in this world is thus to come to terms *positively* with a world in which gaps, breaks, dissonances, events, dangers and messy intersections unfold. (emphasis in original)[101]

Hacking seeks to enable the unfolding of the Anthropocene rather than to hold it back; as a mode of governance it necessarily prioritises the process itself as a guide rather than seeking to impose a goal or a telos though directing or 'short-cutting' experimentation towards narrow or instrumental purposes.[102] Thus Hacking is subversive – but not in the modernist sense of enabling free play as an autonomous process of 'doing what you want' – in that it offers 'invitations to turn ground into new figure, even if just temporarily'.[103] In doing this, Hacking does not just transvalue limits from negatives into positives, it also transvalues the lure of autonomy as a freedom from limits, precisely because this 'challenges us to aspire for something other than our reality ... constantly denying rather than accepting [our] circumstances'.[104] The more we recognise our constraints and limitations the more we are free to focus on the reality of the world we actually live in. As Elizabeth Grosz argues, freedom:

> is not fundamentally linked to the question of choice, to the operation of alternatives, to the selection of options outside the subject and independently available to it ... but a freedom above all connected to an active self, an embodied being ... Freedom is not a quality or a property of the human subject, as implied within the phenomenological tradition, but can only characterize a process ... Freedom is not a transcendent quality inherent in subjects but is immanent in the relations that the living has with the material world, including other forms of life.[105]

In removing modernist ideas of 'progress' and of 'futurity', the Anthropocene condition enables the affirmation of what exists rather than seeking to go beyond this. This is the promise of the 'great outdoors', where human experience can become much richer in the affirmation of the creativity of a world which, in the Holocene, was treated merely as 'ground', 'background' or 'environment' rather than as agential in its own right. In discourses of Hacking, creativity does not stem from human initiation but is rather a process which humans can become part of through the realisation that the world is a world of restraints – that Gaia cannot be bargained with or challenged, only composed with.[106] Hacking, as a mode of governance, emancipates or liberates the human, once the Anthropocene as a condition of being is embraced. To hack successfully, the world has to be revered despite the fact that it is no longer there 'for us' in the meaning-making sense of modernity: the familiar has to become strange and what seems fixed therefore open to adaptation and repurposing through creative interaction.

Notes

1 Colebrook, 2014: p.52.
2 Ibid.: p.55.
3 Ibid.: p.57.
4 Ibid.: p.71.
5 Burke et al., 2016.
6 Tsing, 2015.
7 Berlant, 2011: p.262.
8 Grove, 2015.
9 Galloway, 2004: pp.146–72.
10 Ibid.: p.165.
11 Ibid.: p.169.
12 Povinelli, 2016a: p.56.
13 Ibid.: p.142.
14 See, for example, Burke et al., 2016, and, for a critique, Chandler et al., 2017.
15 Povinelli, 2016b: p.119.
16 Colebrook, 2014: pp.161–2.
17 Haraway, 2016.
18 Ibid.: p.31.
19 Wakefield, 2017.
20 See the discussion in Chapter 2, see also Gunderson and Holling, 2002.
21 Haraway, 2016: p.11.
22 Dempster, n.d.: p.4; see also Dempster, 1998.
23 See further, Chapter 2.
24 Bryant, 2014: pp.181–3.
25 Zylinska, 2014: p.32.
26 Ibid.
27 Ibid.
28 Ibid.: pp.32–3; see also Barad, 2007.
29 Tsing, 2015: p.22.
30 Ibid.: p.23
31 Ibid.: p.142.
32 Ibid.: p.258.
33 Ibid.
34 Haraway, 2016: p.33.
35 Morton, 2016: p.65.
36 Connolly, 2017: p.45.
37 Bryant, 2014: p.24.
38 Sharp, 2011: p.77.
39 Ibid.
40 Whereas constituent power seeks to constitute a new governmental regime, destituent power seeks to deactivate the elements of power and release them to the emergent process of potential life without the ends of governance; see Agamben, 2014b; also Wakefield and Braun, 2018; Braun and Wakefield, 2018.
41 Wakefield and Braun, 2018; Braun and Wakefield, 2018.
42 Wakefield and Braun, 2018.

43 Invisible Committee, 2014: Section 4(2).
44 Ibid. p.27.
45 Sharp, 2011: p.183.
46 Braun and Wakefield, 2018.
47 Ibid.
48 Connolly, 2017: p.45.
49 Ibid.: p.46.
50 Famously developed in Charles Darwin's *On the Origin of Species* (1859); see Mindell, 2013.
51 Bryant, 2014: p.80.
52 Grosz, 2011: p.119.
53 Connolly, 2017: p.49.
54 Haraway, 2016: p.1.
55 Ibid.: p.3.
56 Ibid.
57 Ibid.: p.4.
58 Ibid.: p.10.
59 Ibid: p.61.
60 Ibid.
61 Marx, 1983: pp.173–4.
62 Ingold, 2015: p.123.
63 Ibid.: p.122.
64 Bryant, 2014: p.19.
65 Ibid.: p.50.
66 Morton, 2013: pp.164–5.
67 Ibid.: p.174.
68 Ibid.: p.175.
69 Bruno Latour (2004c) uses the phrase 'learning to be affected' for the development of new bodily sensing capacities.
70 Stengers, 2015: p.138.
71 Stengers, 2017: pp.396–7.
72 Stengers, 2015: pp.148–9.
73 Connolly, 2017: p.56.
74 Ibid.: p.60.
75 Ibid.: p.61.
76 Ibid.: p.65.
77 Haraway, 2016: p.14.
78 Ibid.: p.67.
79 Ibid.: p.88.
80 Ibid.: p.127.
81 Ibid.
82 Ibid.: p.128; p.131.
83 Ibid.: p.150.
84 Bogost, 2016: p.x.
85 Ibid.
86 Ibid.: p.xi.
87 Ibid.
88 Ibid.: p.xii.

89 Ibid.: pp.4–5.
90 Ibid.: p.7.
91 Ibid.: p.11
92 Ibid.: p.16.
93 Morton, 2013: p.139.
94 Bogost, 2016: p.72.
95 Ibid.: p.73.
96 Ibid.
97 Ibid.: p.80.
98 Ibid.: p.92.
99 Braun and Wakefield, 2018.
100 Zylinska, 2014: p.14.
101 Connolly, 2017: p.84.
102 Stengers, 2015: p.138.
103 Bogost, 2016: p.111.
104 Ibid.: pp.129–30.
105 Grosz, 2011: pp.67–8.
106 Stengers, 2015: p.53.

PART V

Stakes

8

ONTOPOLITICS AND CRITIQUE

Introduction

This book has analysed the emergence of new modes of governance grounded and enabled by the ontopolitics of the Anthropocene. In developing the categories of Mapping, Sensing and Hacking to distinguish specific modes of governance, it has sought to highlight the increasingly positive affirmation of the new epoch of the Anthropocene. This chapter seeks to draw out further the links between the ontopolitical assumptions of the Anthropocene and new modes of governance. Its subject is the transvaluation of critique. It seeks to emphasise that the affirmation of the Anthropocene is neither driven merely by concerns over climate change and global warming, if anything these concerns would make the Anthropocene problematic, but nor is it driven merely by a critique of modernist modes of political theorising. This chapter focuses on what is unique about the affirmation of the Anthropocene and what makes it distinct from critical, neo-Marxist or cultural critiques of modernity: the fact that the critique of modernity is not built on the basis that modernity was dehumanising, separating man from nature, but its inversion: that modernity was not dehumanising enough. The problem is no longer seen to be the lack of reason of modernist rationalism but the lack of reason of the world itself. The 'Left' critique of modernity is thus transvalued in the affirmation of the Anthropocene. The ontopolitical assumptions which ground the new modes of governance of the Anthropocene do not raise the possibility of alternatives – any alternative would merely reconstitute man as a knowing subject separated from the world – but instead seek to affirm the world as it currently exists. Thus the ontopolitics of the Anthropocene are necessarily hostile to critique – they ontologise politics, seeking to ground a new metaphysical set of assertions of the limits of governance.

This may seem counterintuitive considering the emphasis which is put upon the alternative possibilities which are alleged to emerge once the modernist vision of the human and the world is rejected. This chapter therefore seeks to engage with how it is possible that the threat or indeed the promise of planetary extinction – or at the very least the humbling and decentring of the human as the meaning and value-giving subject of modernity – can be greeted with such affirmation. What could have happened to enable so many commentators to find affirming the ontopolitical assumption that the world is not amenable to human desires or aspirations of progress and development? What drives contemporary thought to the belief that the human is not distinct from the natural world, except perhaps in its destructiveness and capacities for self-delusion? What is it that explains how radical political aspirations for modernist progress have so failed to capture the hearts and minds of contemporary theorists?

This book is not a study or a history of the defeats of radical political struggles over the last century, it does not seek to dwell on battles long over or seek to revive a politics from the past. Instead, the preceding analysis has sought to engage with the consequences of these historical failures in the realm of contemporary theory and consciousness, as reflected in the ontopolitical understandings that inform our imaginaries of governance in the Anthropocene. A key problematic has been that of contemporary sensitivities which seem to affirm the idea that 'there is no happy ending'.[1] What is it about the imputed impossibility of a happy ending that is held to liberate thought and practice in the Anthropocene? As Danowski and Viveiros de Castro note, today we appear surrounded by a cacophony of contemporary voices, with new and sophisticated arguments, all determined to 'end the world' and even advocating that the 'real' world, 'in its radical contingency and purposelessness, has to be "realized" against Reason and Meaning'.[2] There is little doubt that even if these views do not always directly feed into substantiating new modes of governance, they are powerfully expressive of the underlying sentiments driving the ontopolitical assumptions of the Anthropocene.

Firstly, though, it is important to clarify that the affirmation of the Anthropocene – as signalling the end of the nature/culture divide and the end of modernist aspirations towards progress – is not the same as an awareness of the importance of addressing problems of climate change or of species extinction, ocean acidification or the loss of biodiversity. This book is about the ontopolitics of the Anthropocene, it is not a direct engagement with questions of *ontology*; it is not the facts of the world that are the subject of this analysis but their ontopolitical interpretation. All the problems of the world could be equally interpreted and engaged with in modernist ways and, of course, confidence in modernist approaches still exists across many diverse fields of life. However, it is the *ontopolitics* of the Anthropocene that are key to explaining the grounds for new modes of contemporary governance. As noted in the introductory chapter, *the facts of climate change, are not ontopolitical, their political interpretation is.* [3]

This book has specifically focused on the implications of approaches and theories, which accept or advocate affirmative approaches to the Anthropocene. These approaches all tend to see the Anthropocene as imposing new limits and enabling new possibilities obscured by modernist assumptions. While not all the commentators and analysts engage with the new epoch of the Anthropocene in the same way, or understand its implications in exactly the same terminology, the chapters above have sought to emphasise how influential Anthropocene thinking has been in shaping contemporary social and political theory and policy understandings, and particularly in the legitimisation of the new modes of governance at the centre of our concern.

One missing element of the analysis has been the broader context, which has enabled the range of contemporary theories and modes of governance, classified here in terms of Mapping, Sensing and Hacking, to cohere as specific responses to the perceived failure of modernity. The affirmation of the Anthropocene thus appears to be over determined. The arrival of climate change and global warming, indicating a new set of problems and potential limits to progress and development, seems to have coincided with an already existing exhaustion of the modernist episteme, creating a potent ontopolitical dynamic. As Claire Colebrook notes: 'The Anthropocene seems to arrive just as a whole new series of materialisms, vitalisms, realisms, and inhuman turns require us to think about what has definite and forceful existence regardless of our sense of world.'[4] This is why, for many theorists, the Anthropocene appears as something that is non-negotiable. Jessi Lehman and Sara Nelson, for example, argue that: 'In the Anthropocene, we are always already living in the aftermath of the event.' The delayed dynamics of climate change mean that its impact is unavoidable while the entanglement of human and geological factors mean that human agency can never again be imagined in modernist ways.[5] Stephanie Wakefield asserts that: 'the crisis is the age. It is on this terrain of an exhausted paradigm – both historical and metaphysical – that a battle is underway.'[6] This sense of modernity as 'an exhausted paradigm' has enabled the ontopolitics of the Anthropocene to rapidly cohere and appear to be powerfully vindicated in every extreme weather event or unexpected accident or disaster.

In answer to the question of 'Why affirm the Anthropocene?' the same ready-made explanation is repeated over and over, regularly wheeled out everywhere from newspaper articles to graduate presentations, conference papers and scientific journal articles: the Anthropocene is alleged to liberate us from the prison and constraints of modernist or Enlightenment thought, which has been revealed to be too linear, too binary, too abstract, too reductionist, too subject- or human-centred, too rationalist, too instrumentalist, too hubristic, too Euro-centric, too anthropocentric, too totalising … add any other popular trope of your choice. The speed and ease of the (at least rhetorically asserted) rejection of modernist understandings is something that takes more explanation than merely the finding that the earth might be entering a new geological epoch.

This book has sought to go beyond any simplistic or binary contra positioning of modernist or Enlightenment framings and those of the Anthropocene, drawing out three specific modes of governing on the basis of Anthropocene ontopolitics. However, the articulation of the new sensitivities of the Anthropocene is not just a rejection of modernity. It is argued here that this rejection takes a particular and highly contemporary form. Unlike earlier critiques of modernity,[7] the ontopolitical framings of the Anthropocene do not seek to return the human to the world, to 're-enchant' the world after modernity's passing. The three governance modes of Mapping, Sensing and Hacking affirm the Anthropocene not in terms of a return to a relational unity, a return to a pre-modern set of sensitivities or interconnections and interdependencies but rather as affirmation of the radical contingency of relational interaction and entanglement. Rather than becoming 'at home' in the Anthropocene, the opposite movement is at play: the earth is understood to be more alien to us, more inaccessible and stranger than we could have imagined. Counterintuitively, it is this alienation from the world, the world as lacking in meaning for man (the world as a 'desert' in Arendtian terms),[8] which provides the affirmation of the Anthropocene and distinguishes it from alternative critiques of the modernist paradigm. The Anthropocene is not merely the recognition of the importance of climate change or global warming; but neither is it merely a critique of modernity: it is affirmed as a new framework for understanding and acting in a world, which can never be considered a 'home'.

This chapter is organised in four sections, which draw towards a conclusion this research project into the affirmation of the ontopolitics of the Anthropocene and its emerging modes of governance. The next section introduces the problematic of critique in the Anthropocene, highlighting that critical theory approaches tend to see the Anthropocene within a discourse of modernist critique. The second section draws out the importance of understanding the distinct mode of contemporary critique, which rather than seeking to return man to the world, emphasises the impossibility of finding meaning in the world. It is this inverting of critical understandings that enables the ontopolitics of the Anthropocene to be seen affirmatively rather than problematically. The third section expands on this point to consider how contemporary theoretical approaches articulate the transvaluation of critique as the guide to progress. The final section summarises five key aspects of Anthropocene ontopolitics, which enables this framing to have such a powerful appeal, independently of either an appreciation of the importance of climate change or a critical approach to the modernist episteme.

Critique and the Anthropocene

If the facts of climate change do not alone explain the ontopolitics of the Anthropocene, it would perhaps be comforting to think that the affirmation of the Anthropocene is driven by the fact that it provides a convenient framing with which to challenge modernist or Enlightenment assumptions. If so, this raises the obvious question: Why couldn't we have liberated ourselves from modernity without the Anthropocene? Why is the Anthropocene able to do what intellectuals and critical activists couldn't do? Why didn't previous critiques of modernist thought, for its rationalist subject-centredness and human/nature binaries, not achieve this already? This point is often raised in a self-congratulatory manner; for example, by Timothy Morton and Bruno Latour, who both point out that climate scientists and climate change itself have done more to shake the modern episteme than critical theorists and the entirety of continental philosophy.[9] The affirmation of the Anthropocene cannot be properly understood without a clarification of its relationship to the critical thought of modernity. It is suggested here that the Anthropocene is affirmed precisely because it does something that critical theory had not merely not achieved but, more importantly, had not attempted.

For the modernist world, especially for the Marxist Left, there was always the possibility of a 'happy ending', through the development and extension of the productive forces, with the removal of capitalist forms of exploitation and oppression, instituting an alternative future based on reason and technological development.[10] This level of confidence in the promise of modernist progress increasingly dwindled throughout the twentieth century, with the experience of fascism, the purges of Stalin's Russia, world war, the Holocaust and the atomic bombings of Hiroshima and Nagasaki. This critical disillusionment was expressed well in the critical theory of the neo-Marxist Frankfurt School, whose approach was much more pessimistic than the Marxism of the late nineteenth and early twentieth century, shifting focus to (psycho)analytical problems of the instrumentalisation of knowledge and social construction of meaning.[11]

The new epoch of the Anthropocene can be seen as a continuation of a trend towards a more pessimistic view of the possibility of progress on behalf of radical or critical theorists and commentators. To the point where, today, it is no longer necessary for critical approaches to promise even the possibility of an alternative 'happy ending'.[12] This radical malaise is captured well in Fredric Jameson's often-cited observation 'that the end of the world is more easily imaginable than the end of capitalism'.[13] Thus to understand the ontopolitical assumptions of the Anthropocene it is necessary to understand how this observation could have been turned from a negative into a positive. As far as there is a shift from a critical focus on capitalism as a specific system of social relations to the problem of reflection upon human forms of social existence more generally, the affirmation of the Anthropocene seems both to build on and, importantly, to differ from the critical theory tradition of the Frankfurt School.

There is a consensus that the end of capitalism would not be a solution to problems of climate change. In fact, as analysed in the introductory chapter, according to Mackenzie Wark,[14] Christophe Bonneuil and Jean-Baptiste Fressoz,[15] Dipesh Chakrabarty,[16] Amitav Ghosh[17] and many others, the development of productive forces and a wider distribution of wealth under any successes for socialism would have merely speeded up the contemporary crisis. Capitalism may be problematic but it is no longer *the* problem: it is sometimes a catalyst or at least partly to blame but, more often than not, it is seen as merely a symptom or perhaps even an evasion of the problem, which is now cast in terms of the human, or rather the modernist construction of the human, itself.

Perhaps one of the most 'political' or traditionally 'critical' approaches to the Anthropocene is that of Bonneuil and Fressoz's *Shock of the Anthropocene*, [18] in which they argue that the problematic of the Anthropocene should not be captured by the scientific and technical expertise of eco-modernisers with their conceptions of 'spaceship earth' or 'interplanetary boundaries'. The Anthropocene is understood to be a product of centuries of conscious political choices, rather than an accidental or unknowable effect: it has been brought about by specific regimes of power. Bonneuil and Fressoz seek to draw those with Left sensibilities into an appreciation of the need to develop an ecological awareness and to resist the 'technological totalitarianism' of both the Left and the Right.[19] They particularly emphasise the importance of the legacy of the Frankfurt School, who first popularised a Left-leaning and critical understanding that the problem was not capitalism per se but rather the modernist episteme itself, in its development of technological and instrumentalist reason at the expense of relational and communal sensitivities.[20]

Is the affirmative ontopolitics of the Anthropocene thereby best understood as the fulfilment of the aspirations of critical theory, deposing the instrumentalist, rationalising, reductionism of liberal modernity? I think that the answer is not so straightforward. For the inheritors of neo-Marxist critical theory, the Anthropocene is necessarily problematic rather than liberating. Critical theory approaches are forced to evade the ontopolitical claims of the Anthropocene and the modes of governance they call forth (focusing on the Anthropocene as a modernist framing of politics and governance). What is interesting about Bonneuil and Fressoz's 'left' critique of the Anthropocene is precisely the way they tie it to modernist drives and understandings in order to maintain a critical approach. While critical of modernity, Bonneuil and Fressoz seek to follow the critical theorists of the Frankfurt School in returning man to a human-centred world of meaning and progress.

This is a point of fundamental importance regarding a critical stance to the ontopolitics of the Anthropocene. It would appear that to take a 'left' approach of critique the Anthropocene has to be seen as a modernist problematic, calling forth modes of governance of top-down 'command-and-control'. This book has taken a different approach, engaging critically with discourses of the Anthropocene which advocate for a clear break from the ontopolitical assumptions of modernity. The critical contemporary theorists who affirm the new ontopolitics of the Anthropocene may share some of Bonneuil and Fressoz's distain for modernity and their more psychotherapeutic and cultural critique of hegemonic ideas, but they take a fundamentally different ontopolitical stance. Rather than mourning man's separation from the world, Anthropocene ontopolitics celebrates it and wishes to take this as its ontological starting point. The modernist episteme is critiqued from the opposite aspect today, that it is too humanist or human-centred, not that it is alienating and dehumanising. It is for this reason that in the ontopolitical grounding of new modes of governance, considered in the chapters above, there is no demand for the human to be returned to a world of meaning, allegedly denied it by modernist rationalism and instrumentality, but rather for the human to be expunged further.

The work of Bonneuil and Fressoz is important as an example to highlight that while the critique of the modern episteme is a necessary precondition for the affirmation of Anthropocene ontopolitics, it is not in itself sufficient. In fact, the implication of the analysis presented in the previous chapters is that the discussion and debates on new modes of governance have turned the assumptions of critical theory inside out or transvalued critique. It is not the problematic or dehumanising nature of the modernist episteme which is central to the emergent ontopolitics of the Anthropocene. If this were the case, then the Anthropocene would still be construed negatively and critical theory and its post-Marxist inheritors would still provide a dominant framework for contemporary critical understanding.

Frankfurt School redux?

Perhaps the classic critical work on the problem of modernity is the one that established the reputation of critical theory and the Frankfurt School, Theodor Adorno and Max Horkheimer's (1947) *Dialectic of Enlightenment*. [21] For them, modernist thinking was dehumanising: the Enlightenment was problematic in denaturalising the world and the human, and reducing, universalising and equalising the experience of the world. For critical theory, the Enlightenment was problematic and oppressive rather than liberating. The Enlightenment view of reason contained its own seeds of destruction. Enlightenment was seen as a history of the separation of humanity from nature through the power of rationality – based on the subsumption of difference to the rule of equivalences, casting the Enlightenment as a totalitarian project with no inherent limits:[22] 'Bourgeois society is ruled by equivalence. It makes the dissimilar comparable by reducing it to abstract quantities.'[23] For Adorno and Horkheimer:

What was different is equalized. That is the verdict which critically determines the limits of possible experience. The identity of everything with everything else is paid for in that nothing may at the same time be identical with itself. Enlightenment ... excises the incommensurable ... [u]nder the levelling domination of abstraction.[24]

Rather than a process of progress and reason, the Enlightenment was seen as a machinic, deadening reduction of the world and of the human individual. For Adorno and Horkheimer, this was a world with no possibility of an outside as everything was subsumed into equivalence through conceptual abstraction.[25] In other words, this meant that nothing new could ever occur as 'the process is always decided from the start'; even unknown values could still be put into equations, dissolving the world into mathematics. Everything new was thus already predetermined, producing a world of 'knowledge without hope'.[26]

Thus the history of civilisation was the attempt to bring the outside under control through the extension of equivalence, Mauss's gift economy and pre-modern magic and sacrifice being early versions of the exchange of non-equivalents.[27] The performative exchange of non-equivalents then led to the reflection of equivalence in thought – conceptual subsumption – through the ratio, i.e. the proportion of conceptual equivalence. Under capitalism this process was formalised further, in both practice and in thought, through money as the universal equivalent of exchange and through the abstractions of democracy and universal rights and the development of science and the digital.[28] The modernist project was thus one of the extension of the imaginary of control, with the development of subject/object and human/nature binaries. Critical theory and its inheritors thereby sought to challenge the dominance of this modernist imaginary, questioning hierarchies of reason and progress and contesting the grounds upon which equivalences and subsumptions of difference were established.

The Frankfurt School sought to address the crisis of modernist thinking understood as a crisis for the Left, i.e. for those who aspired to critically advocate alternative worlds and social progress. The question at the heart of their work was that of the possibility for critical thought after the Holocaust and Hiroshima. If the Holocaust and Hiroshima were symptoms of rationalist thinking and technological progress, what possibility was there for critique? Bonneuil and Fressoz take up the Left approach of critiquing modernist/Enlightenment thought from within the critical theory tradition, seeing modernity as the failure to appreciate humanity as part of a material, natural world and seek to heal the 'metabolic rift'[29] caused by the extraction of 'cheap nature',[30] restoring a more holistic framework for politics. For these critical thinkers it is the political struggle against modernist thought which is the emancipatory aspect of the Anthropocene. The critical approach, which reduces the separation of man from the world to political problems of perception and projection, seeks to resolve the problem through bringing man back to the world, through its emphasis on lived experience, the body, affect, ethical entanglements etc. In the words of leading posthumanist theorist Rosi Braidotti, developing a posthumanism that can 'actualize the virtual possibilities of an expanded, relational self that functions in a nature–culture continuum', expressing an 'affirmative, ethical dimension of becoming-posthuman' as a community bound 'by the compassionate acknowledgement of their interdependence with multiple others'.[31]

Perhaps, in his more recent work, Bruno Latour could be seen to symbolise the last gasp of the critical attempt to return man to a world of meaning, with his conception of the earth in terms of the complex adaptive system of Gaia, where there is nothing 'natural' about the interactive agencies of the planet, which together produced life.[32] For Latour, like Bonneuil and Fressoz, the problem is the divide between culture and nature: a product of modernist human invention.[33] Like other critical theorists, and despite his claim that 'critique has run out of steam',[34] Latour seeks to heal the rift that modernity is held to have opened and restore the 'Earthbound' to their true home.[35] However, if the affirmation of the ontopolitics of the Anthropocene was merely about the limits of modernist imaginaries of universal and timeless knowledge, linear causality and autonomous rational subjects then it would already have arrived in the 1970s with the panopoly of neoliberal, neo-institutionalist policy framings (as analysed in Chapter 2).

The affirmation of the ontopolitics of the Anthropocene is the transvaluation of critical theory and thereby should not be confused with neo-Marxist and cultural critiques of classical Enlightenment or modernist thought. Something else is at stake. In order to illustrate this and to draw out the underlying sentiments behind the ontopolitics of the Anthropocene it is useful to highlight the role played by the imagination of extinction: the assumption that there can be 'no happy ending'.[36] To my mind, this provides a clear intimation of the desire to free social and political thought not just from its modernist legacies but also from any human-centred instrumentalism. As we have already seen above, particularly in the chapters analysing Hacking as a mode of governance, as long as climate change is viewed as a problem to be mitigated, adapted, managed, controlled or 'solved' in some way, then contemporary theorists argue that the Anthropocene is not properly understood or affirmed.

Extinction: after critique ... after failure ...

It is important to emphasise that critical theory and its inheritors highlight the critique of Cartesian rational man in order to have a happy ending – in order to save humanity and the planet rather than to affirm the Anthropocene.[37] The new relational, embodied and entangled subject of late modernity is thus sometimes seen as an extension of the modernist will to govern and problem-solve on the basis of intervening, adapting and being resilient in the face of non-linear or complex life, which is seen to set new norms for governance and problem-solving. Thus, the early iterations of the three ontopolitical modes of governance in the Anthropocene can be seen to bear the traces of this modernist or critical resistance, as drawn out in the chapters above. The non-linear tracing of Mapping, as a mode of autopoietic adaptation after the event, and even the Sensing mode of governance, with its discourses of equilibrium and homeostatic governance, highlight the difficulties of becoming at home in the Anthropocene. It is only the open and playful governance mode of Hacking that seems to fully affirm the Anthropocene and to be at home in a world without meaning 'for us', where what is important is the lack of stable relation and the lack of intentionality. Claire Colebrook would appear to hit the nail on the head:

> Humanism posits an elevated or exceptional 'man' to grant sense to existence, then when 'man' is negated or removed what is left is the human all too human tendency to see the world as one giant anthropomorphic self-organizing living body ... When man is destroyed to yield a posthuman world it is the same world minus humans, a world of meaning, sociality and readability yet without any sense of the disjunction, gap or limits of the human.[38]

For Colebrook, these approaches offer a narrative of redemption: after the detour of modernity, man is returned to the world. The Anthropocene would thus be no different to the critical response to the horrors of the Holocaust or Hiroshima, seen as products of modernist rationalism. In which case, the rejection of the foundational assumptions of modernity would enable man to find other modes of reasoning in the world. Colebrook asserts powerfully that:

The problem with humanism, so it seems, is that it is deemed to be rather inhuman. The Cartesian subject of calculative reason, along with computational theories of mind or representation, including both older humanisms of man as supreme moral animal and posthumanisms envisioning a disembodied world of absolute mastery, cannot cope with the complexity and dynamism of affective life.[39]

The response to the Anthropocene would, for critical theory, be to learn our lesson and to assert 'never again' on the basis of overcoming modernity's detachment from entangled and affective life. 'All our talk of mitigation and stability maintains a notion of stabilized nature, a nature that is ideally there for us and cyclically compatible with production'.[40] The affirmation of the Anthropocene is, in this respect, the inverse of critical theory. For affirmative approaches the slogan of 'never again' still places the human at the centre of the world. 'Never again' is always therefore just the prelude to the next hubristic assertions of human-centred solutions, leading to the next claims of 'never again' in an ever repeating cycle of imaginaries of human mastery.

For affirmative approaches to the ontopolitics of the Anthropocene, this cycle can be broken, and declarations of 'never again' become an impossibility, precisely through the imagination of the extinction of the human as a securing subject. As Audra Mitchell states, it is 'because IR [international relations] is so invested in human survival that it renders the assumption of its possibility unquestionable – and therefore renders extinction unthinkable'.[41] Following Colebrook, she argues that rather than seeing the problems as solvable on the basis of alternative forms of securing, it is the drive to secure itself which is problematic; 'only questioning the dogma of survival can enable us to critique this condition, and possibly (although not necessarily) to transcend it'.[42]

It seems clear that the positive affirmation of the ontopolitics of the Anthropocene completes the process of the rejection of modernist and Enlightenment thought but only through the inversion or transvaluation of the Frankfurt School's critical project. The Frankfurt School was caught in the trap of modernist thinking, in that they looked for reason in the world rather than looking to the world to critique the possibility of reason. Thus the framing of the affirmation of Anthropocene ontopolitics as a fulfilment of the aspirations of critical theory would fail to capture the transvaluation of thought which is increasingly at the centre of radical 'post-critical' approaches to the Anthropocene and (as all critical thought must) falls into the trap, increasingly highlighted by alternative radical approaches, of repeating a subject-centred attempt to 'restore' humanity to a world of meaning. Thus the conceptual focus upon extinction is post-nihilistic, freeing, as Mitchell argues, 'the political possibilities of becoming [that] are precluded by the imperative to survive "as we are" at all costs', enabling 'new modes of ethico-political action and forms of life'.[43]

The affirmation of the ontopolitics of the Anthropocene is an inversion of this focus upon finding reason or meaning in the world, instead seeking to push or enlarge the rift between the human and the world. The rift is naturalised or reified: the world is not and never was there for us, so there can be nothing to be healed or to be overcome. Any imagination of a scientific, a technological or a political solution to the problematic of the Anthropocene would be to nihilistically reject the world that exists and to reproduce the modernist failure to confront reality. This framing of the inversion of critical nihilism is presented by Bruno Latour through the example of Benjamin's 'Angel of History', which Latour compares to the 'Modern', flying backwards but, in this case, not able to see the rubble of destruction piling up in his wake, until the ecological crisis makes him realise, too late, that it was precisely 'His flight that has created the destruction He was trying to avoid in the first place'.[44] It is precisely the flight from reality of modernity that the Anthropocene is held to bring to an end.

For the new metaphysicians of Anthropocene ontopolitics, the Anthropocene is not a problem to be solved: it is an opportunity to be grasped. While, for the critical theorists of the Frankfurt School, the Enlightenment resulted in a failure that needed to be addressed. It seems there is a very different set of sensibilities at work today. The affirmation of the Anthropocene is captured well in the work of Laurent Berlant, in her study of *Cruel Optimism*.[45] After the promise of progress and the 'good life' has waned, the new assumptions of ontopolitics speak to the desire to give coherence and meaning to conditions of precarity and contingency, which in turn dramatise the instability of the present. For this reason, the Anthropocene is a self-amplifying condition of negotiating 'adaptation to the adaptive imperative'.[46]

Modernity has only failed if the reader still holds on to the promise of a happy ending. The ontopolitics of the Anthropocene free us from the promise of a happy ending and in so doing transvalue the aspirations of modernity and the Enlightenment, especially the promise that critical reason could liberate or emancipate humanity. The difference between the affirmation of the Anthropocene and the 'failure' of the Holocaust or

Hiroshima is that the latter were based on the presupposition that science would lead to truth and progress whereas the former is held to negate these possibilities entirely. Theorists who affirm the Anthropocene state that science itself has now proven that the world is no longer seen to be there for our benefit, to enable humanity to 'progress' in line with the imaginary of the liberal telos. To put this in another way – science reveals that the world does not care about us, that it is not there for us, to provide us with meaning.

The world is not a set of scientific and political puzzles set for us to solve; it is no longer 'all about us' – i.e. about what cultures, beliefs, politics, institutions, policies, education systems etc. are better to access the world of reason and progress. Without a world that is there for our benefit, problems can no longer be understood as epistemological: problems of the social, cultural, economic or political barriers to our knowing and understanding. The flip side of this is that the modernist or Enlightenment drive to separate the subject from the object of knowledge is revealed to be an error or mistake only in so far as it has not been pushed far enough. There is no such thing as an Enlightenment subject – a subject that imagines itself as separate to other beings, somehow capable of eventually building up more and more universal knowledge of an external world so as to control, direct and to dominate this world in order to live happily ever after. There is no world 'for us', no separate subject and no happy ending. As Ray Brassier puts it: 'Science subtracts nature from experience, the better to uncover the objective void of being.'[47] The only thing certain is the 'necessity' of contingency itself.[48]

The ontopolitics of the Anthropocene

The affirmative ontopolitics of the Anthropocene pose a fundamental break with modernist conceptions of the human subject and with critical theory attempts to posit alternative possibilities for finding meaning in the world. While assertions of the 'necessity of contingency' and of the 'objective void of being' sound radical in their opposition to any ontological foundations for the establishment of new forms of hegemony over life, they come at a cost of ontopolitically grounding new modes of governance, where there appears to be no choice apart from submission, or in Berlant's words: 'adaptation to the adaptive imperative'.[49] As suggested above, the key move in the transvaluation of critique and the affirmation of the world that exists is in the metaphysical assertion that there is no reason in the world, and that the positing of reason in the world prevents rather than enables its governance. It might not appear immediately obvious why this grounding assertion should be so widely accepted by contemporary theorists. I think that there are five logically interlinked reasons for this, and that any challenge to the ontopolitics of the Anthropocene will therefore have to take up these five claims.

1. No more 'never again': the Holocaust/Hiroshima

Firstly, the projection of unreason onto the world itself transforms the modernist/Enlightenment problematic. While critical theory and its inheritors attempted to rescue reason and the world for man, approaches that affirm the ontopolitics of the Anthropocene seek to go beyond this. The assertion that reason can no longer seek to solve problems, or to impose itself upon the world, is the key 'liberating' or 'emancipatory' aspect of the Anthropocene. Instrumentalist thinking is thereby no longer necessary, and if it is no longer necessary there is no longer the danger that reason will be problematic, whether the thinking subject is interpolated as rationalist or entangled. The Holocaust and Hiroshima that loomed so large over critical theory are thereby no longer problems that need to be explained or excused. There is no longer any need for a speculative history of the failure of modernity or the Enlightenment. The transvaluation of critique – its disconnection from the search for 'truth' or for 'knowledge' – means that the spectres haunting modernity are excised at last. This is no small achievement.[50]

When the theorists that affirm Anthropocene ontopolitics emphasise that we are now 'after the end of the world', 'after progress', 'after theory' or 'after critique' they mean that critical theorists are now freed from the tainted baggage of modernist failures. Reason, free from its modernist task of discovering meaning in the world, is free to 'discover the great outdoors';[51] critical theorists are free to explore, to go out and to play:[52] to discover a new world of strangeness, hope and possibility. Once critique can no longer be held responsible for the aspirations of reason and science and their failures – whether it is Stalinist gulags, the Holocaust or even the war in Iraq – critique is free of any responsibilities. The discovery that unreason is in the world itself, rather than a product of a lack of human reasoning, thus absolves critique of any and all responsibilities. In a world where, ontopolitically, the Anthropocene has been scientifically ratified as the truth of the end of modernist truth (in all its forms), any attempt to restore critique can only be a sign of a hubristic desire to return to a world of repression and hierarchical exclusions.

2. Everything is appreciated

In a world without the modernist drive to equivalences, to theory and abstraction, everything in the world is finally alleged to be 'given its due'.[53] Everything is treated on its own terms, as identical with itself and as incommensurable, non-reducible. As Deleuze and Guattari suggest, everything is a singularity, 'a continuous variation of variables'.[54] No longer is the rich plurality of the world reduced to constancies and to ratios of equivalences, or to inherent drives of autopoietic ordering from chaos. This, as noted in the chapters preceding, is key to the rise of new modes of governance. This is what gives the affirmation of Anthropocene ontopolitics its real purchase, very much in the spirit of Nietzsche's 'eternal return'.[55] As Brassier notes, Nietzsche's transvaluation of the will to know is crucial to the affirmative force of Anthropocene ontopolitics. Once the idea of knowledge-in-itself is rejected as impossible in a world of becoming, the will is no longer suborned to the world through a process of 'evaluating and interpreting under the aegis of truth and knowledge', whether this is constructed as transcendental or as immanent.[56] The will to know becomes affirmative and creative rather than negative and oppressive. The creative power of affirmation is the will to life itself, 'affirming the invaluableness of meaningless life as an end in itself'.[57]

3. The dissolution of the subject

The third point is that the flipside to everything being appreciated is that the subject dissolves back into the world, without the separations of the process of modernist reason. If there is no God's eye view, there is no God. If there is no ratio of equivalence, there is no knowing *ratio*-nal subject. As Deleuze and Guattari highlighted, the act of abstraction and equivalence-building separates the subject 'implying the permanence of a fixed point of view that is external' to the phenomena,[58] 'constantly reterritorializing around a point of view'.[59] A world in which nothing can be reduced to anything else is a world where the subject can no longer be separate from the world acting according to the hubristic imaginary of the Enlightenment. As decolonial theorist Walter Mignolo argues, the colonial imaginary of the universal subject of knowledge reduces the other to its object, thus the task is a 'new politics of knowledge rather than new contents'.[60] This new politics of knowledge is taken up by contemporary philosophical trends such as speculative realism and object-oriented ontology, Graham Harman and Levi

Bryant providing leading examples of phenomenological understandings of the withdrawn nature of objects from each other and themselves.

Instead of separating itself from the world, or imagining to know itself as the world, the knowing subject of the ontopolitics of the Anthropocene is drawn into the world itself, following the world, being drawn into it, rather than acting above it. It is precisely this division that Tim Ingold makes in the distinction between seeing the world as a maze and seeing it as a labyrinth. Whereas a journey through a maze is a strategic struggle based on sequential intentional decision-making in order to reach a predetermined goal, in a journey through a labyrinth it is the path that leads and there is no goal beyond carrying on the journey.[61] In the maze it is intentionality that is key, whereas in the labyrinth of the Anthropocene it is *attentionality* that is important: the ontopolitical necessity of paying attention to the world in its concrete specificity. This is not the subject at one with nonhuman others but always aware of the infinite depth and contingency of relationality in the world.

4. Keeping it real

The fourth key point I wish to stress, about the affirmative ontopolitics of the Anthropocene, is that though there is no reason in the world, there is still a world external to us, but shorn of its illusory 'solutionism',[62] shorn of its imaginary of a 'happy ending' – whether this is constituted as a technological fantasy or a return to nature's loving embrace. The world is there, it just cannot be thought about in modernist or critical ways, as if there was a truth waiting to be revealed; as if, as US comedian Bill Hicks argued, in another context, there was a 'prankster God' testing our faith.[63] This point is emphasised in the 'non-philosophy' of François Laruelle, who argues that thought is an object of the world; it doesn't represent it but it does tell us things, provides an indication or a sign, like any other object. Although there is no relation between the world and thought, as reality is foreclosed to thought, reality constitutes or determines thought. Thus, while reality cannot be objectified, thought can be.[64]

Thought does not mediate between the subject and the world. There is no such thing as a world in this (modernist) sense. Thus:

> the object is no longer conceived of as a substance but rather as a discontinuous cut in the fabric of ontological synthesis. It is no longer thought that determines the object, whether through thought or

intuition, but rather the object that seizes thought and forces it to think it, or better, according to it ... this objective determination takes the form of a unilateral duality where by the object thinks through the subject.[65]

The object or the world 'seizes thought' once it is realised that the world without reason is not open to the implementation of instrumental calculation. In the ontopolitics of the Anthropocene it becomes clear that policymaking needs to start with the world rather than from hubristic imaginaries of modernity. Like a carpenter, humanity realises that it cannot impose forms upon the world but has to work with rather than against the grain, listening to the object-other, allowing itself to be seized: thus the carpenter, the painter, the musician, even the academic, allow their subject matter to 'think' through them, and so should the town planner, the doctor or the engineer. In fact, it now appears clear that the dangerous world was the modernist one, which the Anthropocene takes us beyond. For many writers, the relationship between thought and world is inversed in the Anthropocene, in the governance mode of Hacking, 'synchronicity confirms that the Anthropocene has become our interlocutor, that it is indeed thinking "through" us'.[66]

5. The return of creativity and innovation

Fifth and finally, the affirmation of Anthropocene ontopolitics is precisely the affirmation of this world 'after the world'. In the modernist world of reason, there was nothing new or creative in the world: the agential power was the human subject's attempt to find or to discover hidden reason in the world. The Anthropocene promises a world without modernist hope; a world that, in its affirmation of what exists, has no more need for hope than for progress towards an alternative future. As Claire Colebrook argues, rejecting hope forces us to 'stay with the trouble' without 'bestowing an epic agential power in "man"'.[67] This is highlighted in comparison with Kantian hope, based upon a hidden reason in nature, which enables human discord, war and aggression to ultimately tend towards a level of stability and harmony: a transcendental telos of progress, which enables order to emerge from disharmony and conflict.[68] For the affirmative ontopolitics of the Anthropocene, hope cannot be found in the imaginary of the world as a complex self-adapting system, as a unified whole or Gaia, somehow being disrupted by human error. The ontopolitics of the Anthropocene finds affirmation not in the human-centred discovery of new 'solutions' but in the inability to ever grasp the world as more than a 'continuous variation of variables'. As Connolly argues:

> the contending senses of belonging to an organic world, being detached masters of a blind world, or sinking into passive or aggressive nihilism in an empty, meaningless world may now devolve toward pursuit of reflective attachments to a multifarious, entangled, dangerous world.[69]

Affirmation becomes an ontological aspect of being rather than a product of human reason. As Morton states, in an object-oriented ontology: 'Appearance is the past. Essence is the future.'[70] The fact that the surface of appearances only tells us the history of past interactions means that the 'future future lies ontologically "underneath" the past',[71] i.e. that it needs to be drawn out through the unfolding of the intra-active processes of the Anthropocene:

> What is left if we aren't the world? Intimacy. We have lost the world but gained a soul – the entities that coexist with us obtrude on our awareness with greater and greater urgency. Three cheers for the so-called *end of the world*, then, since this moment is the beginning of history. We now have the prospect of forging new alliances between humans and nonhumans alike, now that we have stepped out of the cocoon of the world. (emphasis in original)[72]

Conclusion

For neo- and post-Marxist critical theory, the Enlightenment or modernist episteme was problematic because it alienated man from himself and from the world, opening up a separation between nature and culture, which narrowed and reduced the world (including the vast majority of humanity) to passive objects for instrumental manipulation. The modernist regime was problematic because its hierarchies of power and knowledge rationalised and reproduced this desire for regulation and control, excluding and oppressing whatever could not be compliantly included. Both man and nature were excluded from realising their potential and suborned to the rule of technocratic rationality. This critical perspective, of 'rehumanising' critique, can be understood as 'ontological' in that it problematised the modernist assumptions of the autonomous human subject and of the world as object, external to it. As Stephen White notes, the 'ontological turn' in contemporary political theory and its wider influence across the social sciences has reflected the decline of 'modernity's self-confidence', which has increasingly engendered diverse discourses of 'ontological reflection'.[73]

What was distinctive about the ontological turn in Left critical theory was that it was marked by a 'weak ontology'. In the past, when ontology was deployed in discourses of ethics or politics, it was as a 'strong ontology'; its purpose being to enable clear forms of rationalisation and legitimisation. In a strong ontology, 'the whole question of passages from ontological truths to moral-political ones is relatively clear'.[74] Clarity and certainty were not the goals of the advocates of 'weak ontology', often categorised as post-foundationalist or as anti-foundationalist approaches to political theory.[75] The goal was to destabilise the dominant modernist grounds for truth claims: to contest and problematise assumptions, which enabled the passage from ontological claims to moral-political ones, and to remove the possibility of metaphysical certainty. The radical claims of the 'ontological turn' rested precisely on their resistance to 'strong ontology' – the making of ethical or political claims on the basis of particular understandings of nature or life itself – as well as resistance to liberal or modernist paradigms, which were seen to ignore the importance of reflection upon the ontological basis for their ethical and political assumptions.[76] Thus radical approaches to 'weak ontology' were seen to open space for other critical possibilities and alternatives to emerge.

The methodological framing of ontopolitical critique deployed in this book thus can be seen to draw on the critical 'weak ontology' tradition of post-foundationalism. The critical international relations theorist David Campbell, for example, argues that the critical engagement with theories and assumptions in terms of ontopolitics 'enables us to see how dominant accounts of specific situations arrive at their conclusions by injecting ontological presumptions into their claims of actuality without disclosing their complicity in the representational process'.[77] This chapter has argued that there is a pressing problem with contemporary critical approaches, which affirm the ontopolitics of the Anthropocene rather than highlighting its ontopolitical framings in order to critique dominant and hegemonic frameworks. Whereas for theorists, such as Deleuze or Derrida, an ontopolitical ethics of alterity was construed as part of a practical political struggle to continually keep open the possibility of alternative modes of being. Today, there is a real danger of intellectual and critical closure marked by the turn from the post-foundationalist ontopolitics of critique to the uncritical and unreflective ontopolitics of affirmation.

Rather than drawing out and revealing the necessary gaps and aporia between ontological assumptions and ethical and political claims, the ontopolitics of affirmation has resulted in producing a new and unquestioning 'strong ontology' whereby the Anthropocene is seen as ontopolitically affirming new modes of governance.[78] To take one recent example, in the *European Journal of International Relations*, Audra Mitchell makes an explicit claim to be developing a 'weak ontology' critique 'remaining fundamentally open to possibilities' while radically affirming the Anthropocene on the basis that a 'cosmopolitics attuned to extinction and to the inhuman would foster a new mode of future-oriented politics based not on the *continuity* of the present, but rather on the creative possibilities of *discontinuity* and unpredictable difference' (emphasis in original).[79] Upon the basis of this ontological 'openness' (representative of many of the affirmative voices analysed in this book):

> This cosmopolitics would: better attune humans to their planetary conditions; dissolve essentialist boundaries that ground regimes of exclusion and oppression; and offer a new form of global ethics rooted in gratitude, experimentation and an ethos of welcome towards new life forms and worlds.[80]

She represents a growing consensus. Elizabeth Grosz, similarly, prioritises the unfolding of life as a process of enabling 'more making and doing, more difference' over juridical or political claims for rights or recognition.[81] For the new metaphysics of the Anthropocene, it would appear that 'renaturalising politics', to make life the ontopolitical grounding of its governance, is only oppressive if nature is seen as fixed and linear rather than as lively excess and creativity. Thus for Grosz, becoming suborned to 'life' is not necessarily a matter of 'a rational strategy for survival, not a form of adaptation, but the infinite elaboration of excess' and experimentation.[82] In a world of becoming, beyond the binaries of 'man' and 'nature', submission can thus be a creative and enabling perspective that sees contingency as an opportunity rather than as a constraint on human freedom.

For Claire Colebrook and other theorists, critical of this appeal to 'life' as an ontopolitical ground, 'this too would be a metaphysics, with the same structure of the subject'.[83] As Lynne Huffer describes in her critique of the trend towards 'renaturalizing politics', there seems to be a slippage towards a new metaphysical construction of 'life', which forgets the 'temporal contingencies through which epistemes emerge and topple'.[84] The Anthropocene affirming discourses of Mapping, Sensing and Hacking all take the contingent flux of 'life' as their starting point, with the sympoietic mode of Hacking being the most affirmative. Thus it would appear that our contemporary condition expresses both the exhaustion of modernist understandings of reason and progress and of critical and post-foundational attempts to keep open alternative possibilities. It is not just that 'the end of the world is more easily imaginable than the end of capitalism': it would appear that 'after the end of the world' it is no longer possible even to imagine any alternative. Thus Levinas's claim of the dangers of 'ontological totalitarianism' would seem to be more prescient today than in even his lifetime. This book has therefore been a first attempt to raise the need for an ontopolitics of critique rather than of affirmation.

Notes

1 Tsing, 2015: p.21.
2 Danowski and Viveiros de Castro, 2017: p.3.
3 See also Connolly, 1995.
4 Colebrook, 2017: p.7. In fact, Richard Grusin (2017: p.viii) argues that 'the concept of the Anthropocene has arguably been implicit in feminist and queer theory for decades'.
5 Lehman and Nelson, 2014: p.444.
6 Wakefield, 2014: p.451.
7 Bennett, 2011.
8 See Arendt, 2005: pp.201–4.
9 See, for example, Latour, 2013b: p.77; Morton, 2013: p.181.
10 Pachter, 1974.
11 See, for example, Jeffries, 2016.
12 Tsing, 2015.
13 Jameson, 2003: p.73.
14 Wark, 2015.
15 Bonneuil and Fressoz, 2016.
16 Chakrabarty, 2009.
17 Ghosh, 2016.
18 Bonneuil and Fressoz, 2016.
19 Ibid.: p.280.
20 Ibid.: 281.
21 Adorno and Horkheimer, 1997.
22 Ibid.: p.6.
23 Ibid.: p.7.

24 Ibid.: pp.12–13.
25 Ibid.: p.16.
26 Ibid.: pp.27–8.
27 Mauss, 2002.
28 See also Sohn-Rethel, 1978.
29 Wark, 2015.
30 Moore, 2015.
31 Braidotti, 2017: p.34; p.39.
32 Latour, 2013b: pp.62–3.
33 Ibid.: p.67.
34 Latour, 2004b.
35 Latour, 2013b.
36 Tsing, 2015; Brassier, 2007.
37 See, for example, Burke et al., 2016.
38 Colebrook, 2014: pp.163–4.
39 Ibid.: p.173.
40 Colebrook, 2017: p.18.
41 Mitchell, 2017: p.12.
42 Ibid.: p.17.
43 Ibid.: p.18.
44 Latour, 2010c: pp.485–6.
45 Berlant, 2011.
46 Ibid.: p.195.
47 Brassier, 2007: p.25.
48 Meillassoux, 2008.
49 Berlant, 2011: p.195.
50 Considering the centrality of the Holocaust in discussions of the limits of modernist reason, its absence from the Anthropocene problematic is quite striking.
51 Meillassoux, 2008.
52 Bogost, 2016.
53 Latour, 2013b: p.126.
54 Deleuze and Guattari, 2014: p.434.
55 Nietzsche, 1997: p.312.
56 Brassier, 2007: p.215.
57 Ibid.: p.216.
58 Deleuze and Guattari, 2014: p.433.
59 Ibid.: p.434.
60 Mignolo, 2011: p.58.
61 Ingold, 2015: pp.130–3.
62 Morozov, 2013.
63 Hicks, 1992.
64 See, Galloway, 2014.
65 Brassier, 2007: p.149.
66 Ghosh, 2016: p.83.
67 Colebrook, 2015: p.176.
68 See also, Colebrook, 2014: p.106.
69 Connolly, 2017: p.120.
70 Morton, 2013: p.91.

71 Ibid.
72 Ibid.: p.108.
73 White, 2000, p.4.
74 Ibid.: p.6.
75 See Strathausen, 2009; Marchart, 2007.
76 See further, for example, Connolly, 1995.
77 Campbell, 2005: p.128.
78 See Chandler and Grove, 2017: pp.85–86.
79 Mitchell, 2017: p.21.
80 Ibid.: p.23.
81 Grosz, 2011: p.71. See also the previous chapter.
82 Ibid.: p.119.
83 Colebrook, 2012: p.192.
84 Huffer, 2017: p.67.

9

CONCLUSION

All three governance modes heuristically mapped in this book – Mapping, Sensing and Hacking – start on the basis that the world is not there for us; that the world is immune to modernist reason. Rather than starting from a subject-centred or hylomorphic imaginary of 'solutionism' – the biopolitical drive to govern life according to its laws – they start from the recalcitrant being of the world itself. In the ontopolitics of the Anthropocene the world is to be followed and affirmed rather than forced to reveal its 'truths' (which could then be understood and acted upon independently or bent to human needs and desires). The Anthropocene is even seen to lack the hope of a new science of complexity or of complex adaptive systems, through which order emerges from chaos without external or centralised direction.[1] While humanity may still be physically on the planet, the ontopolitics of the Anthropocene suggest that we should govern through the imaginary that we do, in fact, live in a 'world without us':[2] without a modernist view of the human as a knowing subject capable of transforming themselves and their conditions of existence.

The different modes of governance on the basis of the ontopolitical assumptions of the Anthropocene all privilege the world over thought or theorising. The key demand of contemporary modes of governance is that the world be followed, despite its lack of meaning for us: i.e. that we develop new attributes for attentiveness, adaptation, responsivity, sensitivity, surprise and wonder. However, living after the 'end of the world', after the 'end of critique' and after the 'end of theory' does not mean that the human cannot be at home in a world that can never be a home in the modernist sense. Paying attention to the world understood as not a world of hidden relation or meaning makes submission itself the only meaningful thing. As Timothy Morton states:

> Futurality is reinscribed in the present ... The end of teleology is *the end of the world*. The end is precisely not an instant vaporization, but rather a lingering coexistence with strange strangers. For the end of the world is the end of endings, the end of telos, and the beginning of an uncertain, hesitating furturality. (emphasis in original)[3]

The Anthropocene has no past and no future: it is merely a world without meaning to which humanity can no longer be suborned in modernist ways. This new form of 'submission', to the meaningless void of the real, like that of the controversial dystopian Michel Houellebecq novel,[4] seems to be much more affirming than we could have previously imagined.

If we do now truly live after modernity – and the ontopolitics of the Anthropocene inform our political imaginary, enabling the new modes of governance of Mapping, Sensing and Hacking – then the question of critique (as we saw in the last chapter) is sharply posed. It seems unsatisfactory to critique claims made for these modes of ontopolitical governance on the basis that they remove the world of modernist possibilities of progress. The non-modern ontopolitical assumptions, informing the modes of governing in the Anthropocene, are attractive precisely because of the perceived failure of modernity: they are legitimised and rationalised on the basis that the politics of modernity (of top-down, cause-and-effect understandings) is dangerous, false and hubristic and does nothing to remove the hierarchies, inequalities, injustice and suffering of the world. New Anthropocene understandings of governance cannot really be critically engaged with on the basis that they reject the ontological and epistemological assumptions of human-centred or Enlightenment thought. This rejection today is regarded as a positive sign of conceptual and political sophistication and ethical awareness.

Perhaps the best that can be done – and this book should be seen as a step towards this – is to use the insights of contemporary critical approaches, that affirm the ontopolitics of the Anthropocene, to problematise the assertions that the world we live in today is immune to theory and causal understandings and that alternatives are not only impossible but, quite literally, unimaginable. Perhaps the world is no more necessarily complex and contingent today than it was necessarily linear and universal in the recent past? Perhaps the human subject is no more necessarily relationally embedded and materially entangled than it was necessarily constructed in the modern ontology of the universal, autonomous and abstract individual? If modernity and the modern human were ontopolitical constructs then, this book has argued, so is the Anthropocene condition and its ontopolitical groundings of new modes of governance.

Anthropocene ontopolitical perspectives agree that it took a lot of work to construct the world in linear ways and to construct the human as separable from the world and to imagine the modernist binaries and cuts which enabled modernist forms of governance. Perhaps, advocates of Anthropocene ontopolitics might be equally willing to undertake the painstaking approaches of genealogical reconstruction necessary to reveal the processes at play in the construction of the world as complex and without meaning for us. Modernist conceptions of knowledge and of governance, agency and the human subject have not just collapsed as if by magic, as if the world revealed its true self to science and technology; their demise is the contingent reflection of real material and subjective processes. The world could therefore be otherwise. Even if we live 'after the end of the world' this does not necessarily mean that we live 'after the end of endings' as Morton asserts above. This is merely, as Lynne Huffer notes, the ontopolitical 'universalizing [of] the historically contingent frames of our present world as a new metaphysics of life'.[5]

It seems to me that a future-oriented research project of international relations could be that of critically engaging the ontopolitical assumptions of complexity and emergent causality which are held to necessitate new constructions of governance through the modes of Mapping, Sensing and Hacking. The insights of critical and speculative realist thought should enable a thorough engagement and deconstruction of the assertion that we have no choice but to affirm only 'what is'. The research hinterlands or assemblages, which have enabled Anthropocene ontopolitics to become the new doxa or commonsense of the world, need to be brought into clear view and contested.[6] Karen Barad's insights about the social materiality of ways of seeing, doing and being in the world can also be enrolled into the project, questioning easy assumptions that minimise the challenge posed by the ontopolitics of the Anthropocene. Recent shifts to affirming contingency and complexity cannot be reduced either to the technological advances of computational algorithms and sensing technologies or to the political or subjective motivations of either funders or researchers.[7]

The fact that the ontopolitics of the Anthropocene may be constructed or contingent does not make it any less real, or the affirmative appeal of its discourses any less powerful, nor its modes of governance any less attractive to policy-makers, managers and regulators. Now that Anthropocene onto-politics have become a coherent framework of theory informing distinct modes of governance, there is a danger that the confinement of intellectual enquiry to the production of situated and embedded knowledge, whether through high tech algorithms or through ethnographic methods, will make the world politically and intellectually a sterile place. For those of us who do not wish to merely describe the world in forms amenable to Mapping, Sensing and Hacking as modes of governance, the task of revitalising a new critical approach to ontopolitics has never been more urgent.

Notes

1 See Chandler, 2014a
2 Weisman, 2008.
3 Morton, 2013: p.95.
4 Houellebecq, 2015.
5 Huffer, 2017: p.84.
6 See Law, 2004.
7 Barad, 2007.

REFERENCES

Abrahamsen, R. and Williams, M. C. (2011) *Security beyond the State: Private Security in International Politics*. Cambridge: Cambridge University Press.

Acuto, M. and Curtis, S. (eds) (2014a) *Reassembling International Theory: Assemblage Thinking and International Relations*. Basingstoke: Palgrave Macmillan.

Acuto, M. and Curtis, S. (2014b) 'Assemblage thinking and international relations' in M. Acuto and S. Curtis (eds) *Reassembling International Theory: Assemblage Thinking and International Relations*. Basingstoke: Palgrave Macmillan, 1–15.

Adorno, T. and Horkheimer, M. (1997) *Dialectic of Enlightenment*. London: Verso.

Agamben, G. (1998) *Homo Sacer: Sovereign Power and Bare Life*. Stanford, CA: Stanford University Press.

Agamben, G. (2005) *State of Exception*. Chicago, IL: University of Chicago Press.

Agamben, G. (2014a) 'For a theory of destituent power', *Chronos* 10, February. Accessed at: www.chronosmag.eu/index.php/g-agamben-for-a-theory-of-destituent-power.html.

Agamben, G. (2014b) 'What is a destituent power?' *Environment and Planning D: Society and Space* 32: 65–74.

Ahrens, J. and Rudolph, P. M. (2006) 'The importance of governance in risk reduction and disaster management', *Journal of Contingencies and Crisis Management* 14(4): 207–220.

Allouche, G. (2014) 'Spy craft and disease: Big Data's impact on the global stage', *Smart Data Collective*, 30 April. Accessed at: http://smartdatacollective.com/gilallouche/197721/spy-craft-and-disease-big-datas-impact-global-stage.

ALNAP (2016) 'Active learning network for accountability and performance' in *Humanitarian Action, Establishing Early Warning Thresholds for key Surveillance*

Indicators of Urban Food Security: The Case of Nairobi. Accessed at: www.alnap.org/p ool/files/thresholds-paper-final-february-2016.pdf.

Anderson, C. (2008) 'The end of theory: the data deluge makes the scientific method obsolete', *Wired Magazine* 16(7), 23 June. Accessed at: http://archive. wired.com/science/discoveries/magazine/16-07/pb_theory.

Anderson, B., Kearnes, M., McFarlane, C. and Swanton, D. (2012) 'On assemblages and geography', *Dialogues in Human Geography* 2(2): 171–189.

Anggakara, K., Frederika, M. and Rahwidiati, D. (2016) 'Reconnecting the state with its citizens: from talk to action', *Pulse Lab Jakarta*, 2 June. Accessed at: https://m edium.com/@PLJ/reconnecting-the-state-with-its-citizens-from-talk-to-action-5e84 4c81427d#.

Aradau, C. and Blanke, T. (2015) 'The (big) data-security assemblage: knowledge and critique', *Big Data and Society* 2(2).

Aradau, C. and Blanke, T. (2017) 'Politics of prediction: security and the time/space of governmentality in the age of big data', *European Journal of Social Theory* 20(3): 373–391.

Arendt, H. (2005) *The Promise of Politics.* New York: Schocken Books.

Bahadur, A. and Doczi, J. (2016) 'Unlocking resilience through autonomous innovation', *Overseas Development Institute Working Paper.* London: ODI.

Baldwin, D. A. (1997) 'The concept of security', *Review of International Studies* 23(1): 5–26.

Barad, K. (2007) *Meeting the Universe Halfway: Quantum Physics and the Entanglement of Matter and Meaning.* London: Duke University Press.

Bargues-Pedreny, P. (2016) 'From promoting to de-emphasizing "ethnicity": rethinking the endless supervision of Kosovo', *Journal of Intervention and State-building* 10(2): 222–240.

Barnett, M. and Weiss, T. (2008) *Humanitarianism in Question: Politics, Power, Ethics.* Cornell, NY: Cornell University Press.

Barry, A., Osborne, T. and Rose, N. (eds) (1996) *Foucault and Political Reason: Liberalism, Neoliberalism and Rationalities of Government.* Chicago, IL: University of Chicago Press.

Baudrillard, J. (1994) *Simulacra and Simulation.* Ann Arbour: University of Michigan Press.

Bays, J. (n.d.) 'Harnessing big data to address the world's problems', *McKinsey on Society.* Accessed at: http://voices.mckinseyonsociety.com/harnessing-big-data -to-address-the-worlds-problems/.

Beck, U. (1992) *Risk Society: Towards a New Modernity.* London: Sage.

Beck, U. (2009a) *World at Risk.* Cambridge: Polity Press.

Beck, U. (2009b) 'World risk society and manufactured uncertainties', *IRIS: European Journal of Philosophy and Public Debate* I(2): 291–299.

Beck, U. (2015) 'Emancipatory catastrophism: what does it mean to climate change and risk society?', *Current Sociology* 63(1): 75–88.

Beck, U. (2016) *The Metamorphosis of the World.* Cambridge: Polity Press.

Bennett, C., Foley, M. and H. B. Krebs (2016) 'Learning from the past to shape the future: lessons from the history of humanitarian action in Africa', *Humanitarian Policy Group Working Paper*. London: Overseas Development Institute.

Bennett, J. (2010) *Vibrant Matter: A Political Ecology of Things*. London: Duke University Press.

Bennett, J. (2011) 'Modernity and its critics', in R. E. Goodin (ed.) *The Oxford Handbook of Political Science*. Oxford: Oxford University Press.

Berkes, F., Colding, J. and Folke, C. (eds) (2003) *Navigating Social–Ecological Systems: Building Resilience for Complexity And Change*. Cambridge: Cambridge University Press.

Berlant, L. (2011) *Cruel Optimism*. Durham: Duke University Press.

Bertolucci, J. (2014) '10 Powerful Facts About Big Data', *Information Week*, 10 June. Accessed at: www.informationweek.com/big-data/big-data-analytics/10-power ful-facts-about-big-data/d/d-id/1269522.

Bhaskar, R. (1998) *The Possibility of Naturalism: A Philosophical Critique of the Contemporary Human Sciences*, 3rd edn. Abingdon: Routledge.

Blaser, M. (2013) 'Ontological conflicts and the stories of peoples in spite of Europe: toward a conversation on political ontology', *Current Anthropology* 54(5): 547–568.

BNPB (The Indonesian National Agency for Disaster Management) (2014) *Indonesia: National Progress Report on the Implementation of the Hyogo Framework for Action (2013–2015)*. Accessed at: www.preventionweb.net/files/41507_IDN_Nationa lHFAprogress_2013-15.pdf.

Bogost, I. (2012) *Alien Phenomenology or What It's Like to Be a Thing*. Minneapolis: University of Minnesota Press.

Bogost, I. (2016) *Play Anything: The Pleasure of Limits, The Uses of Boredom, & the secret of Games*. New York: Basic Books.

Bonneuil, C. (2015) 'The geological turn: narratives of the Anthropocene', in C. Hamilton, C. Bonneuil and F. Gemenne (eds) *The Anthropocene and the Global Environmental Crisis: Rethinking Modernity in a New Epoch*. Abingdon: Routledge, 17–31.

Bonneuil, C. and Fressoz, J.-B. (2016) *The Shock of the Anthropocene*. London: Verso.

Bourbeau, P. (2015) 'Resilience and international politics: premises, debates, agenda', *International Studies Review* 17(3): 374–395.

Bowker, G. C. (2000) 'Biodiversity datadiversity', *Social Studies of Science* 30(5): 643–683.

boyd, d. and Crawford, K. (2012) 'Critical questions for big data: provocations for a cultural, technological, and scholarly phenomenon', *Information, Communication & Society* 15(5): 662–679.

Braidotti, R. (2013) *The Posthuman*. Cambridge: Polity Press.

Braidotti, R. (2017) 'Four theses on posthuman feminism', in R. Grusin (ed.) *Anthropocene Feminism*. Minneapolis: University of Minnesota Press, 21–48.

Brand, F. S. and Jax, K. (2007) 'Focusing the meaning(s) of resilience: resilience as a descriptive concept and a boundary object', *Ecology and Society* 12(1): art.23.

Brassier, R. (2007) *Nihil Unbound: Enlightenment and Extinction*. Basingstoke: Palgrave Macmillan.

Bratton, B. (2015) *The Stack: On Software and Sovereignty*. Cambridge, MA: The MIT Press.

Braun, B. and Wakefield, S. (2018) 'Destituent power and common use: reading Agamben in the Anthropocene', in M. Coleman and J. Agne (eds) *Geographies of Power*. Georgia: University of Georgia Press.

Brenner, N. and Theodore, N. (2002) 'Cities and the geographies of "Actually Existing Liberalism"', *Antipode* 34(3): 349–379.

Brigg, M. and Muller, K. (2009) 'Conceptualising culture in conflict resolution', *Journal of Intercultural Studies* 30(2): 121–140.

Brillembourg, A. (2015) 'Learning from slums', *Economist Intelligence Unit*, 28 January. Accessed at: www.economistinsights.com/infrastructure-cities/opinion/learning-slums.

Bryant, L. (2011) *The Democracy of Objects*. Ann Arbour: Open Humanities Press.

Bryant, L. (2012) 'Thoughts on posthumanism', *Larval Subjects*, 10 November. Accessed at: https://larvalsubjects.wordpress.com/2012/11/10/thoughts-on-p osthumanism/.

Bryant, L. (2014) *Onto-Cartography: An Ontology of Machines and Media*. Edinburgh: Edinburgh University Press.

Burhaini, F. E. (2011) '"Kampung kota" offers solution to urban living', *The Jakarta Post*, 20 April. Accessed at: www.thejakartapost.com/news/2011/04/20/kamp ung-kota'-offers-solution-urban-living.html.

Burke, A., Fishel, S., Mitchell, A., Dalby, S. and Levine, D. J. (2016) 'Planet politics: a manifesto from the end of IR', *Millennium: Journal of International Studies* 44(3): 499–523.

Campbell, D. (2005) 'Beyond choice: the onto-politics of critique', *International Relations* 19(1): 127–134.

Campbell, S., Chandler, D. and Sabaratnam, M. (eds) (2011) *The Liberal Peace?* London: Zed.

Caquard, S. (2013) 'Cartography I: mapping narrative cartography', *Progress in Human Geography* 37(1): 135–144.

Carrithers, M., Candea, M., Sykes, K., Holbraad, M. and Venkatesan, S. (2010) 'Ontology is just another word for culture: motion tabled at the 2008 Meeting of the Group for Debates in Anthropological Theory, University of Manchester', *Critique of Anthropology* 30(2): 152–200.

Castree, N. (2007) 'Neoliberal environments: a framework for analysis,' *Manchester Papers in Political Economy*, working paper no. 04/07, 10 December.

Castroni, M. (2009) 'Learning from the slums: literature and urban renewal', *Arch Daily*, 8 March. Accessed at: www.archdaily.com/15271/learning-from-the-slum s-12literature-and-urban-renewal/.

Chakrabarty, D. (2009) 'The climate of history: four theses', *Critical Inquiry* 35(2): 197–222.

Chakrabarty, D. (2015) 'The Anthropocene and the convergence of histories', in C. Hamilton, C. Bonneuil and F. Gemenne (eds) *The Anthropocene and the Global Environmental Crisis: Rethinking Modernity in a New Epoch*. Abingdon: Routledge, 44–56.

Chandler, D. (2010) 'Neither international nor global: rethinking the problematic subject of security', *Journal of Critical Globalisation Studies* 3: 89–101.

Chandler, D. (2013) *Freedom vs Necessity in International Relations: Human-Centred Approaches to Security and Development*. London: Zed Books.

Chandler, D. (2014a) *Resilience: The Governance of Complexity*. Abingdon: Routledge.

Chandler, D. (2014b) 'Beyond good and evil: ethics in a world of complexity', *International Politics* 51(4): 441–457.

Chandler, D. (2014c) 'Beyond neoliberalism: resilience, the new art of governing complexity', *Resilience: International Policies, Practices and Discourses* 2(1): 47–63.

Chandler, D. (2014d) 'The onto-politics of assemblages', in M. Acuto and S. Curtis (eds) *Reassembling International Theory: Assemblage Thinking and International Relations*. Basingstoke: Palgrave Macmillan, 99–105.

Chandler, D. (2015) 'A world without causation: big data and the coming of age of posthumanism', *Millennium: Journal of International Studies* 43(3): 833–851.

Chandler, D. (2017) *Peacebuilding: The Twenty Years' Crisis: 1997–2017*. Basingstoke: Palgrave Macmillan.

Chandler, D. and Grove, K. (2017) 'Introduction: resilience and the Anthropocene: the stakes of "renaturalising" politics', *Resilience: International Policies, Practices and Discourses* 5(2): 79–91.

Chandler, D. and Reid, J. (2016) *The Neoliberal Subject: Resilience, Adaptation and Vulnerability*. London: Rowman & Littlefield International.

Chandler, D. and Sisk, T. (2013) *Routledge Handbook of International Statebuilding*. Abingdon: Routledge.

Chandler, D., Cudworth, E. and Hobden, S. (2017) 'Anthropocene, Capitalocene and Liberal Cosmopolitan IR: a response to Burke et al.'s "Planet Politics"', *Millennium: Journal of International Studies*, https://doi.org/10.1177/0305829817715247.

Chardronnet, E. (2015) 'McKenzie Wark: "You don't just need to hack to be a hacker"', *Makery*, 9 February. Accessed at: www.makery.info/en/2015/02/09/m ckenzie-wark-il-ne-suffit-pas-de-faire-du-hack-pour-etre-hacker/.

Cilliers, P. (1998) *Complexity and Postmodernism: Understanding Complex Systems*. Abingdon: Routledge.

Clark, L. (2013) 'No questions asked: big data firm maps solutions without human input', *Wired Magazine*, 16 January. Accessed at: www.wired.co.uk/news/a rchive/2013-01/16/ayasdi-big-data-launch.

Clark, N. (2010) *Inhuman Nature: Sociable Life on a Dynamic Planet*. Sage Publications, Kindle Edition.

Clark, N. (2014) 'Geo-politics and the disaster of the Anthropocene', *The Sociological Review*, 62(S1): 19–37.

Clough, P. (2009) 'The new empiricism: affect and sociological method', *European Journal of Social Theory* 12(1): 43–61

Club of Rome (1972) *The Limits to Growth*. London: Earth Island Limited.

Cohen, M. P. (2000) 'Risk, vulnerability, and disaster prevention in large cities', *Lincoln Institute of Land Policy Working Paper*. Accessed at: www.alnap.org/pool/ files/1348-666-perlo00pc1-final.pdf.

COIC (2016) *After the World Humanitarian Summit: A Thinkpiece Drawing on Colla-boration by OCHA, UNDP, UNHCR, UNICEF, WFP and the World Bank*. New York: Center on International Cooperation.

Colebrook, C. (2012) 'Not symbiosis, not now: why anthropogenic change is not really human', *The Oxford Literary Review* 34(2): 185–209.

Colebrook, C. (2014) *Death of the Posthuman: Essays on Extinction, Vol. 1*. Ann Arbour: University of Michigan.

Colebrook, C. (2015) 'Introduction: Anthropocene feminisms: rethinking the unthinkable', *philoSOPHIA* 5(2): 167–178.

Colebrook, C. (2017) 'We have always been post-Anthropocene: the Anthropocene counterfactual', in R. Grusin (ed.) *Anthropocene Feminism*. Minneapolis: University of Minnesota Press, 1–20.

Collier, S. (2005) 'The spatial forms and social norms of "actually existing neoliber-alism": toward a substantive analytics', *International Affairs Working Paper 2005–2004*, June.

Collinson, S. (2016) 'Constructive deconstruction: making sense of the international humanitarian system', *Humanitarian Policy Group Working Paper*. London: Overseas Development Institute.

Commons, J. R. (1936) 'Institutional economics', *American Economic Review* 26, Supplement: 237–249.

Concern Worldwide (2015a) 'The role of technology at Concern Worldwide', *Knowledge Matters*, 15 December. Accessed at: www.concern.net/resources/knowledge-matters-role-technology-concern-worldwide.

Concern Worldwide (2015b) *Responding Early to Urban Crisis: Concern Worldwide's Research on Indicators for Urban Emergencies: Implications for Policy and Practice in Kenya*. Accessed at: www.alnap.org/pool/files/concern-idsue-brief-2015.pdf.

Connolly, W. E. (1995) *The Ethos of Pluralization*. Minneapolis: University of Min-nesota Press.

Connolly, W. E. (2013) *The Fragility of Things: Self-Organizing Processes, Neoliberal Fantasies, and Democratic Activism*. London: Duke University Press.

Connolly, W. E. (2017) *Facing the Planetary: Entangled Humanism and the Politics of Swarming*. Durham, NC: Duke University Press.

Coole, D. and Frost, S. (2010) *New Materialisms: Ontology, Agency, and Politics*. London: Duke University Press.

Cornell, D. and Seely, S. (2016) *The Spirit of Revolution: Beyond the Dead Ends of Man*. Cambridge: Polity Press.

Cox, R. (1981) 'Social forces, states and world orders: beyond international relations theory', *Millennium – Journal of International Studies* 10(2): 126–155.

Coyle, D. and Meier, P. (2009) *New Technologies in Emergencies and Conflicts: The Role of Information and Social Networks*. Washington, DC: United Nations Foun-dation and Vodafone Foundation. Accessed at: www.globalproblems-globalsolutions-files.org/pdf/UNF_tech/emergency_tech_report2009/Tech_EmergencyTechReport_full.pdf.

Crawford, K. (2014) 'The anxieties of big data', *The New Inquiry*, 30 May. Accessed at: http://thenewinquiry.com/essays/the-anxieties-of-big-data/.

Crawford, K., Faleiros, G., Luers, A., Meier, P., Perlich, C. and Thorp, J. (2013) *Big Data, Communities and Ethical Resilience: A Framework for Action*. Accessed at: http://poptech.org/system/uploaded_files/66/original/BellagioFramework.pdf.

Crutzen, P. J. (2002) 'Geology of mankind', *Nature* 415: 23.

Crutzen, P. J. and Steffen, W. (2003) 'How long have we been in the Anthropocene era?' *Climatic Change* 61: 251–257.

Crutzen, P. J. and Stoermer, E. (2000) 'The "Anthropocene"', *Global Change News* 41: 17–18.

Cudworth, E. and Hobden, S. (2011) *Posthuman International Relations: Complexity, Ecologism and Global Politics*. London: Zed Books.

Cukier, K. and Mayer-Schönberger, V. (2013) 'The rise of big data: how it's changing the way we think about the world', *Foreign Affairs*, May/June. Accessed at: http://m.foreignaffairs.com/articles/139104/kenneth-neil-cukier-and-viktor-ma yer-schoenberger/the-rise-of-big-data.

Dalby, S. (2013) 'Biopolitics and climate security in the Anthropocene', *Geoforum* 49: 184–192.

Dalby, S. (2017) 'Autistic geopolitics/Anthropocene therapy', *Public Imagination* 10 (42), 22 June. Accessed at: www.21global.ucsb.edu/global-e/june-2017/autis tic-geopolitics-anthropocene-therapy.

Danowski, D. and Viveiros de Castro, E. (2017) *The Ends of the World*. Cambridge: Polity.

Davies, J. (2016) *The Birth of the Anthropocene*. Oakland, CA: University of California Press.

Davis, M. (2006) *Planet of Slums*. London: Verso.

Dean, M. (2010) *Governmentality: Power and Rule in Modern Society*. London: Sage.

Defert, D. (1991) '"Popular life" and insurance technology', in G. Burchell, C. Gordon and P. Miller (eds) *The Foucault Effect: Studies in Governmentality*. Chicago, IL: University of Chicago Press, 211–233.

DeLanda, M. (2006) *A New Philosophy of Society: Assemblage Theory and Social Complexity*. London: Continuum.

Deleuze, G. (1988) *Spinoza: Practical Philosophy*. San Francisco, CA: City Lights.

Deleuze, G. (1995) 'Postscript on control societies', in G. Deleuze, *Negotiations: 1972–1990*. New York: Columbia University Press, 177–182.

Deleuze, G. and Guattari, F. (2014) *A Thousand Plateaus*. London: Bloomsbury Academic.

Dempster, B. L. (1998) 'A self-organizing systems perspective on planning for sustainability', Masters thesis, Environmental Studies in Planning, University of Waterloo, Ontario, Canada. Accessed at: www.bethd.ca/pubs/mesthe.pdf.

Dempster, B. L. (n.d.) 'Sympoietic and autopoietic systems: a new distinction for self-organizing systems'. Accessed at: http://citeseerx.ist.psu.edu/viewdoc/down load?doi=10.1.1.582.1177&rep=rep1&type=pdf.

Department for International Development, Foreign and Commonwealth Office and Ministry of Defence (2011) *Building Stability Overseas Strategy*. London: DfID, FCO, MoD.

Dewey, J. (1991) *The Public and Its Problems*. Athens: Ohio University Press.

Dill, J. G. (2003) 'Lodestone and needle: the rise of the magnetic compass', *Ocean Navigator*, 1 January. Accessed at: www.oceannavigator.com/January-February-2003/Lodestone-and-needle-the-rise-of-the-magnetic-compass/.

Dillon, M. (2008) 'Underwriting security', *Security Dialogue* 39(2–3): 309–332.

Duffield, M. (2013) 'Disaster-resilience in the network age: access-denial and the rise of cyber-humanitarianism', *Danish Institute for International Studies (DIIS) Working Paper*, 23. Accessed at: www.diis.dk/files/media/publications/import/extra/wp 2013-33_disaster-resilience-cyber-age_duffield_web.pdf.

Duffield, M. (2016) 'The resilience of the ruins: towards a critique of digital humanitarianism', *Resilience: International Policies, Practices and Discourses* 4(3): 147–165.

Economist (2010) 'Data, data everywhere', *Economist*, 15 February. Accessed at: www.economist.com/node/15557443.

Economist (2011) 'Welcome to the Anthropocene', *Economist*, 26 May. Accessed at: www.economist.com/node/18744401.

Epstein, C. (2014) 'The postcolonial perspective: an introduction', *International Theory* 6(2): 294–311.

Esposito, E. (2013) 'Digital prophecies and web intelligence', in M. Hildebrandt and K. de Vries (eds) *Privacy, Due Process and the Computational Turn: The Philosophy of Law meets the Philosophy of Technology*. Abingdon: Routledge.

Esposito, R. (2008) *Bios: Biopolitics and Philosophy*. Minneapolis: University of Minnesota Press.

Esposito, R. (2013) *Terms of the Political: Community, Immunity, Biopolitics*. New York: Fordham University Press.

Evans, B. and Reid, J. (2014) *Resilient Life: The Art of Living Dangerously*. Cambridge: Polity Press.

Ewald, F. (1991) 'Insurance and risk', in G. Burchell, C. Gordon and P. Miller (eds) *The Foucault Effect: Studies in Governmentality*. Chicago, IL: University of Chicago Press, 197–210.

Fagan, M. (2017) 'Security in the Anthropocene: environment, ecology, escape', *European Journal of International Relations* 23(2): 292–314.

Federici, S. (2012) *Revolution at Point Zero: Housework, Reproduction and Feminist Struggle*. Oakland, CA: PM Press.

Finkenbusch, P. (2016) 'Expansive intervention as neo-institutional learning: root causes in the Merida Initiative', *Journal of Intervention and Statebuilding* 10(2): 162–180.

Folke, C. (2006) 'Resilience: the emergence of a perspective for social–ecological systems analyses', *Global Environmental Change* 16: 253–267.

Forest, J. and Mehier, C. (2001) 'John R. Commons and Herbert A. Simon on the concept of rationality', *Journal of Economic Issues* 35(3): 591–605.

Foucault, M. (1981) *The History of Sexuality, Volume 1: An Introduction*. London: Penguin.

Foucault, M. (2003) *"Society Must Be Defended": Lectures at the Collège de France 1978–1979*. London: Allen Lane.

Foucault, M. (2008) *The Birth of Biopolitics: Lectures at the Collège de France 1978–1979*. Basingstoke: Palgrave.

Fuller, M. and Goffey, A. (2012) *Evil Media*. Cambridge, MA: MIT Press.

Galloway, A. (2004) *Protocol: How Control Exists After Decentralization*. Cambridge, MA: MIT Press.

Galloway, A. (2012) *The Interface Effect*. Cambridge: Polity Press.

Galloway, A. (2014) *Laruelle: Against the Digital*. Minneapolis: University of Minnesota Press.

GFDRR (2015) *World Bank Global Facility for Disaster Reduction and Recovery, Stories of Impact: Building Resilient Communities across Indonesia*. Accessed at: www.gfdrr. org/sites/default/files/publication/Indonesia.pdf.

Ghosh, A. (2016) *The Great Derangement: Climate Change and the Unthinkable*. Chicago, IL: University of Chicago Press.

Gibson Graham, J. K. and Roelvink, G. (2010) 'An economic ethics for the Anthropocene', *Antipode* 41(s1): 320–346.

Giddens, A. (1994) *Beyond Left and Right: The Future of Radical Politics*. Cambridge: Polity Press.

Gillings, M. (2015) 'Comment: how modern life has damaged our internal ecosystems', *SBS News*, 12 October. Accessed at: www.sbs.com.au/news/article/2015/ 10/09/comment-how-modern-life-has-damaged-our-internal-ecosystems.

Gratton, P. (2014) *Speculative Realism: Problems and Prospects*. London: Bloomsbury.

Greenfield, A. (2014) 'The smartest cities rely on citizen cunning and unglamorous technology', *Guardian*, 22 December. Accessed at: www.theguardian.com/cities/ 2014/dec/22/the-smartest-cities-rely-on-citizen-cunning-and-unglamorous-tech nology.

Grosz, E. (2011) *Becoming Undone: Darwinian Reflections on Life, Politics, and Art*. London: Duke University Press.

Grothoff, C. and Porup, J. M. (2016) 'The NSA's SKYNET program may be killing thousands of innocent people', *Ars Technica*, 16 February. Accessed at: http://a rstechnica.co.uk/security/2016/02/the-nsas-skynet-program-may-be-killing-thou sands-of-innocent-people/.

Grove, J. (2015) 'Of an apocalyptic tone recently adopted in everything: The Anthropocene or peak humanity?' *Theory & Event* 18(3).

Grove, K. (2018) *Resilience*. Abingdon: Routledge.

Gunderson, L. and Holling, C. S. (eds) (2002) *Panarchy: Understanding Transformations in Human and Natural Systems*. Washington, DC: Island.

Grusin, R. (2017) 'Introduction: Anthropocene feminism: an experiment in collaborative theorizing', in R. Grusin (ed.) *Anthropocene Feminism*. Minneapolis: University of Minnesota Press, xii–xix.

Haas, M. (2015) *Bouncing Forward: Transforming Bad Breaks into Breakthroughs*. New York: Enliven.

Hacking, I. (1990) *The Taming of Chance*. Cambridge: Cambridge University Press.

Haldrup, S. V. and Rosén, F. (2013) 'Developing resilience: a retreat from grand planning', *Resilience: International Policies, Practices and Discourses* 1(2): 130–145.

Halevy, A., Norvig, P. and Pereira, F. (2009) 'The unreasonable effectiveness of data', *IEEE Intelligent Systems* 24(2): 8–12; 9. Accessed at: https://static.google usercontent.com/media/research.google.com/en//pubs/archive/35179.pdf.

Halpern, O. (2014) *Beautiful Data: A History of Vision and Reason since 1945*. London: Duke University Press.

Hamilton, C. (2013) *Earthmasters: The Dawn of the Age of Climate Engineering*. London: Yale University Press.

Hamilton, C. (2015) 'Human destiny in the Anthropocene', in C. Hamilton, C. Bonneuil and F. Gemenne (eds) *The Anthropocene and the Global Environmental Crisis: Rethinking Modernity in a New Epoch*. Abingdon: Routledge, 32–43.

Hamilton, C., Bonneuil, C. and Gemenne, F. (eds) (2015a) *The Anthropocene and the Global Environmental Crisis: Rethinking Modernity in a New Epoch*. Abingdon: Routledge.

Hamilton, C., Bonneuil, C. and Gemenne, F. (2015b) 'Thinking the Anthropocene', in C. Hamilton, C. Bonneuil and F. Gemenne (eds) *The Anthropocene and the Global Environmental Crisis: Rethinking Modernity in a New Epoch*. Abingdon: Routledge, 1–13.

Hamilton, S. (2017) 'Securing ourselves from ourselves? The paradox of "entanglement" in the Anthropocene', *Crime, Law and Social Change*, First Online: 29 July.

Haraway, D. (1988) 'Situated knowledges: the science question in feminism and the privilege of partial perspective', *Feminist Studies* 14(3): 575–599.

Haraway, D. (1991) *Simians, Cyborgs, and Women: The Reinvention of Nature*. London: Free Association Books.

Haraway, D. (2015) 'Anthropocene, Capitalocene, Plantationocene, Chthulucene: making kin', *Environmental Humanities* 6: 159–165.

Haraway, D. (2016) *Staying with the Trouble: Making Kin in the Chthulucene*. Durham: Duke University Press.

Harland, M. (2013) 'Working with not against natural forces – an original permaculture principle', *Permaculture*, 12 April. Accessed at: www.permaculture.co.uk/a rticles/8-working-not-against-natural-forces-original-permaculture-principle.

Harley, J. B. (1989) 'Deconstructing the map', *Cartographica* 26(2): 1–20.

Harman, G. (2005) *Guerrilla Metaphysics: Phenomenology and the Carpentry of Things*. Peru, IL: Open Court.

Harman, G. (2009) *Prince of Networks: Bruno Latour and Metaphysics*. Melbourne, Australia: re:press.

Harman, G. (2010) *Towards Speculative Realism: Essays and Lectures*. Winchester: Zero Books.

Harman, G. (2016) *Immaterialism: Objects and Social Theory*. Cambridge: Polity Press.

Hayek, F. (1945) 'The use of knowledge in society,' *American Economic Review* 35(4): 519–530.

Hayek, F. (1952) *The Sensory Order: An Enquiry into the Foundations of Theoretical Psychology*. Chicago, IL: University of Chicago Press.

Hayek, F. (1960) *The Constitution of Liberty*. London: Routledge.

Hayek, F. (1978a) *The Three Sources of Values*. London: London School of Economics and Political Science.

Hayek, F. (1978b) 'Lecture on a Master Mind: Dr. Bernard Mandeville', in F. Hayek, *New Studies in Philosophy, Politics, Economics and the History of Ideas*. London: Routledge & Kegan Paul, 125–141.

Hayles, K. (1999) *How We Became Posthuman: Virtual Bodies in Cybernetics, Literature, and Informatics*. London: University of Chicago Press.

Heath-Kelly, C. (2016) 'Algorithmic auto-immunity in the NHS: radicalisation and the clinic', *Security Dialogue* 48(1): 29–45.

Heins, V. M., Koddenbrock, K. and Unrau, C. (eds) (2016) *Humanitarianism and Challenges of Cooperation*. Abingdon: Routledge.

Hicks, B. (1992) *Relentless* (DVD). Salem, MA: Rykodisc.

Himelfarb, S. (2014) 'Can big data stop wars before they happen?', *Foreign Policy*, 25 April. Accessed at: www.foreignpolicy.com/articles/2014/04/25/can_big_data_stop_wars_preemptive_peace_technology_conflict.

Hird, M. J. and Zahara, A. (2017) 'The Arctic Wastes', in R. Grusin (ed.) *Anthropocene Feminism*. Minneapolis: University of Minnesota Press, 121–145.

Holderness, T. and Turpin, E. (2015) *White Paper – PetaJakarta.org: Assessing the Role of Social Media for Civic Co-Management During Monsoon Flooding in Jakarta, Indonesia*. Accessed at: https://petajakarta.org/banjir/en/research/.

Holderness, T. and Turpin, E. (2016) 'How tweeting about floods became a civic duty in Jakarta', *Guardian*, 25 January. Accessed at: www.theguardian.com/publi c-leaders-network/2016/jan/25/floods-jakarta-indonesia-twitter-petajakarta.org.

Holling, C. S. (1973) 'Resilience and stability of ecological system', *Annual Review of Ecological Systems* 4: 1–23.

Holling, C. S. (1986) 'The resilience of terrestrial ecosystems: local surprise and global change', in W. Clark and R. Munn (eds) *Sustainable Development of the Biosphere*. Cambridge: Cambridge University Press, 292–320.

Holling, C. S. (2001) 'Understanding the complexity of economic, ecological, and social systems', *Ecosystems* 4: 390–405.

Holling, C. S. and Meffe, G. (1996) 'Command and control and the pathology of natural resource management', *Conservation Biology* 10(2): 328–337.

Houellebecq, M. (2015) *Submission*. London: William Heinemann.

Huffer, L. (2017) 'Foucault's fossils: life itself and the return to nature in feminist philosophy', in R. Grusin (ed.) *Anthropocene Feminism*. Minneapolis: University of Minnesota Press, 65–88.

Ihde, D. (2009) *Postphenomenology and Technoscience: The Peking University Lectures*. Albany: State University of New York.

Ingold, T. (2015) *The Life of Lines*. Abingdon: Routledge.

Invisible Committee (2014) *To Our Friends*. Accessed at: https://theanarchistlibrary. org/library/the-invisible-committe-to-our-friends.pdf.

Jakarta Post (2015) 'Experts defend "kampong" for making Jakarta unique, diverse', *The Jakarta Post*, 16 November. Accessed at: www.thejakartapost.com/news/2015/11/16/experts-defend-kampung-making-jakarta-unique-diverse.html.

Jameson, F. (2003) 'Future city', *New Left Review* 21: 65–79.

Jeffries, S. (2016) *Grand Hotel Abyss: The Lives of the Frankfurt School*. London: Verso.

Johnson, E. R. (2017) 'At the limits of species being: sensing the Anthropocene', *South Atlantic Quarterly* 116(2): 275–292.

Joseph, J. (2013) 'Resilience as embedded neoliberalism: a governmentality approach', *Resilience: International Policies, Practices and Discourses* 1(1): 38–52.

Karlsrud, J. (2014) 'Peacekeeping 4.0: harnessing the potential of big data, social media, and cyber technologies', in J.-F. Kremer and B. Müller (eds) *Cyberspace and International Relations: Theory, Prospects and Challenges*. London: Springer, 141–160.

Kitchin, R. (2014a) *The Data Revolution: Big Data, Open Data, Data Infrastructures & their Consequences*. Sage: London.

Kitchin, R. (2014b) 'Big data, new epistemologies and paradigm shifts', *Big Data and Society* 1(1): 1–12.

Kitchin, R. and Dodge, M. (2007) 'Rethinking maps', *Progress in Human Geography* 31(3): 1–14.

Klein, M. (2014) *This Changes Everything: Capitalism vs. the Climate*. New York: Simon & Schuster.

Koch, W. (2015) 'Could a Titanic seawall save this quickly sinking city?', *National Geographic*, 10 December. Accessed at: http://news.nationalgeographic.com/energy/2015/12/151210-could-titanic-seawall-save-this-quickly-sinking-city/.

Koddenbrock, K. J. (2015) 'Strategies of critique in international relations: from Foucault and Latour towards Marx', *European Journal of International Relations* 21(2): 243–269.

Latour, B. (1986) 'Visualisation and cognition: drawing things together', in H. Kuklick (ed.) *Knowledge and Society Studies in the Sociology of Culture Past and Present*, vol. 6, Amsterdam: Jai Press, 1–40.

Latour, B. (1993a) *We Have Never Been Modern*. Cambridge, MA: Harvard University Press.

Latour, B. (1993b) *The Pasteurisation of France*. Cambridge, MA: Harvard University Press.

Latour, B. (2003) 'Is re-modernization occurring – and if so, how to prove it? A commentary on Ulrich Beck', *Theory, Culture & Society* 20(2): 35–48.

Latour, B. (2004a) *Politics of Nature: How to Bring the Sciences into Democracy*. Cambridge, MA: Harvard University Press.

Latour, B. (2004b) 'Why has critique run out of steam? From matters of fact to matters of concern', *Critical Inquiry* 30(2): 225–248.

Latour, B. (2004c) 'How to talk about the body? The normative dimension of science studies', *Body & Society* 10(2–3): 205–229.

Latour, B. (2005) *Reassembling the Social: An Introduction to Actor-Network-Theory*. Oxford: Oxford University Press.

Latour, B. (2010a) *On the Modern Cult of the Factish Gods*. Durham, NC: Duke University Press.

Latour, B. (2010b) 'Tarde's idea of quantification', in M. Candea (ed.) *The Social after Gabriel Tarde: Debates and Assessments*. London: Routledge, 145–162.

Latour, B. (2010c) 'An attempt at a "Compositionist Manifesto"', *New Literary History* 41(3): 471–490.

Latour, B. (2011) 'Love your monsters', *Breakthrough Journal* 2: 21–28.

Latour, B. (2012) 'Gabriel Tarde and the end of the social', in P. Joyce (ed.) *The Social in Question: New Bearings in History and the Social Sciences*. London: Routledge, 117–132.

Latour, B. (2013a) *An Enquiry into Modes of Existence: An Anthropology of the Moderns*. Cambridge, MA: Harvard University Press.

Latour, B. (2013b) *Facing Gaia, Six Lectures on the Political Theology of Nature: Being the Gifford Lectures on Natural Religion, Edinburgh, 18th-28th of February 2013* (draft version 1-3-13). Accessed at: https://macaulay.cuny.edu/eportfolios/wa kefield15/files/2015/01/LATOUR-GIFFORD-SIX-LECTURES_1.pdf.

Latour, B. (2014) 'Agency at the time of the Anthropocene', *New Literary History* 45: 1–18.

Latour, B. (2016) 'Does the body politic need a new body?' Yusko Ward-Phillips lecture, University of Notre Dame, 3 November 2016. Accessed at: www.bru no-latour.fr/sites/default/files/151-NOTRE-DAME-2016.pdf.

Latour, B., Harman, G. and Erdélyi, P. (2011) *The Prince and the Wolf: Latour and Harman at the LSE*. Winchester: Zero Books.

Latour, B., Jensen, P., Venturini, T., Grauwin, S. and Boullier, D. (2012) '"The whole is always smaller than its parts" – a digital test of Gabriel Tardes' monads', *British Journal of Sociology* 63(4): 590–615.

Lavell, A. and Maskrey, A. (2014) 'The future of disaster risk management', *Environmental Hazards* 13(4): 267–280.

Law, J. (2004) *After Method: Mess in Social Science Research*. Abingdon: Routledge.

Law, J. and Hassard, J. (eds) (1999) *Actor Network Theory and After*. Oxford: Blackwell.

Lazzarato, M. (2014) *Signs and Machines: Capitalism and the Production of Subjectivity*. South Pasadena, CA: Semiotext(e).

Lehman, J. and Nelson, S. (2014) 'Experimental politics in the Anthropocene', *Progress in Human Geography* 38(3): 444–447.

Leigh Geros, C. (2015) 'Does Jakarta have any viable options to defend itself from ocean inundation?', *National Geographic*, 21 December. Accessed at: http://voices. nationalgeographic.com/2015/12/21/a-fine-line-separates-jakarta-from-the-sea/.

Lemke, T. (2011) *Biopolitics: An Advanced Introduction*. New York: New York University Press.

Lewis, S. and Maslin, M. (2015) 'Defining the Anthropocene', *Nature* 519: 171–180.

Lezard, N. (2008) 'Goodbye to all this', *Guardian*, 3 May. Accessed at: www.thegua rdian.com/books/2008/may/03/society1.

MacGinty, R. and Richmond, O. P. (2013) 'The local turn in peace building: a critical agenda for peace', *Third World Quarterly* 34(5): 763–783.

Macfarlane, R. (2016) 'Generation Anthropocene: how humans have altered the planet for ever', *Guardian*, 1 April. Accessed at: www.theguardian.com/books/2016/apr/01/generation-anthropocene-altered-planet-for-ever.

Macrae, J. and Leader, N. (2001) 'Apples, pears and porridge: the origins and impact of the search for "coherence" between humanitarian and political responses to chronic political emergencies', *Disasters* 25(4): 290–307.

Madrigal, A. C. (2014) 'In defense of Google flu trends', *The Atlantic*, 27 March. Accessed at: www.theatlantic.com/technology/archive/2014/03/in-defense-of-g oogle-flu-trends/359688/.

Marchart, O. (2007) *Post-Foundational Political Thought: Political Difference in Nancy, Lefort, Badiou and Laclau*. Edinburgh: Edinburgh University Press.

Marres, N. (2012) *Material Participation: Technology, the Environment and Everyday Politics*. Basingstoke: Palgrave Macmillan.

Marx, K. (1983) *Capital: A Critique of Political Economy*, Vol. 1. London: Lawrence & Wishart.

Massey, D. (2005) *For Space*. London: Sage.

Massumi, B. (2002) *Parables for the Virtual: Movement, Affect, Sensation*. London: Duke University Press.

Mauss, M. (2002) *The Gift: The Form and Reason for Exchange in Archaic Societies*. London: Routledge.

Mayer-Schönberger, V. and Cukier, K. (2013) *Big Data: A Revolution that Will Transform How We Live, Work and Think*. London: John Murray.

Mazenec, C. (2017) 'Will algorithms erode our decision-making skills?' *NPR: All Tech Considered*, 8 February. Accessed at: www.npr.org/sections/alltechconsidered/2017/02/08/514120713/will-algorithms-erode-our-decision-making-skills.

Mbembe, A. (2003) 'Necropolitics', *Public Culture* 15(1): 11–40.

McClure, S., Scambray, J. and Kurtz, G. (2001) *Hacking Exposed: Network Security, Secrets and Solutions* (3rd ed.). Berkeley, CA: McGraw-Hill.

McCormick, T. (2013) 'Hacktivism: a short history: how self-absorbed computer nerds became a powerful force for freedom', *Foreign Policy*, 29 April. Accessed at: http://foreignpolicy.com/2013/04/29/hacktivism-a-short-history/.

McQuillan, D. (2014) 'The countercultural potential of citizen science', *Media/Culture Journal* 17(6). Accessed at: http://journal.media-culture.org.au/index.php/m cjournal/article/view/919.

Meier, P. (2013) 'How to create resilience through big data', *iRevolution*, 11 January. Accessed at: http://irevolution.net/2013/01/11/disaster-resilience-2-0/.

Meier, P. (2015) *Digital Humanitarianism: How Big Data is Changing the Face of Humanitarian Response*. London: CRC Press.

Meillassoux, Q. (2008) *After Finitude: An Essay on the Necessity of Contingency*. London: Continuum.

Merleau-Ponty, M. (1989) *Phenomenology of Perception*. London: Routledge.

Mezzi, P. (2016) 'The Great Garuda, the masterplan to save Jakarta', *Abitare*, 24 January. Accessed at: www.abitare.it/en/habitat-en/urban-design-en/2016/01/24/the-great-garuda-the-masterplan-to-save-jakarta/?refresh_ce-cp.

Mignolo, W. (2011) *The Darker Side of Western Modernity: Global Futures, Decolonial Options*. London: Duke University Press.

Mignolo, W. and Escobar, A. (eds) (2010) *Globalization and the Decolonial Option*. Abingdon: Routledge.

Millennium (2013) *Millennium: Journal of International Studies*, special issue 'Materialism and World Politics', 41(3).

Mindell, D. P. (2013) 'The tree of life: metaphor, model, and heuristic device', *Systematic Biology* 62(3): 479–489.

Mirowski, P. (2002) *Machine Dreams: Economics Becomes a Cyborg Science*. Cambridge: Cambridge University Press.

Mitchell, A. (2017) 'Is IR going extinct?', *European Journal of International Relations* 23 (1): 3–25.

Mitchell, M. (2009) *Complexity: A Guided Tour*. Oxford: Oxford University Press.

Mol, A. (2002) *The Body Multiple: Ontology in Medical Practice*. London: Duke University Press.

Moore, J. W. (2015) *Capitalism in the Web of Life: Ecology and the Accumulation of Capital*. London: Verso.

Moore, J. W. (ed.) (2016) *Anthropocene or Capitalocene: Nature, History, and the Crisis of Capitalism*. Oakland, CA: PM Press.

Morozov, E. (2013) *To Save Everything, Click Here: Technology, Solutionism and the Urge to Fix Problems That Don't Exist*. London: Allen Lane.

Morozov, E. (2014) 'The rise of data and the death of politics', *The Observer*, 30 July. Accessed at: www.theguardian.com/technology/2014/jul/20/rise-of-data-dea th-of-politics-evgeny-morozov-algorithmic-regulation.

Morton, T. (2012) *Ecological Thought*. Cambridge, MA: Harvard University Press.

Morton, T. (2013) *Hyperobjects: Philosophy and Ecology after the End of the World*. Minneapolis: University of Minnesota Press.

Morton, T. (2016) 'All objects are deviant: feminism and ecological intimacy', in K. Behar (ed.) *Object-Oriented Feminism*. Minneapolis: University of Minnesota Press, 65–81.

MSF (2015) *Initial MSF Internal Review: Attack on Kunduz Trauma Centre, Afghanistan*. Geneva: Medicins sans Frontieres. Accessed at: www.doctorswithoutborders.org/ sites/usa/files/msf_kunduz_review.pdf.

Nagel, T. (1974) 'What is it like to be a bat?', *The Philosophical Review* 83(4): 435–450.

Narvaez, R. W. M. (2012) 'Crowdsourcing for disaster preparedness: realities and opportunities', unpublished dissertation. Graduate Institute of International and Development Studies, Geneva. Accessed at: www.academia.edu/2197984/ Crowdsourcing_for_Disaster_Preparedness_Realities_and_Opportunities.

Nelson, S. and Braun, B. (2017) 'Autonomia in the Anthropocene: new challenges to radical politics', *South Atlantic Quarterly* 116(2): 223–235.

Nietzsche, F. (1997) *Thus Spake Zarathustra*. London: Wordsworth.

NIST (US National Institute of Science and Technology) (2016) 'NIST creates fundamentally accurate quantum thermometer', *NIST*, 15 March. Accessed at:

www.nist.gov/news-events/news/2016/03/nist-creates-fundamentally-accura
te-quantum-thermometer.

North, D. C. (1990) *Institutions, Institutional Change and Economic Performance*. Cambridge: Cambridge University Press.

North, D. C. (1999) 'Dealing with a non-ergodic world: institutional economics, property rights, and the global environment', *Duke Environmental Law & Policy Forum*, 10(1): 1–12.

North, D. C. (2005) *Understanding the Process of Economic Change*. Princeton: Princeton University Press.

O'Connor, S. (2016) 'When your boss is an algorithm', *Financial Times*, 8 September. Accessed at: www.ft.com/content/88fdc58e-754f-11e6-b60a-de4532d5ea35? mhq5j=e1.

ODI (Overseas Development Institute) (2016) *Time to Let Go: A Three-point Proposal to Change the Humanitarian System*. Accessed at: www.odi.org/sites/odi.org.uk/ files/resource-documents/10421.pdf.

O'Grady, N. (2016) 'A politics of redeployment: malleable technologies and the localisation of anticipatory calculation', in A. Louise and V. Piotukh (eds) *Algorithmic Life: Calculative Devices in the Age of Big Data*. Abingdon: Routledge, 72–86.

Ogunlesi, T. (2016) 'Inside Makoko: danger and ingenuity in the world's biggest floating slum', *Guardian*, 23 February. Accessed at: www.theguardian.com/cities/ 2016/feb/23/makoko-lagos-danger-ingenuity-floating-slum.

ó Súilleabháin, A. (2014) 'Building urban resilience in Bangkok: Q&A with Apiwat Ratanawaraha', *Global Observatory*, 13 August. Accessed at: http://theglobalob servatory.org/interviews/801-building-resilience-in-bangkok-apiwat-ratanawara ha.html.

Oxfam (2016) *What Are the Practices to Identify and Prioritize Vulnerable Populations Affected by Urban Humanitarian Emergencies? A Systematic Review Protocol of Methods and Specific Tools Used to Target the Most At-need Individuals, Households and/or Communities in Urban Crises*. London: Oxfam. Accessed at: http://policy-practice. oxfam.org.uk/publications/what-are-the-practices-to-identify-and-prior itize-vulnerable-populations-affect-605166.

Pachter, H. M. (1974) 'The idea of progress in Marxism', *Social Research* 41(1): 136–161.

Pagh, J. and Freudendal-Pedersen, M. (2014) 'Projects, power, and politics: a conversation with Bent Flyvbjerg', *Twentyfirst* 3: 62–75.

Paris, R. (2004) *At War's End: Building Peace after Conflict*. Cambridge: Cambridge University Press.

Pelling, M. (2011) *Adaptation to Climate Change: From Resilience to Transformation*. Abingdon: Routledge.

Perrotta, C. (2016) 'Chasing the algorithmic magic: an introduction to the Critical Data Studies Group at the University of Leeds', *Leeds Critical Data Studies Group*, 19 September. Accessed at: http://datastudies.leeds.ac.uk/chasing-the-algorithmic-ma gic-an-introduction-to-the-critical-data-studies-group-at-the-university-of-leeds/.

Pickering, A. (2010) *The Cybernetic Brain: Sketches of another Future*. Chicago, IL: University of Chicago Press.

Perry, W. L., McInnis, B., Price, C. C., Smith, S. C. and Hollywood, J. S. (2013) *Predictive Policing: The Role of Crime Forecasting in Law Enforcement Operations*. Santa Monica, CA: RAND Corporation.

Pietsch, W. (2013) 'Big data: the new science of complexity', 6th Munich-Sydney-Tilburg Conference on Models and Decisions, Munich, 10–12 April, Philsci Archive, University of Pittsburgh. Accessed at: http://philsci-archive.pitt.edu/9944/.

Plehwe, D. (2009) 'The origins of the neoliberal economic development discourse', in P. Mirowski and D. Plehwe (eds) *The Road from Mont Pelerin: The Making of the Neoliberal Thought Collective*. Cambridge, MA: Harvard University Press, 238–279.

Poulin, C. (2014) 'Big data custodianship in a global society', *SAIS Review of International Affairs* 34(1): 109–116.

Povinelli, E. (2016a) *Geontologies: A Requiem to Late Liberalism*. Durham, NC: Duke University Press.

Povinelli, E. (2016b) 'The world is flat and other super weird ideas', in K. Behar (ed) *Object-Oriented Feminism*. Minneapolis: University of Minnesota Press, 107–121.

Povinelli, E. (2017) 'The three figures of geontology', in R. Grusin (ed.) *Anthropocene Feminism*. Minneapolis: University of Minnesota Press, 49–64.

Prigogine, I. and Stengers, I. (1985) *Order out of Chaos: Man's New Dialogue with Nature*. London: Fontana.

Proctor, J. D. (2013) 'Saving nature in the Anthropocene', *Journal of Environmental Studies and Sciences* 3: 83–92.

Protevi, J. (2009) *Political Affect: Connecting the Social and the Somatic*. Minneapolis: University of Minnesota Press.

Radford, T. (2003) 'A brief history of thermometers', *Guardian*, 6 August. Accessed at: www.theguardian.com/science/2003/aug/06/weather.environment.

Ramalingam, B. (2013) *Aid on the Edge of Chaos: Rethinking International Cooperation in a Complex World*. Oxford: Oxford University Press.

Ramalingam, B., Jones, H., Reba, T. and Young, J. (2008) 'Exploring the science of complexity: ideas and implications for development and humanitarian efforts', *ODI Working Paper*, 285. London: Overseas Development Institute.

Read, J. (2017) 'Anthropocene and anthropogenesis: philosophical anthropology and the ends of man', *South Atlantic Quarterly* 116(2): 257–273.

Read, R., Taithe, B. and MacGinty, R. (2016) 'Data hubris? Humanitarian information systems and the mirage of technology', *Third World Quarterly* 37(8): 1314–1331.

Revkin, A. C. (2014) 'Exploring academia's role in charting paths to a "good" Anthropocene', *New York Times*, 16 June. Accessed at: https://dotearth.blogs.nytimes.com/2014/06/16/exploring-academias-role-in-charting-paths-to-a-good-anthropoce ne/?mcubz=2.

Robbins, M. (2016) 'Has a rampaging AI algorithm really killed thousands in Pakistan?', *Guardian*, 17 February. Accessed at: www.theguardian.com/science/the-lay-scientist/2016/feb/18/has-a-rampaging-ai-algorithm-really-killed-thousands-in-pakistan.

Rodin, J. (2015) *The Resilience Dividend: Managing Disruption, Avoiding Disaster, and Growing Stronger in an Unpredictable World*. London: Profile Books.

Rosenberg, J. (2000) *The Follies of Globalisation Theory: Polemical Essays*. London: Verso.

Rowan, R. (2014) 'Notes on politics after the Anthropocene', *Progress in Human Geography* 38(3): 447–450.

Rukmana, D. (2014) 'The megacity of Jakarta: problems, challenges and planning efforts', *Indonesia's Urban Studies*, 29 March. Available at: http://indonesiaurba nstudies.blogspot.co.uk/2014/03/the-megacity-of-jakarta-problems.html.

Sabaratnam, M. (2013) 'Avatars of Eurocentrism in the critique of the liberal peace', *Security Dialogue* 44(3): 259–278.

Salter, M. (ed.) (2015) *Making Things International 1: Circuits and Motion.* Minneapolis, MN: University of Minnesota Press.

Salter, M. (ed.) (2016) *Making Things International 2: Catalysts and Reactions.* Minneapolis, MN: University of Minnesota Press.

Santa Fe Institute (2016) 'How to make slums more resilient to climate change', *Phs.Org*, 28 January. Accessed at: http://phys.org/news/2016-01-slums-resilient-climate.html.

Scheuer, J. (2012) 'What we call "natural" disasters are not natural at all', United Nations Development Programme, 12 October. Accessed at: www.undp.org/content/undp/en/home/ourperspective/ourperspectivearticles/2012/10/12/wha t-we-call-natural-disasters-are-not-natural-at-all-jo-scheuer/.

Scott-Smith, T. (2016) 'Humanitarian neophilia: the "innovation turn" and its implications', *Third World Quarterly* 37(12): 2229–2251.

Sharp, H. (2011) *Spinoza and the Politics of Renaturalization.* Chicago, IL: Chicago University Press.

Shilliam, R. (2015) *The Black Pacific: Anti-Colonial Struggles and Oceanic Connections.* London: Bloomsbury Academic.

Siegler, M. G. (2010) 'Eric Schmidt: every 2 days we create as much information as we did up to 2003', *TechCrunch*, 4 August. Accessed at: http://techcrunch.com/2010/08/04/schmidt-data/.

Sihombing, A. (2004) 'The tranformation of Kampungkota: symbiosys between Kampung and Kota: a case study from Jakarta'. Accessed at: www.housingauthor ity.gov.hk/hdw/ihc/pdf/phhkt.pdf.

Skoglund, A. (2014) 'Homo clima: the overdeveloped resilience facilitator', *Resilience: International Practices, Policies and Discourses* 2(3): 151–167.

Sohn-Rethel, A. (1978) *Intellectual and Manual Labour: A Critique of Epistemology.* Atlantic Highlands, NJ: Humanities Press.

Steadman, I. (2013) 'Big data and the death of the theorist', *Wired Magazine*, 25 January. Accessed at: www.wired.co.uk/news/archive/2013-01/25/big-data -end-of-theory.

Stengers, I. (2015) *In Catastrophic Times: Resisting the Coming Barbarism.* Paris: Open Humanities Press.

Stengers, I. (2017) 'Autonomy and the intrusion of Gaia', *South Atlantic Quarterly* 116(2): 381–400.

Sticzay, N. and Koch, L. (2015) *Slum Upgrading: Global Sustainable Development Report 2015 Brief.* Accessed at: https://sustainabledevelopment.un.org/content/documents/5754Slum%20Upgrading.pdf.

Stockholm Resilience Centre (2014) 'The hidden cost of coerced resilience', Stockholm Resilience Centre, 29 November. Accessed at: www.stockholmresi lience.org/21/research/research-news/11-29-2014-the-hidden-cost-of-coerced-r esilience.html.

Stockholm Resilience Centre (2017) 'The nine planetary boundaries', *Stockholm Resilience Centre*. Accessed at: www.stockholmresilience.org/research/planetary-bounda ries/planetary-boundaries/about-the-research/the-nine-planetary-boundaries.html.

Stoner, A. M. and Melathopoulos, A. (2015) *Freedom in the Anthropocene: Twentieth-Century Helplessness in the Face of Climate Change*. Basingstoke: Palgrave Macmillan.

Strathausen, C. (ed.) (2009) *A Leftist Ontology: Beyond Relativism and Identity Politics*. Minneapolis: University of Minnesota Press.

Sukardjo, S. (2013) 'Jakarta under constant threat of flooding and rising sea levels', *Jakarta Post*, 23 January. Accessed at: www.thejakartapost.com/news/2013/01/ 23/jakarta-under-constant-threat-flooding-and-rising-sea-levels.html.

Sunstein, C. (2002) 'The paralyzing principle', *Regulation* (Winter): 32–37. Accessed at: http://object.cato.org/sites/cato.org/files/serials/files/regulation/2002/12/v25 n4-9.pdf.

Swyngedouw, E. (2011) 'Whose environment? The end of nature, climate change and the process of post-politicization', *Ambiente & Sociedade* 14(2). Accessed at: www.scielo.br/scielo.php?script=sci_arttext&pid=S1414-753X2011000200006.

Thrift, N. (2008) *Non-Representational Theory: Space, Politics, Affect*. Abingdon: Routledge.

Thrift, N. (2014) 'The "sentient" city and what it may portend', *Big Data & Society* 1 (1): 1–21.

Tierney, K. (2014) *The Social Roots of Risk: Producing Disasters, Promoting Resilience*. Stanford, CA: Stanford University Press.

Tkacz, N. (2018) 'In a world of data signals, resilience is subsumed into a design paradigm', *Resilience: International Policies, Practices and Discourses*, forthcoming.

Tsing, A. L. (2015) *The Mushroom at the End of the World: On the Possibility of Life in Capitalist Ruins*. Princeton, NJ: Princeton University Press.

Tuhus-Dubrow, R. (2009) 'Learning from slums', *Boston Globe*, 1 March. Accessed at: www.boston.com/bostonglobe/ideas/articles/2009/03/01/learning_from_slums/?p age=full.

Turpin, E. (2015) 'Aerosolar infrastructure: polities above & beyond territory', in T. Saraceno, *Becoming Aerosolar*. Vienna: Österreichische Galerie Belvedere, 169–200.

Turpin, E., Bobette, A. and Miller, M. (2013) 'Navigating postnatural landscapes: Jakarta as the city of the Anthropocene', paper presented at the European Council of Landscape Architecture Schools Annual Conference, The Netherlands.

UN (2010) 'International Strategy for Disaster Reduction: Resolution adopted by the General Assembly on 21 December 2009', United Nations General Assembly, 25 February. Accessed at: www.un.org/en/ga/search/view_doc.asp?symbol=A/ RES/64/200.

UN (2014) *A World that Counts: Mobilizing the Data Revolution for Sustainable Development*. Accessed at: www.undatarevolution.org/wp-content/uploads/2014/12/A-World-That-Counts2.pdf.

UN (2015a) *The Millennium Development Goals Report 2015*. New York: United Nations.

UN (2015b) *Report of the High-level Independent Panel on Peace Operations in Uniting Our Strengths for Peace: Politics, Partnership and People*. New York: United Nations.

UN (2015c) *Challenges of Sustaining Peace: Report of the Advisory Group of Experts on the Review of the Peacebuilding Architecture*. New York: United Nations.

UN (2015d) *Transforming Our World: The 2030 Agenda for Sustainable Development: Resolution Adopted by the General Assembly on 25 September 2015*. New York: United Nations.

UN (2016a) *One Humanity: Shared Responsibility: Report of the Secretary-General for the World Humanitarian Summit*. New York: United Nations.

UN (2016b) *Outcome of the World Humanitarian Summit: Report of the Secretary-General*. New York: United Nations.

UN (n.d.) *United Nations, 'Cities: Vital Statistics', UN Resources for Speakers on Global Issues*. Accessed at: www.un.org/en/globalissues/briefingpapers/cities/vitalstats.shtml.

UN-Habitat (2014) *Pro-Poor Urban Climate Resilience in Asia and the Pacific*. Nairobi, Kenya: UN-Habitat.

UNISDR (UN Office for Disaster Risk Reduction) (2014) *Progress and Challenges in Disaster Risk Reduction: A Contribution towards the Development of Policy Indicators for the Post-2015 Framework on Disaster Risk Reduction*. Geneva: UNISDR.

Venturini, T. and Latour, B. (2010) 'The social fabric: digital traces and quali-quantitative methods', in E. Chardronnet (ed.) *Proceedings of Future En Seine 2009: The Digital Future of the City*. Paris: Cap Digital, 87–101.

Voss, J.-P. and Bornemann, B. (2011) 'The politics of reflexive governance: challenges for designing adaptive management and transition management', *Ecology and Society* 16(2): art.9.

Wakefield, S. (2014) 'The crisis is the age', *Progress in Human Geography* 38(3): 450–452.

Wakefield, S. (2017) 'Field notes from the Anthropocene: living in the back loop', *The Brooklyn Rail*, 1 June. Accessed at: http://brooklynrail.org/2017/06/field-notes/Field-Notes-from-the-Anthropocene-Living-in-the-Back-Loop.

Wakefield, S. and Braun, B. (2018) 'Oystertecture: infrastructure, profanation and the sacred figure of the human', in K. Hetherington (ed.) *Infrastructure, Environment, and Life in the Anthropocene*. Durham, NC: Duke University Press.

Walker, J. and Cooper, M. (2011) 'Genealogies of resilience: from systems ecology to the political economy of crisis adaptation', *Security Dialogue* 42(2): 143–160.

Wark, M. (2004) *A Hacker Manifesto*. Accessed at: http://monoskop.org/images/8/85/Wark_McKenzie_A_Hacker_Manifesto.pdf.

Wark, M. (2015) *Molecular Red: Theory for the Anthropocene*. London: Verso.

Weinberger, S. (2017) 'The graveyard of empires and big data', *Foreign Policy*, 15 March. Accessed at: http://foreignpolicy.com/2017/03/15/the-graveyard-of-empires-and-big-data/.

Weisman, A. (2008) *The World Without Us*. New York: Picador.

Weiss, T. (2013) *Humanitarian Business*. Cambridge: Polity Press.

White, S. K. (2000) *Sustaining Affirmation: The Strengths of Weak Ontology in Political Theory*. Princeton, NJ: Princeton University Press.

Wilkinson, A. (2015) 'Kenneth Goldsmith's poetry elevates copying to an art, but did he go too far?', *New Yorker*, 5 October. Accessed at: www.newyorker. com/magazine/2015/10/05/something-borrowed-wilkinson.

Williams, M. (2014) 'Will big data have a direct impact on patient care?', *Business Solutions*, 18 August. Accessed at: www.bsminfo.com/doc/will-big-data-have-a -direct-impact-on-patient-care-0001.

Wistrom, B. (2017) 'CityCop aims to crowdsource crime like Waze does with traffic', *AustinInno*, 15 March. Accessed at: http://austininno.streetwise.co/2017/03/15/a ustin-neighborhood-crime-maps-app-citycop-crowdsources-and-uses-police-data/.

Wolfendale, P. (2014) *Object-Oriented Philosophy: The Noumenon's New Clothes*. Falmouth: Urbanomic Media.

Working Group on the Anthropocene (2017) 'What is the "Anthropocene"? – Current definition and status', *Quaternary Stratigraphy*. Accessed at: https://qua ternary.stratigraphy.org/workinggroups/anthropocene/

World Bank (2010) *Natural Hazards, Unnatural Disasters: The Economics of Effective Prevention*. Washington, DC: World Bank.

World Bank (2011) *Climate Change, Disaster Risk, and the Urban Poor: Cities Building Resilience for a Changing World*. Washington, DC: World Bank.

World Bank (2015) *Managing Disaster Risks for a Resilient Future: A Work Plan for the Global Facility for Disaster Reduction and Recovery 2016–2018*. Washington, DC: World Bank.

Wynter, S. (2003) 'Unsettling the coloniality of being/power/truth/freedom: towards the human, after man, its overrepresentation – an argument', *CR: The New Centennial Review* 3(3): 257–337.

Zwitter, A. J. and Hadfield, A. (2014) 'Governing big data', *Politics and Governance* 2 (1): 1–2.

Zylinska, J. (2014) *Minimal Ethics for the Anthropocene*. Ann Arbor: Open Humanities Press.

INDEX